The Human Edge

MW00990150

The Human Edge

Analogy and the Roots of Creative Intelligence

Keith J. Holyoak

The MIT Press
Cambridge, Massachusetts
London, England

© 2025 Massachusetts Institute of Technology

This work is subject to a Creative Commons CC-BY-NC-ND license.

This license applies only to the work in full and not to any components included with permission. Subject to such license, all rights are reserved. No part of this book may be used to train artificial intelligence systems without permission in writing from the MIT Press.

[cc] BY-NC-ND

The MIT Press would like to thank the anonymous peer reviewers who provided comments on drafts of this book. The generous work of academic experts is essential for establishing the authority and quality of our publications. We acknowledge with gratitude the contributions of these otherwise uncredited readers.

This book was set in Stone Sans and Stone Serif by Westchester Publishing Services. Printed and bound in the United States of America.

Library of Congress Cataloging-in-Publication Data

Names: Holyoak, Keith James, 1950- author.
Title: The human edge : analogy and the roots of creative intelligence / Keith J. Holyoak.
Description: Cambridge : The MIT Press, [2025] | Includes bibliographical references and index.
Identifiers: LCCN 2024017302 (print) | LCCN 2024017303 (ebook) | ISBN 9780262550901 (paperback) | ISBN 9780262381321 (epub) | ISBN 9780262381338 (pdf)
Subjects: LCSH: Intellect. | Analogy.
Classification: LCC BF431 .H558 2025 (print) | LCC BF431 (ebook) | DDC 153.9—dc23/eng/20240508
LC record available at https://lccn.loc.gov/2024017302
LC ebook record available at https://lccn.loc.gov/2024017303

10 9 8 7 6 5 4 3 2 1

for the next generation

Jim, Jessica, Neil, Vanessa, Dylan, Kai

and beyond

Leo, Ari, Oona, Nico

Contents

Acknowledgments

In writing this book I benefited from the advice and encouragement of several cognitive scientists who served (sometimes unwittingly) as my loose band of consultants. I'm particularly grateful to Hongjing Lu, my wife and closest colleague, who supported the effort in ways large and small, both theoretical and practical. This book (and a great deal more) would not have been possible without her. Miriam Bassok helped me explore the implications of semantic alignment for understanding analogy; Fred Schauer provided insights into the ways analogy is used in the law; Idan Blank, Silvia Bunge, Barbara Knowlton, Matt Lieberman, and Martin Monti guided me through the intricate networks of the human brain; Derek Penn and Danny Povinelli revisited our comparisons of the thinking capacities of human versus nonhuman animals; Nick Ichien and Dušan Stamenković joined me in thinking through the connections between analogy and metaphor; Maureen Gray advised me on best practices for using analogy in teaching; Hongjing Lu and Shuhao Fu helped me consider how vision is connected to thinking; Taylor Webb led our collective effort to understand whether and how large language models can reason by analogy; and Adam Green and Bob Morrison shared in my explorations of the roots of creativity. Hongjing Lu and other collaborators (John Hummel, Martin Monti, and Taylor Webb), as well as my son Jim Holyoak, helped prepare illustrations.

The book also benefited greatly from the advice of three anonymous reviewers for the MIT Press. I owe special thanks to my editor, Philip Laughlin, for his guidance and long-standing support. While writing this book, my lab at UCLA was supported by grants from the National Science Foundation, a Google Faculty Research Award, and a gift from Canon Inc.

Preface

To see a World in a Grain of Sand
And a Heaven in a Wild Flower
Hold Infinity in the palm of your hand
And Eternity in an hour
—William Blake

As long as I can remember, I've been fascinated by the way the mind creates new ideas by seeing one thing as another. Like Blake in the opening lines of his poem "Auguries of Innocence," we might stare at a grain of sand and find a new world there, and go on to imagine space and time without limits. Myths and metaphors, symbols and symmetries—these are manifestations of the human ability to draw *analogies* between concepts the mind can readily grasp and others, more mysterious, that it aims to grasp. Out of knowledge rooted in perception and action, we form concepts of things that can't be seen or touched by mere mortals—ideas such as quarks, democracy, and God. This ability, I will argue, is the human "edge" that enables members of our species (unlike any other that still walks the earth) to generate new ideas—including abstractions—by transforming old ones.

Growing up as a farm boy in British Columbia, I aspired to become a poet—a weaver of symbols within a web of words. But after I entered university (first the University of British Columbia, then Stanford), I was instead drawn to cognitive psychology (though my earlier aspiration was not altogether abandoned). Over the ensuing half century, together with many students and colleagues, my research has examined a constellation of cognitive processes related to analogy. These include the representation of semantic relations between words, the operation of human memory, the special properties of cause-and-effect relations, and the bases for moral judgments and decisions. Along the way I wrote, coauthored, or coedited several books that dealt with analogy. As my editor, Philip Laughlin, recently pointed out to me, the MIT Press has published one of these books in each decade from the 1980s on. The first was *Induction* (1986, with John Holland, Dick Nisbett, and Paul Thagard), in which we examined analogy in the context of induction, defined broadly as mechanisms by which knowledge can be expanded in the face of uncertainty. Next came *Mental Leaps: Analogy in Creative Thought* (1995, with Paul Thagard), which focused on analogy and its contributions to human thinking (in science, philosophy, and general culture). This was followed by *The Analogical Mind* (2001, coedited with Dedre Gentner and Boicho Kokinov), a "state of the art" collection of papers on analogy written by a stellar set of cognitive scientists. The following decade brought *The Spider's Thread: Metaphor in Mind, Brain, and Poetry* (2019), in which I examined the nature of literary metaphors, for which analogy plays an important (though by no means exclusive) role.

The Human Edge is my effort to synthesize what has been learned about the cognitive and neural basis of human analogy. The topic has been discussed extensively over the years by philosophers, linguists, psychologists, neuroscientists, and computer scientists, but a number of relatively recent scientific developments have made possible a deeper and more comprehensive understanding of the constellation of processes that enable people to draw analogies. Ideally, a cognitive theory of analogy will take the form of a model that actually performs analogical tasks in much the same way as people do. A model should operate on realistic inputs (ideally "raw materials" such as texts describing situations or pixel-level representations of pictures) and generate outputs that match human analogical judgments in some detail. Typically, a proposal of this sort takes the form of a computer program that can perform specific analogical tasks. The models developed so far only approximate human analogy, but we can learn from their shortcomings as well as their successes. The time seems right to sketch a "big picture" of the human ability to draw analogies. Here's a preview of some of the questions that I'll examine (or reexamine) in the fourteen chapters of the book.

1) What is analogy, and why is it important? How does it relate to different aspects of intelligence, as well as to creativity?

2) Analogy depends on seeing the *relations* between things, including relations that aren't directly observable (e.g., increasing mortgage interest

rates might *cause* a dip in housing prices; the meaning of "fast" is *opposite* to that of "slow"). What *are* relations, and how are they represented in the human mind?

3) How do we decide what information is *relevant* to deciding whether an analogy counts as evidence for some conjecture—in science, math, law, or everyday reasoning?

4) What mental processes are involved in thinking by analogy?

5) How is analogical reasoning realized in the human brain?

6) Is analogy a unique property of human cognition, or is it shared in important ways with the minds of some nonhuman animals? At what point do children acquire the ability to think by analogy?

7) How is analogy related to language (including metaphor) as well as the ability to understand the minds of other people?

8) How can analogy be used as a teaching tool?

9) Is it possible to construct computer programs that capture the way people use analogies?

10) Can computer models shed light on how semantic relations are learned and used to solve verbal analogies?

11) How do people (and how can computer models) use vision to "see" analogies between objects and scenes?

12) Can artificial intelligence (AI) reach or exceed human analogical ability?

13) What role does analogy play in creative thinking?

14) What surprises have we encountered along the way?

To seriously address these questions, we'll need to take a careful look at relevant research findings. My aim is to provide a general introduction and synthesis, broadly accessible to readers interested in analogy. Accordingly, I've kept formalisms and other technical material to a minimum. At the same time, the notes provide pointers to the extensive body of scientific research from which I've drawn ideas and evidence. Students and researchers who wish to delve more deeply into particular topics will be able to use the notes and references to trace back to original research articles.

Over the past fifty years, it has been my privilege to collaborate with a great many brilliant students and colleagues who contributed immensely to our joint research projects on analogy and allied topics. I won't try to list them all—many of their names appear on papers listed in the references at the end of the book. However, a few people played special roles that warrant mention at the outset. The first is Mary Gick, who as a PhD student at the University of Michigan managed to overcome my initial reluctance to change my research direction. Together we went back to the Gestalt psychology of the early twentieth century, an exploration that led us to create a paradigm for studying analogical problem-solving in the lab.[1] Yet earlier, my fellow graduate student in the 1970s at Stanford, Arnold Glass, collaborated with me on studies of how people evaluate semantic relations, such as *opposite*.[2] At the time I didn't see any connection to analogy; half a century later, I consider the representation of semantic relations to be foundational.

One of the most significant changes in my view of analogy was triggered by an intense collaboration with Derek Penn and Danny Povinelli, cognitive scientists focused on cognition in nonhuman primates.[3] I had previously viewed the development of analogy, both phylogenetic and ontogenetic, as a basically continuous process tied to expansion of working memory. Derek and Danny led me through a detailed examination of research on primate cognition, which highlighted a critical gap between the minds of humans and those of our closest extant relatives, the great apes.

Finally, my aspiration to create computational models of human analogy would have come to nothing without the aid of colleagues who brought to bear formal skills that I lamentably lack. My understanding of analogy has been shaped by a succession of computer models, each developed jointly with an indispensable collaborator: with Paul Thagard, *Analogical Constraint Mapping Engine* (ACME);[4] with John Hummel, *Learning and Inference with Schemas and Analogies* (LISA);[5] and with Hongjing Lu, *Bayesian Analogy with Relational Transformations* (BART)[6] and *Probabilistic Analogical Mapping* (PAM).[7] I hasten to add that none of my collaborators are responsible for anything I've written here—nor is any one of them likely to agree with all (or even most!) of it.

1 What Is Analogy?

You see, wire telegraph is a kind of a very, very long cat. You pull his tail in New York and his head is meowing in Los Angeles. Do you understand this? And radio operates exactly the same way: you send signals here, they receive them there. The only difference is that there is no cat.

—attributed (probably falsely) to Albert Einstein

Over four centuries ago, William Shakespeare wrote *Hamlet*, a tragic play about a prince of Denmark of that name. Before Hamlet was born, his father was murdered by his own brother, Claudius, who poured poison in his ear. Claudius was able to hide his crime, marry his brother's widow, Gertrude, and claim the throne as the new king. Then one dark night, Hamlet is visited by his father's ghost, who tells Hamlet how he had been murdered by Uncle Claudius. Hamlet swears to seek vengeance for his father. But Hamlet is unsure of himself. Struggling to decide on a course of action, he feigns madness and contemplates life and death ("To be, or not to be?"). He drops hints to Claudius and Gertrude that he suspects Claudius of the crime. In an unhappy accident while intending to confront his mother, Hamlet stabs and kills the father of his betrothed, Ophelia.

Things go from bad to worse. Hamlet is exiled to England, and meanwhile Ophelia becomes mad with grief over her father's death and drowns. Hearing that his uncle is plotting to kill him, Hamlet returns to Denmark, meeting his good friend Horatio along the way. A final duel ensues, and the play ends with almost everyone dead—not only the evil uncle Claudius but also Gertrude and Hamlet himself. Only Horatio lives to tell the tale. *Hamlet* became a prototype of the "tragedy of blood," in which the protagonist's pursuit of revenge leads not only to their enemies' death but to their own.

Much closer to the present day, the Walt Disney Company launched a franchise that began with a full-length animated movie, followed by multiple spin-offs (most notably an award-winning Broadway musical), all based on the story of *The Lion King*. Set in a kingdom of lions in Africa, the young cub Simba is destined to succeed his beloved father, Mufasa, as king of the Pride Lands. But Mufasa is killed through machinations of his evil brother Scar, who then manipulates Simba into believing he was the one responsible. Simba flees into exile in the desert, where he is rescued by Timon (a meercat) and Pumbaa (a warthog). Simba grows up on an oasis with his two new friends, living a carefree life according to their motto, "hakuna matata" (Swahili for "no worries"). Meanwhile, Uncle Scar rules and pillages the Pride Lands with the help of his minions, a trio of hyenas, while trying (unsuccessfully) to woo his brother's widow, Queen Sarabi.

Then things take a new turn. Simba is reunited with a grown-up lioness, his childhood friend Nala. They fall in love. Nala tells him that Scar is devastating the Pride Lands and urges Simba to return home. At first, he refuses. But Rafiki (a monkey who's a shaman) tells Simba his father's spirit lives on in him. Then Simba is visited at night by the spirit of his father, who convinces Simba that it's his duty to return home. Simba returns, and after a confrontation Scar reveals himself as the one who had caused Mufasa's death. Simba overcomes Scar, and though he spares his life, Scar is then killed by his own gang of hyenas. Simba becomes king with Nala as his queen. The Pride Lands are restored, and a new heir is born to Simba and Nala. Rafiki presents the cub to the denizens of the kingdom, and the "circle of life" continues unbroken.

So, here we have two stories laid out side by side—the prince of Denmark and of the Pride Lands, "To be, or not to be?" and "hakuna mutata," the tragedy of blood and the circle of life. Do they form an analogy?

Before trying to answer this question, we need to consider what it even means. First a bit of basic terminology: I'll freely use the term "analogy" to refer either to a special type of connection between two situations (the sense intended here) or to the constellation of cognitive and neural mechanisms by which people create or evaluate that sort of connection. Thus, "seeing an analogy" (in the first sense) is the *product* of the *process* of analogy (in the second sense). The context will usually make clear which sense of "analogy" is intended (often either one fits fine), but occasionally I'll spell it out.

In an analogy, there is typically an asymmetry between the two situations being compared. The analog that is initially more familiar, better understood, or simply first (as in the case of *Hamlet*) is termed the *source*; the one that is less familiar, harder to grasp, or created later (like *The Lion King*) is termed the *target*. To a first approximation, the source and target are considered analogous if they are similar in important ways. Of course, this lame excuse for a definition just raises more questions. How do we decide what is "similar"? How do we count the "ways" in which situations might be similar (or not)? What makes some similarities and differences more "important" than others?

Much of this book is devoted to untangling these loose threads. Let's make a start by thinking through how we might compare *Hamlet* with *The Lion King*. If you're familiar with the actual plays/movies, it will be obvious that my plot synopses have left out a myriad of details from both stories, especially from the more complex of the two, *Hamlet*. (Where are Rosencrantz and Guildenstern? And alas for you, poor neglected Yorick!) In writing my synopses, I had to tacitly decide which characters and plot points were especially important in giving a sense of what each story is "mainly about." In making these selections, I put limits on the "ways" in which the two stories can be related to one another.

Despite my simplifications, the synopses are still quite complex. As a warm-up to evaluating the potential analogy, let's simplify further. Here's my *Hamlet for Dummies*:

Hamlet's father was king of Denmark. Claudius was Hamlet's uncle. He poisoned Hamlet's father. Hamlet missed his father. The result was trouble. Claudius was killed in the end.

And here's a comparable bowdlerization of *The Lion King*:

Simba's father was king of the Pride Lands. Scar was Simba's uncle. Scar caused Simba's father to be killed. Simba missed his father. The result was trouble. Scar was killed in the end.

Now, if *this* were all there was to the two stories, they would certainly seem to be analogous. We can readily place the elements of the two stories into one-to-one correspondence, with nothing left over—a standard criterion for a sound analogy. A bit more technically, we can find an *isomorphism* between the two based on a sensible *mapping* between elements:

Hamlet → Simba

Hamlet's father → Simba's father

Claudius → Scar

king → king

poison → cause to be killed

We could go on to spell out further mapping details (uncle → uncle, trouble → trouble), but I'm sure you get the idea. Everything important (i.e., everything included in my minimalist descriptions of the source and target) can be matched. Notice the mapping mainly depends on *relations* between characters—who is related to who, who does what to who, and why. The mapped elements don't have to be similar in every way (humans are mapped to lions!), but they play the same *roles*. It's very natural to say that Scar is the "Claudius character" in *The Lion King*. Not even the mapped relations have to be identical—"poisoned" isn't exactly the same as "cause to be killed," but close enough. We have a very solid analogy.

Now let's return to my longer synopses. Here things look murkier. But there are still many relational parallels linking the characters. If asked to provide a mapping for them, I'd go with:

Hamlet → Simba

Hamlet's father → Mufasa

Claudius → Scar

Gertrude → Queen Sarabi

Ophelia → Nala

Horatio → Timon and/or Pumbaa, or maybe even Rafiki

Ophelia's father → ??

?? → hyenas

The two stories have clear similarities. Hamlet and Simba are both princes deprived of their rightful thrones because of the nefarious acts of an evil uncle, who was responsible for the death of the former king, their father. After an exile during which they are distracted from achieving retribution (by contemplating life and death, or by partying with buddies), they each return to claim their rightful position in their kingdom. Looks like an analogy.

But wait a minute! Isn't it an *important* difference that Hamlet and Ophelia end up dead, whereas Simba and Nala live happily ever after as king and queen? Nala is a much stronger character than Ophelia. And how about the fact that Gertrude remarries with Claudius, whereas Queen Sarabi will have none of that with Scar? The one-to-one correspondences obviously start to crumble for Hamlet's sole best friend, Horatio, who seems to spread his mapping across Simba's larger set of compadres. Ophelia's father is left unmapped (Nala's parentage is murky). Who are *"Hamlet's* hyenas"? (For Shakespeare afficionados, this might be the cue to bring Rosencrantz and Guildenstern back in.) And most troublesome of all, can a tragedy of blood really be analogous to a celebration of the circle of life?

At this point we might simply conclude that the two stories are *partially* analogous. The resemblances are imperfect, as is the isomorphism, but the mapping is not simply random. *The Lion King* is surely more analogous to *Hamlet* than to *A Midsummer Night's Dream* (even though the jungle story, like the latter play, offers considerably more humor than does *Hamlet*). But are *The Lion King* and *Hamlet* analogous enough to meet some threshold that would make them a *useful* analogy?

Before we tackle this new question, we again need to think about what it means. What makes an analogy "useful"? Let's step back and take a broader look at the wild menagerie of analogies that humans have contemplated and consider the range of purposes that analogies may serve.

A Menagerie of Analogies

It's time to get a bit more serious about defining what makes a comparison an analogy.[1] Let's try this as a provisional definition:

> Human analogy involves an overall assessment of important similarities and differences between a source and target perceived to be distinct from one another, where the comparison at least in part depends on explicit relations between entities.

Note that this definition refers to analogy as a *process*, and in particular as a process of mature human thinking. Exploring this process is the central focus of this book. For now, we'll set aside questions about whether thinkers other than adult humans (children at different ages, nonhuman animals, various AI programs) employ a process comparable to that of human adults—later chapters will explore these possibilities. The general tack I'm taking is to first seek clarity about analogy as a process in the mature human mind and then consider how that process develops in childhood and relates to nonhuman varieties of intelligence.

My definition of analogy excludes many types of similarity-based comparisons. "Overall assessment" implies a comparison based on representations of entire situations (modulated by perceived importance of their various

aspects), rather than some more limited comparison. This is the difference
between metaphor and simile. "Judy is a diamond" (metaphor) invites an
overall comparison of Judy to a diamond, and at least possibly involves analogy; "Judy is like a diamond" (simile) simply suggests there is some specific
resemblance to be found, without mandating a global comparison.

The definition also restricts analogy (in my intended sense—a process
operating in an individual human mind) to cases in which the thinker per-
ceives the source and target to be distinct from one another. This condition
means that comparing something to itself doesn't count as analogy (even
though in that case the source and target will be extremely similar—in fact
identical). Moreover, "The Taylor-Burton Diamond is a famous diamond" is
true, but it is not an analogy: unlike Judy, the Taylor-Burton really *is* a diamond. In general, analogy involves a sense of incongruity: the thinker aims
to "superimpose" one situation on another, yet at some level remains aware
that the two situations are not actually the same thing, nor is one simply an
instance of a category specified by the other. As we'll see, fuzzy cases arise in
which thinkers may vary in whether they perceive two situations as distinct.

Finally, "explicit relations" must be involved. We'll unpack what this
means in chapter 2, but for now it's enough to point out that when a honey-
bee finds nectar on a yellow flower, and later shows a preference for alighting
on other yellow flowers, that's not analogy at work. No explicit relations (in
the intended sense) are involved.

In proposing this definition, my aim is to "cut nature at the joints": I
will argue that the human mind and brain in fact provide special processes
for dealing with analogy as I am defining it. I claim, in fact, that my definition of analogy is closely tied to the operation of a specific neural network
(to be described in chapter 5). Some will object that my definition is too
restrictive. Indeed, it excludes many varieties of similarity-based comparisons. Some enthusiasts argue for the ubiquity of analogy—elevating it perhaps to the "core of cognition."[2] In promoting the general importance of
analogy across biological cognition, theorists may embrace such "examples"
of it as bees selecting flowers based on similarity of color, or of someone treating two different things alike because they're hard to tell apart. It might be
claimed that any and all influences of past experience on current behavior
(perhaps even classical conditioning) should be counted as analogy. Analogy has been alleged to operate in all judgments of category membership
and across the entire range of utterances that some trained linguists consider

to be metaphors.[3] But (in my humble view) such generous bestowal of the term "analogy"—intended to glorify the concept—risks trivializing it instead. Analogy is important not because it forms the core of biological cognition, but because it extends it to provide the "human edge."

So, if not all comparisons involve analogy, what's left? Here are a few examples drawn from the wild menagerie of human analogies.

My wife, Hongjing, wanted to reuse a math book belonging to our older son, Dylan, with our younger son, Kai. It contained multiple-choice questions, for which the correct answer had been circled in pencil back when Dylan had used it. So Hongjing erased the circles. But eagle-eyed Kai persisted in using the faint traces of erased circles to select his answers. Today Hongjing showed me (with a smile) her new and more cunning solution: she went through the book and circled *all* the answers, foiling Kai's non-mathematical shortcut. A few seconds later, I was reminded of the scene in the old Kirk Douglas movie where all the rebel Roman slaves shout together, "*I* am Spartacus!" Many comparable anecdotes of analogical reminding in everyday life have been reported.[4]

More rare but more impactful than such everyday examples, we have analogies that provided the seeds for new scientific theories (and perhaps more often, after-the-fact explanations of them).[5] The ancient Greeks and Romans laid the basis for the earliest analogy-inspired theory that is still accepted today: the transmission of sound is analogous to the motion of water waves after a disturbance. Many centuries later, the wave theory of sound became the source analog for the wave theory of light. The mappings are roughly these:

echo → reflection

loudness → brightness

pitch → color

ear → eye

air → "ether"

Light waves indeed have many parallels to sound waves, though there are also important differences (for example, motion of light waves is transverse, whereas that of sound waves is longitudinal). The most spectacular difference involves the supposed mapping of air (the medium through which sound waves move) to "ether" (the hypothetical medium through which light waves were once assumed to move). The "ether" concept, motivated by a sensible analogical inference (sound waves require a medium in which to travel, so light waves must need one too), turned out to be a fiction—there is no "ether," and light waves can actually travel in a vacuum. This example highlights a general principle to keep in mind: *Reality trumps analogy*. But it also illustrates a second principle: *An imperfect analogy can still be useful*. (*Hamlet* and *The Lion King*, perhaps?)

Analogies are used not only to help generate scientific theories but also to create the varied physical objects constructed by humans. Architecture has often been influenced by analogies and metaphors. For example, the roof of the famous Sydney Opera House was inspired by the billowing sails of ships in the harbor.[6] The biological world has inspired many inventions. In one recent case in which engineering built upon marine biology, a new type of suction cup was created by analogy to the mechanism that allows a clingfish (native to the Pacific coast of North America) to adhere to both smooth and rough surfaces in the intertidal zone.[7] By reverse-engineering the clingfish's suction disk, researchers developed devices that cling well to wet and dry objects both in and out of water. These advanced suction cups have potential applications for tasks as varied as industrial production, surgery, and whale tagging.

Analogies abound in mathematics (which is all about relations of number, quantity, and space). In fact, the word "analogy" is derived from the ancient Greek "analogia," which means *proportion*—a basic mathematical relation. Two ratios are said to be "in proportion" when they are equal. So, if a cake recipe calls for three cups of flour and two cups of sugar, the ratio of ingredients is $\frac{3}{2}$. If we want to bake two cakes, then we should double both the flour and the sugar, maintaining the same ratio: $\frac{3}{2} = \frac{6}{4}$. The absolute quantities of the ingredients differ from the single-cake to the two-cake recipe, but the ratios are in proportion (which implies the corresponding quantities are analogous).

Staying with math, here's an example of a mathematical conjecture that can be derived by exploring an analogy between two-dimensional and three-dimensional geometric forms. Let's use x and y to stand for the lengths of the two pairs of opposite sides in a rectangle. The perimeter of any rectangle is $2(x + y)$, and its area is the product xy. Lengths x and y are usually different, but a square is the special case of a rectangle for which $x = y$. It can be proved that *of all rectangles with a fixed perimeter, the square has the maximum area*.

Now consider a box—basically a three-dimensional rectangle—with parallel edges of lengths x, y, and z. Much like a rectangle, a box has a perimeter (the sum of the lengths of all its edges). And much like the area of a rectangle, a box has a volume (the amount of space it occupies), calculated as the product xyz. By analogy with rectangles, mathematicians hypothesized (correctly) that *of all boxes with a fixed perimeter, the cube (for which $x = y = z$) has the maximum volume.*[8]

While mathematicians make use of analogies between different mathematical cases, *non-math* analogies are commonly used by teachers to help students grasp new math concepts. Often the source analog is from some familiar situation in real life: an equation is likened to a balance scale; assigning a number to a variable is analogized to placing an object in a physical location; collecting like terms is compared to sorting mixed fruits into separate piles.[9]

The spatial aspect of math underlies the interpretation of graphs. These often take the form of an analogy between the pattern in an image (the source analog, often lines or bars) and a quantitative concept (the target). Figure 1.1 shows a temperature-precipitation graph for Cairo that combines two analogies: a curved line that shows average temperature over the twelve months of a year (it gets very hot in summer) and a set of bars indicating average precipitation (little rainfall, especially in the summer). Graphs take advantage of the power of our visual system to see patterns in images, exploiting this capacity to convey more abstract conceptual patterns by analogy.[10]

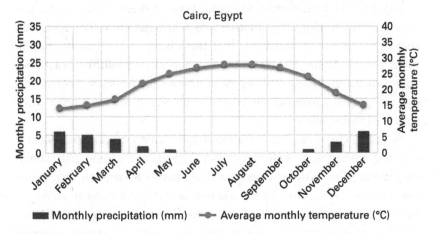

Figure 1.1
A temperature-precipitation graph for Cairo. Credit to NASA Earth Observatory.

Beyond the realms of math and science, analogies also play a role in legal decision-making.[11] Once a case has been decided, it can potentially provide a *precedent* for a later case: The new case, it can be argued, should be decided in the same way as the old one because the two cases are essentially "the same." Of course, no two cases are ever exactly alike, and so what it means to be the "the same" is often contended by the opposing sides. For example, suppose it has been established that a certain law applies to "marine vessels," such as freighters, fishing boats, and yachts. Does the law also apply to a new case involving a stationary houseboat (which is kept at one particular dock and would have to be towed to move it anywhere else)? The outcome of the case may hinge on an *argument* over competing analogies: Is the houseboat basically the same as a yacht, or is it more fundamentally a house? Similar analogical arguments swirl in debates about the legal responsibilities of social media—should a social media company be considered analogous to a traditional publisher, a public forum, a private forum, or none of these?

Analogies aren't only used to convey serious information or make consequential decisions—sometimes they're just a joke. Here's an analogy joke found on the internet:

Question: "Why is proctology called 'proctology'"?

Answer: "Because 'analogy' was already taken."[12]

(If you don't get it, check a dictionary—you'll expand your knowledge of medical specialties!)

Analogies lend themselves to humor because there's always some sort of incongruity lurking. Take another look at the quotation that began this chapter ("The only difference is that there is no cat"). Here the humor stems from the flagrant badness of the analogy as a scientific explanation—we've learned absolutely nothing about how a radio works by comparing it to a cat. (Like any joke vaguely related to physics, it sounds funnier when attributed to Einstein.)

Because pictures can convey a lot of information quickly and without requiring much cognitive effort, visual analogies can be used to make absurd (and therefore amusing) comparisons. The internet teems with images that have become *memes*, often by the addition of text that triggers an analogy.[13] Figure 1.2 shows an example of this genre. Notice how the verbal labels affixed to each person in the picture make the analogical mapping extremely

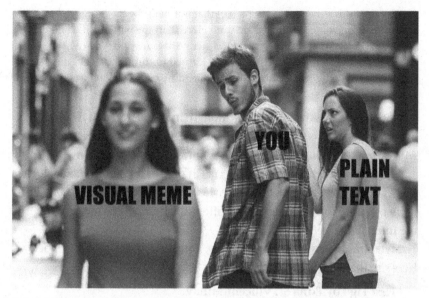

Figure 1.2
A visual meme that comments on the seductive power of visual memes. Credit to
Antonio Guillem for base image; reproduced under license from Shutterstock.

transparent: plain text maps to the underappreciated girlfriend, while a visual
meme maps to the attractive stranger.

Turning back to language, we find hosts of metaphors that depend on
analogical comparisons. Here's an analogical metaphor from an article in
the *Economist*, in the form of a witty remark: "Unity among the nations of
Europe is like a French *soufflé*. First comes the impressive puff, then, inexo-
rably, a graceless sagging as the dish is tested by time and cutlery. Both the
diplomat and the diner are then left wondering whether the whole thing
was worth whipping up in the first place."[14] While overtly commenting on
European unity, the comparison manages to slip in subtle digs at both France
(one of the most important, and most cuisine conscious, nations of Europe)
and diplomats (who at least by stereotype spend much of their time at fancy
formal dinners).

Metaphors can, of course, elicit a wide range of emotional responses, of
which humor is but one. Here's Ernest Hemingway's poignant characterization of F. Scott Fitzgerald in later life:

His talent was as natural as the pattern that was made by the dust on a butterfly's wings. At one time he understood it no more than the butterfly did and did not know when it was brushed or marred. Later he became conscious of his damaged wings and of their construction and he learned to think and could not fly anymore because the love of flight was gone and he could only remember when it had been effortless.[15]

Notice how this metaphor does more than map Fitzgerald to a butterfly: it subtly blends the two so that we have a great but fading writer melded with a beautiful but fragile insect—a butterfly that has learned to think and therefore suffer. Also notice that (as in many metaphors and analogies) the source is not simply an "off the shelf" analog retrieved from memory. Rather, Hemingway has carefully crafted this human-like butterfly to "fit" the intended target.

Metaphor, often based on analogy, finds a natural home in poetry.[16] Here's a small but evocative example:

"First Fig" by Edna St. Vincent Millay
My candle burns at both ends;
   It will not last the night;
But ah, my foes, and oh, my friends–
   It gives a lovely light![17]

A simple mapping—the poet is a candle burning quickly. Her life may be short, but she lives it to the fullest, despite whatever foe or friend (why that order?) may think. For a reader who knows something about Millay's life, the poem might be seen as an allusion to her bisexuality; and her sudden death at a relatively young age seems to add an eerie aura of prescience. But the "creative vagueness" of the metaphor allows each reader the possibility of arriving at their own individual interpretation.

Doing Things with Analogies

Now that we have a diverse set of analogies to compare and contrast, we can step back and ask again: What are they used for? Our examples are all *functional* analogies—they serve a purpose beyond simply "solving an analogy problem" for its own sake. An analogical reminding simply lets us notice that two different situations, despite their separation in time and space, are actually similar somehow—a curious connection that might trigger deeper reflection on what the commonalities mean. We have examples of the use of analogy in the *generation* of plausible hypotheses and innovative inventions, *prediction* of future (or unobservable) properties and events, and the *explanation* of novel or difficult concepts (particularly those involving science and math). Analogies are used to guide *decision-making*, both in the formal setting of law courts and in other professions (economics, politics, medicine) and in everyday life.[18] A close cousin of decision-making is *persuasion*, especially by rational *argument*—calling attention to a compelling analogy can sometimes change peoples' minds about what action should be taken. The special properties of visual perception make graphs, pictures, and other types of images particularly effective as source analogs for more abstract concepts, especially those that depend on quantitative relationships. Because analogies involve an element of incongruity—two things are treated as if they were the same, while we remain aware that they're actually distinct and different—they lend themselves to making *jokes*. Particularly when couched as literary *metaphors*, analogical comparisons can evoke nuanced understanding coupled with emotional impact. At larger textual scales, such as entire stories, analogies become *allegories* in which one set of events stands for or is interpreted in terms of another. It has been argued, for example, that the author of the Gospel of Matthew structured the story in a way that emphasizes parallels between the life of Jesus and that of Moses.[19]

Across its varied functions, an analogy uses a source to help understand a target: on the basis of some initial similarities, additional ones are found or created. I find the metaphor of *superimposition* to be helpful: the source is superimposed on the target, often after some adjustments to improve their "fit" to one another. Our conception of each analog (but especially the target) is likely to change when viewed through the lens of the other—some aspects are foregrounded, others set aside, and new ones added.

Functional analogies come in two broad varieties (and some analogies exhibit aspects of both). An *evidential* analogy offers evidence regarding the truth of an analogical inference with respect to the external world (or some formal system such as math) or regarding its consistency with some moral or legal code. An *evocative* analogy offers a subjective point of view that is meant to evoke a response (perhaps an idea, often tinged with emotion), but it doesn't provide substantive evidence for an inference and is not meant to be seriously questioned or verified. The analogy between sound and water waves is evidential—it's an imperfect analogy, but it aimed to support a scientifically sound theory of light, which makes testable predictions. When the inferred concept of "ether" failed its experimental test, that analogical conjecture was cast aside. In contrast, the metaphor of a fading writer as an injured butterfly is evocative—it provides a point of view with intellectual and emotional overtones, but it's more a comment than an explanation or prediction. An evidential analogy suffers if the mapping is ambiguous; an evocative analogy (often a metaphor) may generate new insights by merging multiple mappings. In somewhat different ways, evidential and evocative analogies can both be used for persuasion.

Even evidential analogies at best lead to plausible conjectures, not deductive certainties. Philosophers argue about whether analogical reasoning should be considered a form of *induction* (reasoning from the particular to the general) or *abduction* (using established knowledge to understand something novel). Reasoning with an evidential analogy probably involves a combination of these two logical processes, both of which deal with reasoning under uncertainty.[20] By abduction, the source analog can generate inferences about the target; then by induction, the two analogs can be used together to form a *schema*—a representation of a new category that captures commonalities linking the source and target.[21] If further examples are encountered that fit the emerging schema, the reasoning process will shift from full-blown analogy between a source and target to recognition that a new target case belongs to the same category as previous ones. In later chapters, we'll consider more carefully how analogy can provide the seed for learning a more abstract schema.

The analogies we've considered generally relate analogs drawn from domains that on the surface seem quite different—sound and light, fish and suction cups, European unity and a *soufflé*. Analogies can also be drawn between situations that appear more similar. When the analogs are drawn from similar domains, they are more likely to share *causal* relations (which, as we will see in chapter 3, serve as the backbone of evidential analogies). For example, a new political crisis may share causal relations with some prior historical episode.[22] But paradoxically, sometimes distant analogies may provide clearer explanations than near ones, and they may be more likely to trigger creative solutions to problems. If we don't understand a target well, then it's quite likely we also won't understand a very similar source—a distant source analog that we *do* understand may have more to offer. Of course, a deep problem is how to decide what similarities—and what differences—are actually important in deciding whether or not an analogy is likely to be useful.

We left *Hamlet* and *The Lion King* dangling with the dubious status of a flawed analogy. Did this analogy have a discernable function? Was the Disney movie actually based on *Hamlet*? Not according to its codirectors, Roger Allers and Rob Minkoff.[23] The film was under development for six years before its release in 1994 and was initially conceived as a kind of "*Bambi* in Africa" (a very different analogy!). But the emerging plot seemed quite original, to the extent that the writers felt a need to anchor it to something familiar. Here's an interesting problem for a creative work—if it's *too* original, it may not appeal to a mass audience. The early version shared a couple of plot points with *Hamlet* (notably, the pivotal death of a father). Then at a project meeting, someone pointed out a resemblance to *Hamlet*. Others responded favorably, and from that point the story evolved to take on additional parallels. Of course, no one at Disney thought that parents would take their kids to watch a big-screen tragedy of blood! On the other hand, with a bit of deft marketing to call attention to the Shakespearean connection, parents might be more likely to take in the movie themselves—the classic recipe for a successful family movie. Funny animals, singing and dancing, plus a sprinkle of Will's classic—the result was Disney magic! There's a lesson here: an imperfect analogy can be much more useful than a gory isomorphism.

2   Relations between Things

Contemplate not *things* only, but likewise and chiefly the *relations* of things.[1]
—Samuel Taylor Coleridge

Suppose you're looking at two stationary balls, one red and the other green, with some distance between them. Now the red ball moves in a straight line until it reaches the green one, at which point the red ball stops moving and the green one starts to move along the same trajectory. When shown a simple movie of this scene, people reliably report that the red ball has *caused* the green one to move. Between two things, something has been added—a *relation* connecting them.

Now suppose you see a blue and a yellow triangle, both stationary, some distance apart. The blue triangle begins to move in a straight line toward the yellow one. Before blue reaches yellow, yellow begins to quickly move away from blue in a random direction, then stops. Blue changes course to again approach yellow, which again moves quickly away, then stops. This sequence repeats a few times. When shown this movie, people often report that the two triangles are both *alive*, that blue *wants to catch* yellow, and yellow *wants to escape from* blue. Between two things, a *pattern of relations* has been added, which changes how the things themselves are interpreted.[2]

These examples are particularly striking because they show how human perception can operate on minimal displays of objects in motion and generate impressions of abstract relations and properties, like *cause* and *alive*. Moreover (when the input is a movie showing an animation), these relations don't actually exist in the world—pixels displayed on a screen don't cause anything, and they aren't alive. In these cases, the relations we perceive only exist in the mind of the observer. Of course, we have good reasons to believe the external world is "real," but we know it through our *mental representations* of it. Seeing an analogy won't change the external world—it will just change your mental representation of it (which might lead *you* to change the world).

The human mind comes with a repertoire of types of concepts it can think about.[3] What is a "thing" anyway? A thing seems to be some sort of object, somehow bounded so as to be potentially identifiable in some way—perhaps by pointing it out with a finger, or by giving it a name, or at least a verbal description. Balls and triangles are certainly things, as are apples and aardvarks. But beyond physical objects, people just keep making up new "things"—gratitude, meditation, quarks, black holes, the multiverse. We love to talk about things that have no real names, and the vaguest of boundaries. "Things are looking up," someone says; "Things are going to hell," replies another. What things are these? "Meeting you was the best thing that ever happened to me." "I read the book but couldn't get a thing out of it." "She just wants to do her own thing." It seems like a thing can be—any*thing*. But we also have that sardonic putdown, "Why is that even a thing?"

It seems as if humans have extended the notion of an object to encompass all kinds of things, which we think of *as if* they were somehow object-like. We can talk about the latest fashion trend, or post-capitalist society, as if that were something we could potentially point to or hold in our hand. This isn't thinking by analogy—at least not in the mind of a typical person discussing such matters—it's just the basic conceptual apparatus we all inherit as normal human beings. But if we step back and imagine how, on an evolutionary timescale, the human mind might first have added an extended "thing as object" to its repertoire of concept types, analogy may have played a role.

The poet Coleridge reminds us (in fact urges us) to also consider the *relations* between things. And indeed, it's hard to even imagine a mind devoid of relations. It would consist, I suppose, of a suite of "thing" concepts, each situated in splendid isolation—no individual thing would have anything to do with any other thing. But people can hardly avoid pondering the relations between things. Whenever we attend jointly to two or more things—perhaps because they're close to each other in space or time, or because seeing one triggers a memory of the other—we tend to consider how these things are related. Even noticing that two things are jarringly *un*related creates a kind of relation between them. Just today, a casual skim of news on the internet brought up a photo of a man paddling down the Mississippi in a carved-out pumpkin—a novel pairing to me, though apparently "longest journey by pumpkin boat" is already an entry in Guinness World Records. This candidate for "most surprising relation of the day" was immediately bested by a video of a girl casually walking an alligator on a leash through a Philadelphia park. WallyGator, billed as an "emotional support animal," is said to enjoy sleeping in bed with his owner. (And oddly, his owner reciprocates!) More than ever in the internet age, the human mind must be prepared to deal with unexpected relations between things.

The Core of Cognition

Contrary to the claims of its extreme enthusiasts, analogy is *not* the core of cognition. Rather, the ability to think about relations and analogies is a human edge built *on top of* more basic and evolutionarily older cognitive systems. Before we begin to seriously discuss relations and analogy, I'll set the stage with a quick sketch of core aspects of human cognition that I'll be referring to repeatedly. Readers with a background in cognitive psychology will already be familiar with these.

The core of cognition embraces *perception, memory,* and *attention.* Across all aspects of perception and memory, attention modulates the processing of information so as to focus on what is most relevant to the current context and goals. Selective attention often involves inhibiting less relevant information. Memory involves multiple systems, with a major division between *long-term memory,* which can maintain information in a passive state for indefinitely long periods, and short-term or *working memory* in which information can be actively manipulated. Long-term memory includes separable systems for *episodic memory*—memory for personal experiences and when and where they happened—and *semantic memory*—memory for ideas, concepts, and facts that constitute general knowledge. Semantic memory includes our knowledge of words and what they mean. Because such knowledge is preserved indefinitely (even into old age), it is sometimes referred to as *crystallized intelligence.* Both episodic and semantic memory involve maintaining knowledge of relations, and both provide inputs that support analogical reasoning.

Analogical processing requires the active manipulation of relations, and hence depends on working memory and attentional processes that modulate it. Working memory is critical to what are termed *executive functions*—core components of cognition required for explicit thinking. These components include the ability to hold multiple pieces of information in working memory at the same time, the ability to focus attention on what is important to a task while inhibiting salient but task-irrelevant information, and also the ability to shift attention as needed. Executive functions largely depend on neural networks with major hubs in subareas of the prefrontal cortex.[4] We use these functions every day to learn, work, and manage daily life. Individual differences in executive functions underlie what is termed *fluid intelligence*—the ability to reason using novel information. Analogy is a prime example of fluid intelligence in operation, as the process requires holding source and target analogs (including the relations involved in each) in working memory while performing systematic comparisons. Because the capacity of working memory is limited, the complexity of the analogies people can grasp is also bounded.

At the neural level, these core components of cognition are supported by partially dissociable networks. As we will explore further, analogy depends on coordinated activity involving a constellation of cognitive processes.

Relations as the Core of Analogy

Suppose we begin with a girl and an alligator—two objects. Then when the girl *walks* the alligator, something new is created—an *event* (an action unfolding over some period of time). If the girl *likes* the alligator, we have a *state* (a static situation that doesn't involve any overt action or change). In either case, a relation (for which a verb provides a name) transforms a pair of isolated objects into a richer concept in which each object plays a distinct *role*.[5] We can't arbitrarily switch around role assignments without changing the meaning (the alligator walking the girl would be a seriously different event!).

An *explicit* relation—the kind that in chapter 1 I placed at the center of our definition of human analogy—is one that we can treat as an object of thought. The relations we can think about, and sometimes give names to, are explicit. This fact makes it hard for people to imagine a relation that is *not* explicit. But animals (including humans) can *react* to a relation without necessarily being able to think about it explicitly. To take an extreme example, if your hand touches a hot stove, within a fraction of a second, you'll withdraw it (and probably yell "ouch" or something stronger). You can later reflect on the fact that "my hand touched a hot stove that caused pain," but the immediate reflex only required reacting to neural activity that *implicitly* encoded the relation between your hand and the stove. Similarly, many animals show an instinctive avoidance response to a *looming* stimulus: a symmetrical expansion of a closed contour in the field of view, which signals an impend-ing collision.[6] There's no need to stop and ponder the relation, "Oh, maybe something big is about to hit me." It's smarter to just duck.

The ability to react to implicit relations is extremely important for an ani-mal's survival, but it's not the basis for human analogy. More fundamental than analogy itself is the capacity to form *explicit* representations of relations: *a mental representation in which the relation is distinct from, yet bound to, repre-sentations of the entities it relates.*[7] For example, consider the spatial relation *on*, as in "The cat is *on* the mat." An explicit relation representation makes it possible to systematically link concepts to roles, thus keeping straight that "The cat is on the mat" is distinct from "The mat is on the cat." If features of the relation *on* were simply muddled together with features of the concepts *cat* and *mat*, it would be impossible to see the similarity between a cat being *on* a mat and snow being *on* a roof. An explicit representation of *on* allows the relation to be recognized as "the same" across situations in which very different entities fill its roles. More generally, explicit relations make it possi-ble to detect (and sometimes represent) relations *between* relations—a critical building block for analogy.

Consider the metaphor of a strong marriage. When they marry, two indi-viduals form a new union, in which each plays a specific role. At the same time, each maintains their separate identity as an individual. The marriage has a *relational structure*, defined by the way two individuals are bound together to create a new social unit. Notice that by calling attention to the similarity of their respective relational structures, I'm able to draw an analogy between a marriage (source) and the way explicit relations work (target). Without the relational structure, there would be no analogy at all.

From now on, I'll simply use "relation" to refer to the explicit variety (unless specifically talking about the explicit/implicit distinction). Relations are the basis not only for human analogy but also for a wide-ranging suite of abilities characteristic of humans. For example, we use relations to form *rules*. These range from the rules that define a game (try explaining to a four-year-old—or even a forty-year-old—what makes a player "offside" in soccer!) to those that underpin mathematics and logic. Relations carry information about roles, which underpin human cooperation to achieve mutual goals. ("You lure the enemies into the woods, where my warriors will set up an ambush. If there's too many in the enemy party, send someone ahead to warn us.") And of course, human language depends in large part on "linking expressions" such as verbs (*chase, remind*), prepositions (*on, through*), and comparative adjectives (*larger, less reliable*), all of which serve as names of relations.

Relations make mental representations *compositional*: a limited pool of elements can be recombined to fill different roles in many possible relations so as to express a much larger pool of possible thoughts. One of the signatures of compositional representations is *recursion*: the ability to embed a structure in another structure of the same kind. Human language (as well as music, mathematics, and other systems) allows recursive constructions, such as the center-embedded sentence, "The cat the dog chases meowed." Meaningful relations make it much easier to learn recursive structures and to generate novel examples of them.[8]

What makes analogy special is that it fundamentally depends on judgments of *similarity* between relations. The ability to respond on the basis of similarity for physical features, such as color of flowers, is evolutionarily primitive—bees do it, birds do it, we all do it. Once humans added explicit relations to their mental repertoire, we became capable of making more sophisticated judgments of similarity in which relations play a key role. Analogy, at its most basic level, depends on *similarity of relations*. Mapping—a process of *alignment* that identifies correspondences between elements of more complex situations—depends on *similarity of patterns of relations*. As we'll see in later chapters, cognitive scientists have developed a variety of computational models of analogy, most of which compute some version of relational similarity. Explicit relations provide a critical "human edge" separating our minds from other forms of biological intelligence.

Decomposing Mental Comparisons

Most situations can be thought about in terms of two different kinds of information: the features or properties of individual entities, and relations between entities. For example, a person has properties, such as their weight and hair color, and may also play roles in relations such as working for a certain boss or being a fan of a particular soccer club. When we think about mental comparisons, it's critical to distinguish two "pools" of similarity: *entity similarity*, based on overlap of features and properties, and *relational similarity*, based on overlap of relations that link entities. Let's consider some of the evidence for why this distinction is so important.

The process of finding the relation(s) linking specific entities is called the *eduction of relations*.[9] As we saw with the examples that opened this chapter, we can quite directly *perceive* a few privileged relations, such as physical causality. But at the cognitive level of *explicit* relations, more mental effort is required. Given a pair of entities, a person may think about how they might be related, using some sort of mental calculation (or possibly memory retrieval) to generate a relational link. This process will take time and attention. The entities must be processed first (or at least have a head start) before eduction of a relation between them can begin. It follows that when people make similarity judgments or analogical comparisons, entities will have an impact early on, whereas relational similarity will show its influence only after some delay. More generally, it should be possible to dissociate the contributions of entities versus relations to mental comparisons. Let's take a look at the evidence from a few experimental studies.

Rob Goldstone and Doug Medin performed a series of elegant experiments that demonstrated the time course of relational similarity.[10] They created simple pictures varying in different features, such as color, shading, or shape. As illustrated by the example in figure 2.1, the pictures varied in relational similarity, defined as a "match in place" (MIP), and also feature-only similarity, defined as a "match out of place" (MOP). In figure 2.1, the cross-like pictures consist of four squares with various shadings. When compared to the standard at the top, the four squares composing the left option share two MIPs (squares in matching positions that have the same shading) with no MOPs. In contrast, the four squares composing the right option don't share any MIPs with the standard, but they do share three MOPs (squares in *mis*-matching positions that have the same shading). The basic question that Goldstone and Medin investigated was whether MOPs and MIPs differed in their influence on perceptual judgments. Both types of matches would have equal weight if only entity similarity matters, whereas MIPs will be more important than MOPs if relations matter (because a MIP is defined by the relational correspondences between pictures).

The task the experimenters asked college students to perform did not overtly require analogy, or even a similarity comparison. Rather, the task was just a simple perceptual judgment: Are two pictures the same or different (ignoring spatial position)? The trials of interest were those in which the two pictures were not identical, so the correct answer was "different."

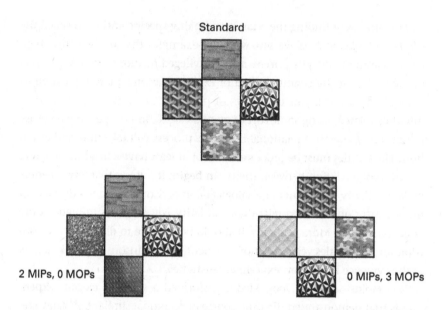

Figure 2.1
An example illustrating the distinction between relational matches ("match in place," or MIP) versus feature-only matches ("match out of place," or MOP). Here a MIP requires that squares with identical shading appear in the same spatial location (i.e., a matching feature in matching spatial relation). When compared to the standard at top, the left option has two MIPs and no MOPs, whereas the right option has no MIPs and three MOPs.

A general phenomenon in perception and memory is that two different items are more likely to be falsely judged as the same if they seem highly similar to one another. So, people's errors can provide a covert assessment of what factors make items appear "similar."

Goldstone and Medin created many displays that varied the numbers of MIPs and MOPs involved in the picture comparisons. In addition, they imposed different deadlines to control the amount of time people were allowed to process a display before having to respond (from one second to a bit more than 2.5 seconds). Using error rates (incorrectly responding "same") as a measure of similarity, both MIPs and MOPs increased similarity, but MIPs increased similarity more. Most critically, longer deadlines *decreased* the influence of MOPs and *increased* the influence of MIPs. At the longest deadline, a single MIP was always more influential than two MOPs. These findings show that relations are very important in determining similarity, but extra time is required to encode relations that depend on identifying overall correspondences between objects.

More generally, a wide range of evidence shows that when people judge similarity or find analogical mappings between situations, they make use of two distinct pools of information: similarity of entities (typically based on features or properties of individual objects or their parts) and similarity of relations. Many kinds of manipulations impact the relative impact of the two pools. A method developed by Dedre Gentner and her collaborators, called *cross-mapping*, has been particularly informative in teasing apart entity and relational similarity.[11] Figure 2.2 shows an example of the kind of stimuli used to create a cross-mapping. In this experiment, Markman and Gentner showed college students pairs of pictures such as these. After studying both pictures for a few seconds, the experimenter pointed to an object in the top picture and the participant was asked to point to the object in the bottom picture that "went with it." The critical object (always tested first) was cross-mapped: entity similarity supported one answer, but relational similarity supported a different choice. In figure 2.2, the woman in the top picture is cross-mapped: she could either correspond to the woman in the bottom picture (based on entity similarity) or to the squirrel in the bottom picture (based on relational similarity—both are recipients of food). Cross-mapping thus creates a competition between entity and relational similarity. Because people prefer one-to-one mappings (and because the instructions encouraged it), participants chose only one of the two rival answers.

Markman and Gentner manipulated what participants did or were told prior to making the mapping, and they identified several factors that affected the preferred choice for the cross-mapped object. In all conditions, the college students split, with sizeable numbers picking each of the rival responses (and almost never making any other response). When simply asked to make a choice for the cross-mapped object without any prior task, about 40 percent selected the relational match. But the relational match was chosen by over 60 percent of participants if they first evaluated the overall similarity of the two pictures, *or* if they were told they would have to find matches for three different objects. Both of these manipulations likely encouraged people to consider the relations among multiple objects within each picture, making the relevant relation involving the cross-mapped object more salient.

Figure 2.2
A pair of pictures illustrating a cross-mapping. Based on entity similarity, the woman in the top picture corresponds to the woman in the bottom picture. But based on relation similarity, the woman in the top picture (who's receiving food) corresponds to the squirrel in the bottom picture (also receiving food). Reprinted from *Cognitive Psychology*, *25*(4), A. B. Markman and D. Gentner, "Structural Alignment during Similarity Comparisons" (pp. 431–437), copyright © 1993, with permission from Elsevier.

We saw earlier that relations typically take longer than individual entities to have their impact. This isn't surprising given the basic fact that a relation requires entities to relate (whereas an entity can stand alone). Because a relation requires holding at least two entities "in mind" at once, relations place an extra burden on our limited working memory. When a cross-mapping is involved, any manipulation that "uses up" working memory (for example, having people hold some unrelated items in memory while they do the mapping task) tends to decrease relational choices. Simply making people more anxious (by leading them to anticipate a difficult math test afterwards) also decreases relational responding. The latter finding suggests one way in which anxiety can impair performance on math problems, for which relations are especially important.[12]

Several other factors can shift the balance between entity and relational similarity. If the objects are perceptually richer (e.g., a detailed drawing of a tree rather than a simple geometric form like a circle), then entity similarity dominates: there is "more" entity similarity when the objects are perceptually rich.[13] In general, as the number of feature-based (entity) matches goes up, the tendency to rely on entity similarity also increases. Conversely, as the number of relation-based matches goes up, the balance shifts to favor relational similarity.[14] In other words, the more each pool of similarity contributes to overall similarity, the more weight is placed on that pool.

One of the most intriguing pieces of evidence for separate pools of similarity comes from studies that directly compare judgments of similarity versus *dis*similarity (difference). Doug Medin and his collaborators showed college students triplets of simple line-drawn objects.[15] One of them (the "standard") appeared at the top; the other two (choices A and B) were shown underneath. Two groups of participants were asked one of two questions: Which of the A and B objects is "more similar" to the standard, or else which is "more different" from the standard?

In commonsense terms, similarity and difference seem like inverses. That is, if A is more similar to the standard, then B must be more different. But the experimenters carefully designed the stimuli so that entity and relational similarity were placed in competition. For example, object A might be more relationally similar to the standard, but B might be more similar in terms of entity features. The surprising finding was that participants were more likely to select the relationally similar but featurally different choice (A in our example) as *both* more similar to the standard *and* more different from it. It seems that asking for a similarity judgment orients people to make a more systematic comparison in which relations are highlighted, whereas asking for a difference judgment orients them to make a more piecemeal comparison emphasizing features of entities. This pattern reflects the fact that relations are more cognitively demanding than features of entities, and *difference* is more linguistically complex than *similar* (because *difference* is understood as a kind of negation: "not same"). When relations are used to make a difference judgment, these two sources of difficulty are combined (hence relations tend to be neglected).

One implication of all of these findings is that people can, and usually do, attend to *both* entity and relation similarity but with different emphases depending on the task and context. Moreover, the two types of similarity often interact. When a relation forms part of a more abstract schema, its roles may call for particular types of entities to fill them. For example, the conventional schema for the "assign" relation involves a kind of asymmetric power hierarchy: the less powerful entity is ordinarily assigned to the more powerful. Generally, objects get assigned to people rather than the reverse (so that students get prizes, rather than prizes getting students). It's also more natural to say that assistants are assigned to bosses, rather than for bosses to be assigned to assistants. Miriam Bassok and her colleagues gave college students math problems that depended on the "assign" relation.[16] The students found it very natural to use a source analog about caddies being assigned to golfers to set up an equation for a target problem in which carts are assigned to caddies, because in both cases the less powerful entity is the one being assigned—even though this mapping between source and target required a cross-mapping for "caddies." But given the same source analog, the students usually failed to set up the correct equation for a target in which caddies were assigned to carts—even though the "assigned" role had a straightforward object match ("caddies" in both source and target). The students naturally honored the role constraint based on the "assign" relation—assign less to more powerful—even when it contradicted the direct entity match.

But as we'll see repeatedly, analogy is seldom based *solely* on relations. In fact, cross-mapping is an unusual occurrence, deliberately created by experimenters to tease apart the two pools of similarity. In natural analogies, it's much more common for entity and relational similarity to go hand in hand, collaborating to support a "best" mapping between two situations. At the same time, the fact that so many factors can influence the propensity to form relations and attend to them suggests that people may differ in the degree to which they naturally focus on relations. As we'll elaborate in chapter 6, children undergo a "relational shift" in the course of cognitive development: a six-year-old is much more likely than a three-year-old to make responses based on relations.[17]

Relations and Intelligence

Given all the evidence that creating and attending to relations involves work-ing memory and related cognitive resources, it's natural to expect that people will vary in their capacity (or perhaps propensity) to use relations. Indeed, analogy problems have figured prominently in the *psychometric* tradition of measuring individual differences in human cognitive functioning. Tests designed to measure intelligence often include four-term or "proportional" analogies, in the form *A:B::C:D*, such as *hand: finger:: foot:?*, where the prob-lem is to infer the missing *D* term (*toe*) that is related to *C* in the same way *B* is related to *A*. The pair *A:B* plays the role of source analog, and *C:D* that of target. Proportional analogies were discussed by Aristotle,[18] and in the early decades of modern psychology, they became a centerpiece of efforts to define and measure intelligence. Charles Spearman argued that the best account of observed individual differences in cognitive performance was based on a general or *g* factor (with additional factors specific to particular tasks). He reviewed several studies that found high correlations between performance in solving analogy problems and the *g* factor.[19] Figure 2.3 shows a spatial representation of individual differences in performance on various cognitive tests, segregated by their general content (mathematical, spatial, or verbal). Note that numerical, verbal, and geometric analogies cluster near the center of the figure. This pattern suggests that the cognitive basis for analogy is highly general and can operate across very different problem content.

The very center of the figure is occupied by the Raven's Progressive Matrices test (RPM). Devised by Spearman's student John C. Raven,[20] the RPM requires selection of a geometric figure to fill an empty cell in a two-dimensional matrix (typically 3 × 3) of such figures. An example of this type of problem is shown in figure 2.4. Much like a geometric proportional analogy, the RPM requires participants to extract and apply information based on visuospatial relations. The RPM proved to be an especially pure measure of *g*, which is why it appears at the center in figure 2.3, with the analogy tests nearby.

Raymond Cattell, another student of Spearman, elaborated his mentor's theory by distinguishing between two components of *g*: crystallized intelli-gence, which depends on previously learned information or skills (especially verbal knowledge), and fluid intelligence, which involves reasoning with novel information.[21] Cattell confirmed Spearman's observation that analogy

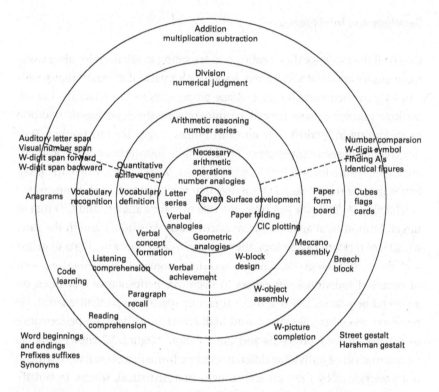

Figure 2.3

An idealized multidimensional scaling solution based on intercorrelations among the Raven's Progressive Matrices test, analogy tests, and other common tests of cognitive functions. Tests that appear close together overlap more in the cognitive processes they engage. The RPM and analogy tests cluster near the center, while tests more dependent on learning are positioned toward the periphery. The entire circle is divided into three triads based on the general content of the tests: mathematical (top), verbal (lower left), and spatial (lower right). From "The Topography of Ability and Learning Correlations" by R. E. Snow, P. C. Kyllonen, and B. Marshalek (Figure 2.9, p. 92); copyright © 1984 by Erlbaum.

tests and the RPM provide sensitive measures of g, clarifying that they primarily measure fluid intelligence.

Earlier I alluded to a *constellation* of cognitive processes that underlie analogy—it's a complex activity that depends on multiple factors. Being able to think with relations is at the center of this constellation, which also includes the executive functions. Of particular note, the ability to *inhibit* salient information is especially important in strategically shifting focus between entity

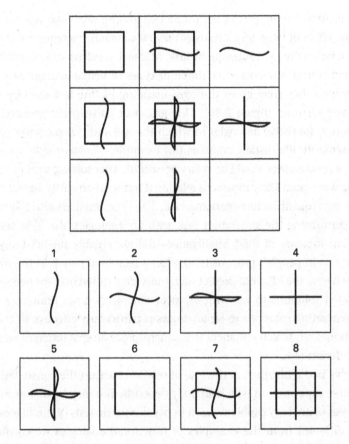

Figure 2.4
An example of a problem similar to those used in the Ravens Progressive Matrices. The task is to select the best completion for the empty square in the 3 × 3 matrix (lower right corner) from the eight options that appear below. (The correct choice is option 4.)

versus relational similarity. Another important idea to keep in mind: as people gain experience reasoning with particular relations and analogies, the mental processes at work may shift from fluid to crystallized intelligence.

People often think their intelligence (which is closely related to relational thinking) is fixed by genetic factors. But in fact, measured intelligence is the product of complex interactions between genes and environment, and is therefore malleable.[22] And relational thinking is certainly *not* fixed—for any particular individual, the task context can encourage or discourage reliance on relations. Besides the manipulations we've already talked about, there is evidence that having people perform a demanding relational task can have the side effect of triggering a transient *relational mindset*: a tendency to think more relationally on a subsequent task. Michael Vendetti and his collaborators had college students solve different types of verbal analogy problems, after which they were given the cross-mapping picture task used by Markman and Gentner (figure 2.2).[23] One group of participants generated the solution to four-term analogies in which the *A:B* and *C:D* pairs were drawn from semantically distant domains (for example, *blindness: sight:: poverty:?*, where a good answer would be *money* or *wealth*). After solving such problems, people were more likely to select a relational (rather than entity-based) match in the subsequent picture-mapping task. The experimenters also found that after performing the generation task with far analogies, the RPM test—an excellent measure of fluid intelligence—did *not* reliably predict individual differences in people's propensity to select a relational match in the transfer task (whereas the RPM did predict such individual differences for people who generated solutions to semantically near analogies). Such findings suggest that generating solutions to far analogies is particularly effective in evoking a relational set, which enhances subsequent processing of different relations in a different task.

We've had a first look at the role of relations within the constellation of cognitive capacities on which analogy depends. You may have noticed that the types of analogy problems used in psychometric tests of intelligence are quite different from the examples of functional analogies we considered in chapter 2—the analogy between sound and light waves has been left far behind. A four-term analogy problem, or an RPM problem like the one shown in figure 2.4, is neither evidential (it doesn't give any clue to how the real world might operate) nor evocative like a metaphor. The problem statement is *closed*, in the sense that all and only the relevant information is provided at the outset. Given the "rules" that define a valid analogy, the "correct" answer follows much like a logical deduction. Basically, the RPM and similar tests measure a person's ability to do a kind of relational pattern completion. We can call such analogies *nonfunctional*, in the sense that they serve no function other than the obvious—"solving an analogy problem" for its own sake.

Depending on your taste, nonfunctional analogies may strike you as interesting puzzles or simply a bore. As we'll see, there's good reason to believe that nonfunctional analogies tap some of the major cognitive processes that also are needed to reason with the functional variety. But functional analogies raise deep issues of their own. More realistic analogies are *open* in the sense that the pool of knowledge relevant to evaluating them is open-ended, so deciding what's *actually* relevant becomes a central focus. When evaluating a functional analogy—in particular, the evidential variety—what makes a similarity (or difference) important? That's our question for the next chapter.

3 What Really Matters?

Analogies, it is true, decide nothing, but they can make one feel more at home.[1]
—Sigmund Freud

About 35,000 years ago, on the walls of a cave on the island of Sulawesi (in present-day Indonesia), people painted what may be the earliest pictures still in existence—hand stencils and depictions of local animals such as the babirusa (a kind of pig). These artistic activities continued, in the same cave, for several millennia. Who were these people, why did they first become artists, and what kept their tradition going so long? The list of such questions about life in the long ago is open-ended. For example, how did ancient Britons haul huge stones more than a hundred miles to construct Stonehenge? What was their purpose in building this megalith? What was daily life like for the Moche people who inhabited Peru centuries before Europeans arrived?

It's natural to wonder about the lives of our truly ancient ancestors, who left us tantalizing but woefully incomplete material traces that beg for explanation. However (barring the invention of time travel), our questions will never be answered with real certainty. But several sciences—notably archeology, and in particular its branch called *ethnography*—aim to develop the best answers possible. Of course, any "best" answer will remain provisional, as new evidence may trigger novel and more promising hypotheses. And unlike physics, chemistry, biology, or psychology—but like astronomy, geology, anthropology, and history—it's virtually impossible to test hypotheses in archeology by running direct, controlled experiments. But scientific progress is still possible using the method of *abduction*, or *inference to the best explanation*.[2] And, as mentioned in chapter 1, an important variety of abduction is reasoning by analogy.

Analogy, of course, is based on comparison. A basic tactic in interpreting prehistory is to compare artifacts of the distant past to similar artifacts of the present (or the better-documented near past). We know something about how and why modern humans create art, so a reasonable explanation of prehistoric cave art is likely to start with the inference that a Late Paleolithic *Homo sapiens* was a lot like a modern human—the human mind has been what it is for a very long time. The stones that form Stonehenge are arranged so as to mark the summer and winter solstices. By analogy to the many known cultures in which the sun has been seen as a god, a reasonable hypothesis is that the ancient Britons worshiped the sun. From knowledge of what it would take to construct a modern version of the megalith, it can be inferred that the Britons had nontrivial knowledge of astronomy and geometry. These are sketchy and incomplete explanations, but more than idle speculation.

Here's a humbler but more detailed example of an ethnographic analogy.[3] At sites associated with the Moche culture (100–800 CE), archeologists have recovered many clay vessels. Some are exquisitely constructed and decorated; others are plain, apparently used for cooking and storing food. About ten percent of the plain vessels (but none of the fancy ones) bear simple but varied marks on one side only, which were incised deliberately before the pots were fired. These marks don't appear to be decorative. What was their function?

In the late twentieth century, it was noted that potters working in an isolated community in Peru, near where the Moche once flourished, have a similar practice. They often travel to make utilitarian pottery in other villages (so as to avoid the need to transport finished pots). After arriving at a new village, individual potters take orders and then multiple potters share the same fire to harden their pots. They first incise marks on each pot to keep track of which potter made it, and which order it fulfills. By analogy, it was proposed that the Moche culture also had traveling potters, who made similar marks for similar reasons. Later, ethnographers proposed an analogous explanation for potters' marks found on utilitarian vessels from the Oyo Empire, which flourished in west Africa for about two centuries (from the early 1600s).

The use of analogy in archeology—and in all the other sciences and mathematics, and in history, politics, and law—raises fundamental questions for cognitive scientists. What makes an analogy compelling (or not)? Is there some way to rationally debate the adequacy of a proposed analogy? These questions are most salient for analogies intended to be *evidential*, in the sense that the analogy-guided hypotheses aim to be true descriptions of the world or of a formal system. In nonexperimental disciplines such as archeology, analogical hypotheses are really "post-dictions"—but even though they can't be tested directly, they can still be evaluated in light of additional evidence. Analogical inferences are never guaranteed to be true descriptions of the world, but some seem more compelling than others. Freud's remark that began this chapter misses this middle ground—indeed, analogy can't decide anything with certainty, but the *right sort* of analogy can provide a degree of rational evidence for or against a conclusion.

Causal Relations as the Cement of Evidential Analogy

How should people decide whether to accept or reject (even provisionally) an inference allegedly supported by an evidential analogy? In this type of analogy, there's always an asymmetry: something is known about the source that isn't initially known about the target. In the most simplistic terms, if the source and target are similar in some known respects, and something else is known to be true about the source only, then the target may share that property. An immediate difficulty with this account is that the core concept of "similarity" is itself murky. It's been argued that any two things are similar in an indefinite number of ways.[4] One might claim a tractor is much like a coconut because both are solid objects, are found more than a million miles from Venus, are less tall than the Eifel Tower, and so on. But I will set aside such objections on the grounds that our concern is with the actual mental representations people use in reasoning—we can ignore hypothetical similarities that no one (who isn't a philosopher) would ever consider. The practical reality is that current models of thinking, both in cognitive science and in AI, owe much of their success to computations of similarity.

Still, "similar things will be similar" doesn't really get us far in understanding how to evaluate analogies. Let's take a couple of very simple cases.[5] Suppose you visit a remote island and encounter an example of a new bird species, the shreeble. This shreeble is blue. How likely is it that the second shreeble you find will also be blue? We can call the first shreeble the source and the second one the target. This looks like a problem of induction, with very weak evidence—from a single example, how can we be confident of anything? Still, you might reason along these lines: bird species tend to be fairly uniform in color (at least for each gender), which has something to do with genetics. So, I guess there's a decent chance (though it's far from certain) that the second shreeble will also be blue.

Now let's tweak the problem a bit. Suppose you encounter a sample of a new metal called floridium and find it burns with a blue flame. How likely is it that a second sample will also burn with a blue flame? On the face of it, this is another case of induction from a single example—neither weaker nor stronger than the inference from a single shreeble. But now you might think: any kind of metal behaves in a uniform way with respect to physical transformations like conducting electricity or changing when heated (something to do with chemistry!)—so I'm actually pretty confident the second floridium sample will burn blue.

In fact, people *do* estimate a higher probability for the floridium analogy than for the shreebles. Notice that the lines of reasoning in each case involve taking what began as a single undifferentiated concept—one shreeble or one sample of floridium—and turning it into a more complex mental representation involving various unobserved relations among internal parts. In an evidential analogy the mental representations are open—we're free to elaborate them with any knowledge we may have that seems relevant to the inference. In particular, both cases evoke the idea that something inside the object is *causing* its external appearance. And though each inference problem is based on a single source analog, the hidden cause seems stronger in the case of the metal than that of the bird, making the floridium analogy more compelling.

Causal relations have famously been called "the cement of the universe."[6] Whether or not causality is a principle of physics (a matter of endless debate), causal relations are central to how people think about the world.[7] We see causes as having some sort of *power* to produce their effects—*generative* causes make things happen, whereas *preventive* causes stop things from happening. We think of certain constant states of affairs as *enabling conditions* that allow causes to operate—the presence of oxygen enables lightning to start a forest fire. If a known cause occurs, we *predict* that its effect will follow—detecting a virus in a patient's blood, a doctor predicts its consequences. We also make *diagnostic* inferences by reasoning backward from observed effects to their possible cause—seeing certain symptoms in a patient, a doctor infers an underlying disease. And if we *want* some effect to occur, we're likely to try to make its cause occur—by manipulating causes, we aim to achieve our *goals*. Because we think of the world as governed by cause-effect relations, we seek explanations grounded in causal stories, and use those stories as guides for *making decisions* and *taking action*.[8]

In general, causal relations are only probabilistic—smoking causes lung cancer, but not always. And the strength of an evidential analogy will necessarily be limited by our incomplete (and possibly erroneous) causal understanding of the source. But despite this inevitable uncertainty, causal relations form the cement of evidential analogy. The centrality of causal relations in evaluating analogies has been recognized by (a few) philosophers and cognitive scientists who have considered the issue. Because causal relevance is inherently sensitive to the context—the reasoner's purpose in using an analogy—this is broadly considered a *pragmatic* constraint on analogy.

One of the earliest and clearest statements of the conditions that govern the credibility of evidential analogies was provided by the philosopher Mary Hesse.[9] She focused on the use of analogies in science, but her basic analysis can be extended to other domains, including law and mathematics.[10] Here's a generalized version of *three conditions for evidential analogy*.

1) *Prior similarity*. Corresponding elements of the source and target should be similar to some degree prior to considering the analogical argument.

2) *Causal overlap*. (a) Causal relations link known aspects of the source to the outcome of interest, (b) at least some of the source elements involved in these causal relations correspond to known elements of the target, and (c) there's a basis for believing the causal relations in the target are of the same general type as those in the source.

3) *Causal differences*. Any inference transferred from source to target must be adjusted to take account of known causal differences (i.e., a relevant causal factor in the source that's absent in the target, or a new causal factor present in the target but absent in the source).

Let's apply these conditions to think about the ethnographic analogies used to interpret ancient pottery marks, starting with the analogy from modern Peru to the unexplained marks on Moche pottery. (1) Prior similarity is strong—potters map to potters, pots to pots, marks to marks. (2) Causal overlap is at least credible: (a) we have definite knowledge of the causal story for the modern source analog; (b) potters, pots, and marks are present in both analogs; (c) human problems and their solutions are likely to involve similar causes; and, more specifically, shared geography and possible cultural transmission across many generations suggest that the same causes of pottery marks may have been present in the Moche culture as for indigenous potters of modern Peru. (3) No obvious causal differences are apparent. The further analogy from the Peruvian pottery marks to those of the Oyo in Africa has much the same basis for support, except there's no apparent causal pathway for cultural transmission, weakening the analogical inference.

Causal relations increase the credibility of an evidential analogy beyond the mere observation that certain aspects of the source occurred together along with the outcome of interest. People grasp that causality is more than association (although patterns of cooccurrence play an important role in establishing a link between a possible cause and effect). And a causal relation between cause and effect is more than just a temporal sequence. We expect a cause to precede (or at least be simultaneous with) its effect. But we don't believe a falling barometer is the cause of a subsequent storm—small changes in human artifacts are not the kind of thing that can trigger large atmospheric events (a violation of condition 2c). Experiments have shown that people judge an analogical inference to be more probable if it's supported by a match between stated causal relations in the source and target, as compared to a match based on the weaker relation *temporally prior*.[11]

A commonsensical prediction (that can be derived from virtually all computational models of analogy!) is that the more similar a source and target are, the stronger any analogical inference must be. However, experiments that Hee Seung Lee and I conducted showed that this prediction fails when causal differences (condition 3) are present.[12] Suppose a source has three causes—two generative and one preventive—and a certain effect occurs. In other words, the two generative causes combine to produce the effect *despite* the preventive cause (like a disease that breaks through despite vaccination). If a target analog shares all three causes, people agree that it's more similar to the source than is a different target sharing only the two generative causes. But people believe that dropping the preventive cause from the target makes the analogous outcome *more* probable (a person might come down with a disease despite vaccination, but failing to get vaccinated makes it even more likely)—even though source-target similarity is reduced.

One of the most striking illustrations of the centrality of causal relations in evidential analogy involves an important distinction drawn in biology between what is termed *homology* and *analogy*.[13] (I will keep using italics here to make it clear that *analogy* in biology is distinct from analogy in general—in fact, *homology* and *analogy* are both varieties of analogy!). Very roughly, organs in different species are *homologous* when they correspond in position and connections relative to the whole organism, regardless of whether they serve the same or different functions. For example, a bat's wing is *homologous* to a human hand. In contrast, organs are *analogous* when they have the same function, regardless of whether they're *homologous*—a bat's wing is *analogous* to a bird's wing. A *homology* is thus an analogy based on structure, whereas an *analogy* is an analogy based on function. In terms of standard analogical mapping, *homology* and *analogy* are simply different ways of using shared relations to define correspondences—neither is inherently preferable. But when considered as evidential analogies, *homology* yields far more compelling inferences about properties of organisms than does *analogy* because structural correspondences have a more direct connection to evolution—bats are more closely related to humans (a fellow mammal) than to birds. In other words, there's a strong causal basis (common ancestry and shared developmental mechanisms) for inferences drawn from mappings based on *homology*; inferences based on *analogy* tend to be weaker.

Prior similarity (condition 1) can include not only "obvious" perceptual features but also more abstract features associated with relational roles. This condition on analogy captures the intuition that near analogies are more likely to share causal structure (dovetailing with condition 2c, which requires that the causal relations in source and target be plausibly of the same type). Continuing with biological examples, a new drug is likely to be first tested on mice (rather than say, turtles) because there's good evidence that mouse physiology is similar in relevant causal respects to that of humans. But before a drug is approved for use with human patients, a follow-up study with human participants is usually required—human trials ensure a closer match of causal factors.

Condition 2c might also be termed the "not-just-a-metaphor" requirement. Recall that an evidential analogy aims not only to suggest a possible hypothesis but to provide some preliminary evidence that the hypothesis is (at least approximately) correct. An analogy such as that between sound and light waves is evidential because the same kind of causal structure (wave motion) operates in both. And indeed, this analogy guided seventeenth-century scientist Christiaan Huygens in developing the wave theory of light.[14] In contrast, many analogies used to teach scientific concepts are basically metaphors—the source and target can be mapped coherently, but they don't share the same type of causal basis. For example, biology teachers often use the operation of a factory as a source analog to explain the structure and functions of a cell. But no one would think that the way a factory works counts as evidence to confirm how a cell operates—the underlying causes are not the same type.

Even the famous Rutherford-Bohr analogy, which uses the solar system as a source for the atom (a standard example for cognitive scientists talking about analogy), is more evocative than evidential. Rutherford apparently offered the analogy "after the fact" to explain the new conception of atomic structure he had already developed on the basis of experimental evidence. And indeed, the underlying force that keeps planets revolving around the sun (gravity) is not the same type that keeps electrons revolving around the nucleus (electromagnetic force). An evocative analogy, often using a source quite dissimilar from the target, can be a fruitful source of hypotheses and explanations. To echo Freud, any good analogy can make us feel at home in unfamiliar territory. But we don't gain confidence in a new drug by running metaphorical trials.

The relation between metaphor and analogy is complex, as I'll explain more fully in chapter 7. In calling condition 2c the "not-just-a-metaphor" requirement, I may well be accused of slighting the impact of metaphor. George Lakoff, Mark Johnson, and others have argued that some metaphors are so foundational that the source seems to almost define the target.[15] Examples include "life is a journey," "time is motion," and "emotion is temperature." In addition to being evocative, such metaphors might be construed as providing evidence about objective facts—a person might well believe that life really *is* a journey and conclude that it involves (for example) movement toward an intended destination.

It is certainly true that such foundational metaphors shape the way we think about the target concepts. But to be coldly objective, I question whether the fact that we talk about life as being a journey actually counts as evidence about the nature of the world. If life were really a journey in all relevant causal respects, we would cheerfully travel from youth to old age, knowing that at any moment we could decide to turn around and retrace our steps back to youth. Alas, life doesn't work that way, and the metaphor provides neither causal force nor magic to change anything. Moreover, I doubt that everyone sees their life as a journey. Many a poor serf has been born in some hamlet, passed their short life laboring at their lord's command, and died there—never imagining they had been on any sort of journey, either literal or metaphorical.

In denying that metaphors count as evidential analogies, I certainly do not mean to imply that they do not often have real-world impact. A person who believes that life is a journey may be more likely to set a long-term goal for themselves—their personal destination—and work to achieve it. Evocative metaphors have the power to shape concepts in ways that guide decisions and actions. For example, a politician might characterize urban poverty as a "blight"—a metaphor that favors taking actions to contain or even eliminate impacted neighborhoods, rather than to provide economic and social support for their residents.[16] But the power to persuade does not constitute actual evidence of how the world works. A literal blight is a plant disease caused by certain fungi. The causes of urban poverty are surely complex, but even more surely are not of the same type as the causes of plant blight—condition 2c on evidential analogy is violated.

It would be a great mistake to imagine that causal structure is only conveyed by the obvious causal verbs, such as *cause* and *prevent*. If a ball *breaks* a window, or a son *persuades* his father to let him borrow the car, or a mudslide *blocks* a highway, or the Federal Reserve *holds* interest rates *steady*, a causal relation is apparent. Nor is it the case that causal relations (or words that name them) are all that matter to causal structure. Causal relations are the cement of evidential analogy—but the basic function of cement is to hold other things together! Causes and effects are themselves events or states, in turn composed of objects (including people) and their relations and properties. All these components of causal structure matter to evidential analogy. These components include other key abstract relations, perhaps most notably *category* and *part-whole* relations. In thinking about shreebles and floridium, it mattered very much that a shreeble *is a bird* and floridium *is a metal*. Indeed, it's been argued that we have the categories we do in part because they capture causal regularities: "Categories are what obey laws."[17] What it means to be "the same kind of cause" (condition 2c) depends on causal knowledge at the level of more abstract categories.[18] In the shreeble case, the relevant causal knowledge involved genetics and the internal parts of biological organisms. Any type of concept—relations of all sorts, objects and their properties, people and their goals—can play a role in causal structure, and therefore matter to evidential analogy.[19]

It's also important to remember that causal structure matters if and only if *it's connected to a source outcome in which we're interested*. In thinking about modern Peru as a source to explain aspects of Moche pottery, we can ignore all sorts of causal knowledge we may have about the source analog—that rain is scarce in the Atacama Desert so food can't be grown there, that the government is based in Lima because the Spanish conquistadors chose it as their capitol, that the popularity of Machu Picchu among foreign tourists is making the once-lost city congested. Our focus is only on a specific causal story that explains the cultural practices of traveling Peruvian potters. In evaluating an evidential analogy, causal relations are relevant just when they relate to the reasoner's *goal* in applying the analogy. Of course, sometimes the reasoner's goal is open-ended—simply to gain greater understanding of the target. In this kind of situation, all causal relations in the source are potentially relevant.

Taking Analogy to Court

An analogy, quite often, amounts to an *argument* for or against some conclusion. And one arena in which argument by analogy is routinely practiced—with immense practical impact—is in courts of law. As previewed in chapter 1, the outcome of a legal case may be determined by which competing analogy prevails—is a houseboat (for legal purposes) a boat or a house? How is a judge supposed to decide? Let's delve a little deeper.

An analogy used as a serious legal argument can be considered to be evidential, in the sense I've been discussing. But unlike the scientific analogies on which we've focused so far, a legal analogy doesn't aim to shed light on how the world "really is" but rather on how it *should be*. The judge (or jury—but I'll focus on the judge as legal expert) doesn't "predict" whether the plaintiff or defendant prevails in a case, but rather *makes it so* in the act of rendering a verdict. Other than taking the case to some higher court of appeal, there's no direct test of whether the verdict was "correct." And (in the American system) once a case has been decided by the Supreme Court, there's no further recourse—the argument has been finally decided (unless some future incarnation of the same court retroactively changes its mind, explicitly overturning its own earlier decision).

Nonetheless, the law (as an ideal, if not always in practice) aims for a collective quality of *coherence*—different decisions should not grossly contradict one another. This means that any particular decision can be justifiably criticized if it doesn't seem consistent with prior decisions (which would violate a principle of fairness). On this basis, judges and legal scholars often assess cases as being "rightly" or "wrongly" decided, even by the Supreme Court. While some judges sometimes are doubtless guilty of what is often alleged—deciding what verdict they want to render and then cherry-picking reasons to confirm their entering bias—most judges most often aim to decide *rightly*, based on the law (so as to maintain their self-respect and that of their peers). In this (admittedly loose) sense, an evidential legal analogy is one that aims to support a "right" verdict—the one that *should* be made so as to cohere with the totality of the law. The same extended sense of evidential analogy applies to its uses in everyday life to argue about moral or ethical questions. As I'll elaborate in later chapters, seeking coherence is a driving force in many aspects of everyday thinking, analogy included.

The role of analogy in the law has been discussed (and sometimes criticized) by many legal scholars, several of whom have influenced my own thinking about evidential analogy.[20] As background, let's assume the general context of the Anglo-American legal system. This "common law" system involves both statutes (written laws established by governing bodies) and *precedents*—the vast set of accumulated cases that have already been decided in courts. An important precedent is accompanied by a written decision, which spells out the reasons—the rationale—for the verdict that was rendered. The store of precedents—decided and "annotated" cases—serves to show how written laws (often vague or unclear) have actually been interpreted, and to fill in the gaps in areas where no statutes apply.

The legal system involves a hierarchy of courts, with the Supreme Court at the top. In general, a precedent from a court at any level is considered binding on all lower courts (and at least a serious consideration for courts at the same level). Suppose the Supreme Court has issued a decision creating a precedent (a source analog) and now a new case (a target analog) comes before a lower court. If the target is "the same" as the precedent (i.e., sufficiently similar in legally relevant ways), then the precedent determines the verdict for the target (the legal principle of *stare decisis*, "to stand by things decided"). Unlike the typical situation in which a source is at best suggestive of what we should infer about a target, an applicable precedent is decisive. This means (as is often lamented!) that a bad precedent can trigger a cascade of wrongly decided cases.

Can we adapt the three conditions on evidential analogy so as to be applicable to the law? What's the role of "causal relations"? All sorts of analogies and more general schemas (some based on scripted legal dramas we've viewed on a screen!) can make an appearance in the courtroom, and often causal relations in the standard sense are what matters. This is particularly so in arguments about the *facts* of a case. Suppose a husband is on trial for the murder of his wife. Did the defendant have motive, means, and opportunity? The prosecution shows that a life insurance policy covering the wife was purchased a month before her death, naming the husband as beneficiary—motive! The defense counters that the policy was purchased by the wife herself and the husband never even knew it existed—motive crumbles! The laws about murder are clear enough—the question is, "Who done it?" Creating a "causal story" in which the defendant is guilty (says the prosecution) or innocent (says the defense) is a standard tactic in courtroom arguments.[21]

Things get more complicated when we consider questions of *law*. There's no doubt about the facts of the houseboat case—it's a houseboat, we all can plainly see! But is it a *vessel* in the sense covered by the relevant maritime law? This is where precedents come into play, and with them an expanded version of the conditions on evidential analogy. Condition 1, *prior similarity*, remains essentially the same. The houseboat clearly has some resemblance to both houses and boats (and not much else), constraining the space of possible precedents. The other two conditions have to be expanded so that rather than simply causal relations, what matters is *relevance* relations—in particular, laws, principles, and facts that were cited as the rationale for the verdicts in precedents. Condition 2 therefore becomes *relevant overlap*, a match in aspects of the source and target that in essence "caused"—by serving as reasons for—the verdict in the precedent. Similarly, condition 3 becomes *relevant differences*—legally relevant aspects of either case that *distinguish* them, and therefore undermine the applicability of the precedent. Mary Hesse's causality principle, first proposed to deal with analogies in science, can thus be usefully generalized as the broader *relevance principle*.

By now the suspense is surely unbearable—what happened to the houseboat? Multiple lower courts decided it was a vessel and subject to the maritime law. But the Supreme Court thought otherwise: a 7–2 majority ruled that the houseboat was more similar to a house (it looked like a house and was lived in like a house) than to a boat. The aspect of the maritime law deemed most relevant was that a vessel is "designed to a practical degree to carry people or things over water"—which the houseboat was not. Verdict for the houseboat![22]

The application of evidential analogy in the law highlights several more general points. Analogies tend to come into play at a kind of intermediate level of theorizing—more abstract than specific details of a case but less abstract than a fully developed theory or set of laws.[23] Evidential analogies play a larger role in ethnography than physics (though in all sciences, evocative analogies are often used to help explain complex concepts). An evidential source analog typically conveys a causal pattern in which multiple factors operate collectively to bring about an outcome (or justify a verdict). Even if we have general knowledge about individual causes, this may not be enough to predict how multiple causes interact. A clear source analog conveys specific knowledge: in *this* situation, *these* causes in combination produced *this* outcome. If the target is similar in relevant respects, its outcome may also be the same or similar.

Perhaps the most important point to stress is that the conditions on evidential analogy don't constitute a "formula" for deciding whether or not an analogy is valid. Rather, they provide a roadmap for developing avenues of investigation in order to rationally debate the credibility of a proposed analogy. Are the source and target similar on the face of it? What really caused the outcome in the source? Are we overlooking relevant factors? Is there something distinctive about the target that undermines the analogical inference? And critically, answering these sorts of questions will usually depend on specific expertise. As Fred Schauer and Bobbie Spellman have argued in regard to law, a legal expert will immediately see the prior similarity between publishing a book, burning an American flag, and conducting a Unite the Right march through the streets of Charlottesville, Virginia—free speech is at play. The same expert will likely detect relevant similarities among true threats, depictions of child sexual abuse, fighting words, libel, fraud, and incitement of a riot—exceptions to the general protection of free speech. What it means to be an "expert" at analogical reasoning is multifaceted, but often a central component is learning what actually matters in a specific field of inquiry.[24]

This chapter has focused on how analogies "ought" to be used as sources of evidence. It's certainly not the case that people always take care to identify relevance relations, or to distinguish evidential from evocative uses of analogies. In fact, all sorts of analogical arguments slip into courtrooms, not to mention Senate chambers, political rallies, and social media. Sometimes evocative analogies masquerade as evidential. To take a controversial social issue, suppose someone claims, "Abortion is murder." The speaker probably means that (in their view) abortion is a very bad thing and should be illegal. But is their comparison simply an evocative metaphor—similar to "my boss is the devil," or "my kids eat like pigs"—or is it intended as a literal, evidential analogy with legal import? If the latter, we can immediately ask whether the speaker *seriously* means that if a doctor performs an abortion, that act constitutes "an unlawful killing of a human being with malice aforethought." If so, we don't need a new law to ban abortion—it's "murder in the first"—life in prison. And the woman involved—clearly a "major participant" in the crime—must therefore also be guilty (according to the law in many states) of felony murder. Such severe crimes and punishments probably seem extreme, except to the most fanatical opponents of abortion. As a general rule, it's unwise to confuse metaphors with laws.

As we'll see in later chapters, people don't cleanly focus on all and only the elements of analogs that actually matter to the outcome of interest. The general rule in human thinking is that available information is used to varying degrees, modulated by *attention*. Relevance relations constrain what people view as pragmatically important to their reasoning goals, and perceived importance is a major (though not the only) factor that controls the allocation of our limited attention.

4   Thinking through Analogy

We can't solve problems by using the same kind of thinking we used when we created them.[1]

—Albert Einstein

Suppose you are a doctor faced with a patient suffering from a malignant stomach tumor. The tumor is inoperable, and the patient will die unless it is destroyed. There is a kind of ray that will destroy the tumor if the rays reach it at a high intensity. But unfortunately, such high-intensity rays will also destroy the healthy tissue they pass through on the way to the tumor. At lower intensities the rays will not damage the healthy tissue, but neither will they remove the tumor. How can the doctor use rays to destroy the tumor while at the same time sparing the healthy tissue?

This "radiation problem" was introduced in the early twentieth century by the Gestalt psychologist Karl Duncker.[2] The crux of the problem is that it seems that the rays will have the same effect on the healthy tissue as on the tumor—high intensity will destroy both, low intensity neither. The key issue is to figure out how the rays can be made to selectively impact the tumor while sparing the surrounding tissue. Duncker recorded and analyzed peoples' proposed solutions. He found (as did later investigators who used the same problem) that people often reach an impasse—basically "stuck" without an idea that seemed at all realistic. This is when a "different kind of thinking" (to follow Einstein's lead) would seem desirable. An analogy, perhaps . . . but how is a good source analog to be found?

Mary Gick and I came up with a simple way to ensure that college students in our experiments would have a possible analog to the radiation problem stored in their memory. In advance of having them tackle the doctor's problem, we presented them with a few stories in the context of what was ostensibly a different experiment. For each story, people were asked to memorize it or write a brief summary. One of these stories was a potential source analog. For example, a version of a story called "The General" went along these lines:

> An evil dictator controlled a fortress situated in the center of a small country. Many roads radiated out from the fortress like spokes on a wheel. A general raised an army at the border, vowing to capture the fortress and overthrow the dictator. The general was about to send his entire army down one road to capture the fortress, when he learned that the dictator had mined each road so that although small groups could still pass, a large army would set off an explosion. The general then had a clever idea: he divided his army into small groups and dispatched each group to the head of a different road. Upon his signal, each group charged down a different road. All the groups passed safely to the fortress, where the entire army attacked the fortress in full strength. In this way the general captured the fortress and overthrew the dictator.

A few minutes after reading this story (plus a couple of irrelevant ones), participants were asked to solve the radiation problem. What we wanted to find out was whether people would notice that the General story—even though it involved a military tactic—could be a useful source analog for the medical problem. Figure 4.1 schematizes four major steps in the use of analogy to solve problems, based on this example.[3] The first step is simply to *retrieve* the source analog from memory and notice its relevance. The second step is to find the *mapping* between the analogs by aligning elements in a coherent way: the general becomes the doctor, the fortress the tumor, and the army the rays. Once the mapping is discovered, the solution to the source can be used to generate *inferences* about how to solve the target problem, making suitable substitutions of mapped elements to produce a parallel "convergence" solution. Just as the general employed small converging groups of soldiers to cross safely to the fortress and capture it, the doctor could use several ray machines positioned around the patient to direct multiple low-intensity rays at the tumor, simultaneously. The key idea is that each beam will pass harmlessly through healthy tissue, but the converging weak rays will summate at the focal point of the tumor, destroying it.

It's not easy to come up with this "convergence" solution (which is actually quite similar to standard medical practice for radiation therapy) without the aid of an analogy. Only about ten percent of the students generated this solution in the absence of the General story. (This estimate turns out to be

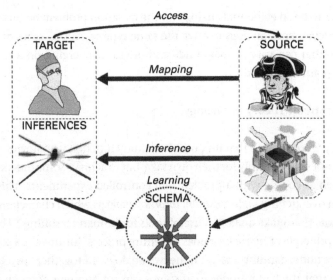

Figure 4.1
The analogy from the General story to the radiation problem, illustrating four major steps in the analogy process: *retrieval* of a source, *mapping* of source to target, generation of new *inferences* about the target, and *learning* of a more abstract schema based on the two analogs.

quite stable—Duncker found the same level of performance decades earlier in experiments he conducted in Germany.) When the students read the story just prior to working on the tumor problem, roughly thirty percent *more* of them generated the convergence problem spontaneously. That is, these students noticed that the General story was relevant and used it to solve the problem. When the experimenters followed up with a simple cue that "a story you read earlier might give some hints," a further thirty percent succeeded in finding the convergence solution. The overall picture is of a glass half full or half empty—a substantial proportion of people spontaneously used the source analog to solve the problem, though about as many initially failed to notice its relevance (yet often succeeded later when given a hint).

The final step in the reasoning process is shown at the bottom of figure 4.1. In the aftermath of exploring an analogy it's possible to *learn* something new, by forming a more abstract schema that captures the commonalities between the source and target. For our example, the "convergence schema" captures the idea that when a large force can't be safely applied to a centrally located object, apply multiple converging small forces instead. The General story turns out to be an evidential analogy for the radiation problem because (at an abstract level) both analogs involve the same type of causes—lines of physical force that can vary in magnitude and origin, converging on a centrally located point of impact.

Multiconstraint Theory of Analogy

Our early work showed that it's possible to study functional analogies—those that are not solved simply for their own sake, but to achieve some independent goal, such as coping with a problem—in controlled experiments. This work led to an overarching *multiconstraint theory of analogy*, which characterizes the key factors that make analogies useful tools for human reasoning.[4] The very general principle of *coherence* guides the entire process. Intuitively, a source is useful for understanding a target if the two analogs "fit together" psychologically, so that the better-understood source can act as a lens through which the less familiar target is seen as similar in ways that matter. Coherence is based on the psychological representations of the source and target, and it will reflect varying degrees of *attention* to different elements depending on relevance relations (as discussed in chapter 3).

A psychologically coherent analogy depends on three criteria, which together constitute the multiconstraint theory. First, the set of correspondences between the source and target should ideally approximate an *isomorphism*. This structural criterion itself has two subparts: each element in the source should map to just one element in the target, and vice versa (*one-to-one correspondence*); and if a certain relation holds between entities in the source, then a corresponding relation should hold between the mapped entities in the target (*structural consistency*). A second aspect of psychological coherence is *similarity*: people aim to find a mapping between the source and target that maximizes the overall similarity of corresponding elements. Both entity and relation similarity are taken into account (although for far analogies, relation similarity is necessarily the major guide). The third aspect of coherence is *relevance*: the mapping should include elements (often causal relations) that appear to be particularly important for generating inferences that would help to achieve the reasoner's goals. These goals may be specific ("How could we destroy this tumor?") or very general ("What causes cancer, and how might different types be treated?"). Relevance operates by guiding attention so that the more important aspects of the analogs receive greater weight in determining their similarity. Putting all the constraints together, *a psychologically coherent analogy approximates an isomorphism that maximizes overall similarity, based on shared elements relevant to the reasoner's goals.* In later chapters I'll consider how these constraints can be incorporated into computer models of analogical reasoning.

Over the past few decades, extensive research has contributed to our understanding of the major steps in the process of analogy. The constraints that make an analogy useful operate in each of the major steps, although their relative impact differs across them. The rest of this chapter provides a quick overview of what has been learned. I've organized it around the four major steps, but as we'll quickly see, these interact in important ways.

Retrieval of a Source Analog from Long-Term Memory

Perhaps the most striking finding from our early work was that people often fail to retrieve and use a potentially useful source analog drawn from a different domain of knowledge, even though it can be applied quite readily once its relevance is pointed out. In other words, the retrieval step is partially dissociable from the mapping step. Later studies using a broad range of materials (stories and problems) and a variety of retrieval-oriented tasks confirmed this "retrieval gap."[5] Far analogs that are relationally similar to a target are often missed, whereas sources with more superficial overlap (similar objects to those in the target) are relatively likely to be retrieved. But once a cue to use the source analog is given, people successfully make use of far analogs. Retrieval can be enhanced by manipulations that encourage a richer representation of the source. For example, the General story is more likely to be used spontaneously to solve the radiation problem if the story is accompanied by an animation, or if people are asked to act out the events in it using simple blocks.[6] Such manipulations likely add vivid perceptual cues to the representation of the source, while also focusing attention on the important causal relations.

Some naturalistic studies found that people more frequently recall far source analogs they had encountered in everyday life (rather than a psychology experiment) when the pragmatic context is a political debate that evokes a goal of persuasion about a controversial topic. However, in the latter studies, the relative number of near and far potential analogs actually available in memory was unknown. When relative availability is taken into account, studies using naturalistic paradigms also find that analog retrieval is heavily influenced by similarity of individual objects.[7] At the same time, experimental evidence indicates that relational similarity does impact retrieval as well, especially if it distinguishes a matching far analog from an otherwise similar competitor in memory.[8]

The retrieval gap is easy to understand given what we know about the normal operation of human memory, coupled with what we've learned about the two pools of similarity (based respectively on entities and relations; see chapter 2). As sketched in chapter 2, human memory includes two major systems.[9] Long-term memory holds our vast store of knowledge about events or episodes (episodic memory) as well as facts and word meanings (semantic memory), accumulated over a range of the last few minutes to decades. The content of long-term memory is stored in a passive state until it becomes active. Working memory (the active memory system) supports the executive functions underlying fluid intelligence.

Analog retrieval, of course, is simply one manifestation of the normal operation of memory processes: it depends on operations that activate source analogs in long-term memory based on cues (typically features of a target analog) that are the current focus of attention in working memory. The details of memory retrieval are complex, but we can get a general sense of what information will be retrieved from a given cue by assuming that memory operates according to a principle of rationality.[10] That is, the probability of retrieving a source is expected to be proportional to an estimate of how likely it's actually needed right now—its current *relevance*. Given a set of potential sources stored in memory, the probability that any one of them is the optimal candidate for retrieval given some target analog depends on the answers to two questions: (1) Is the source in question commonly useful (technically, the *prior*), and (2) Is it likely to be useful given the current context (the *likelihood*)? The prior will favor source analogs that have been useful in the past, so highly familiar sources will tend to be preferentially retrieved. A particularly well-established example is the prevalent use by children of the "person" concept as a source analog in making inferences about other animals and plants. (In chapter 6, we'll see that this tendency is often observed among comparative psychologists interpreting the cognition of apes!) Similarly, people understand new individuals by spontaneously relating them to significant others, such as a parent or close friend.[11]

The likelihood that a particular source analog is optimal to retrieve in a given context can be estimated by the similarity between that source and the current retrieval cues—that is, features of the target. This is where the distinction between the two pools of similarity comes into play. By definition, a far analog is one in which the source and target involve dissimilar objects (low entity similarity) but have at least moderate relation similarity. It follows that retrieval of a far analog will largely hinge on whether or not the shared relations were stored in long-term memory as part of the representation of the source, and whether the corresponding relations in the target are a current focus of attention in working memory. As we discussed in chapter 2, processing relations is in general more demanding than processing individual entities. A relation has to be encoded in terms of what it relates, whereas entities can be encoded separately. Processing relations takes extra time and processing capacity. It follows that a far analog stored in long-term memory may be missed if the person failed to encode its relations into long-term memory when it was encountered earlier, or if the person is not currently attending to the corresponding relations within the target. There is evidence that people who are particularly capable of controlling their attention—and also those better able to find remote semantic associates in memory—are more likely to spontaneously solve the radiation problem by analogy.[12] In addition, memory retrieval is competitive—retrieval probability is reduced if a strong competitor is available—so a far analog will suffer if a more superficial match based on entity similarity is available. In contrast, retrieval of a near analog will be more probable because both pools of similarity favor it.

The situation is quite different once a source has been selected and is being actively compared to a target. At this point, *both* analogs are in working memory, and potential competing sources have been set aside (not retrieved, or else actively inhibited). During mapping, information about both analogs can be actively processed, enabling eduction of relations and strategic allocation of attention to information deemed relevant to the reasoning goal. Basic properties of human memory thus explain the retrieval gap for far analogs. As we'll see shortly, these same properties suggest ways in which the retrieval gap can be reduced: by interventions that focus attention on relations when source analogs are encoded into long-term memory, and/or when new targets are encountered.

Mapping between Source and Target Elements

The process of finding a mapping, or a set of correspondences between elements of the source and target—a process often termed *alignment*—is fundamentally based on comparison of the source and target. The resulting mapping guides the generation of inferences. Often people's mappings can be inferred from their problem solutions—for example, generating the radiation problem implies that elements of a known source were systematically mapped to elements of the target problem. When analogies are used to provide explanations of a target, the mapping depends on the choice of source analog, which in turn constrains the inferences that will be made. For example, to explain how electrical circuits (with batteries and resistors) work, two common source analogs are water flow and moving crowds.[13] It turns out that water flow provides a good mapping for thinking about batteries (which behave like reservoirs) but is less helpful for resistors (serial and parallel resistors both map to impediments in a pipe, but that mapping doesn't illuminate the differences between the two resistor types). Conversely, the moving-crowds analog doesn't provide a good mapping for batteries, but it does provide a clear mapping for resistors (which can be viewed as gates). Depending on which source analog is applied, people's relative accuracy reverses between battery and resistor problems. In addition, misconceptions about the source domain (many people don't fully grasp how water flows through pipes) translate into predictable errors about how electricity behaves. In general, accuracy of analogical mapping and inference is always limited by how well the source analog is understood.

Analogical inferences thus depend on mapping, but, as we'll see shortly, the task of making inferences itself impacts how mapping is done. First let's consider the process of alignment as it operates when people are directly asked to state correspondences between source and target elements. The alignment process is generally straightforward in the case of near analogies in which the objects in each analog are highly distinctive, such as the "traveling potters" example discussed in chapter 3. But alignment becomes challenging when corresponding relations (as well as entities) are significantly dissimilar, when the two analogs each involve multiple elements, and when at least some elements have plausible alternative mappings when considered in isolation. The cases of cross-mappings that we looked at in chapter 2 have this character, as do mappings between relatively complex far analogs, such as the General story and the radiation problem, or water flow and electrical circuits. For novel and complex analogies, alignment involves what has been termed *relational integration*: the mental (and neural) work required to combine information from multiple relations that need to be considered jointly. We'll take a closer look at relational integration in the next chapter.

For now, I'll just give a global overview of how alignment operates, based on the three basic constraints that comprise the multiconstraint theory: isomorphism, similarity, and relevance. Some have questioned whether similarity is really essential to alignment, since it is possible to define an isomorphism without reference to similarity. Particularly in formal domains such as mathematics, similarity might be viewed as irrelevant. But as chapter 2 foreshadowed, similarity is in fact the driving force in the alignment process—sometimes even when math is involved. For many types of mathematical problems, Miriam Bassok and her colleagues showed that people (adults as well as children, across several different nations) are guided by *semantic alignment*: a strong preference to map similar types of relations between real-world situations and mathematical expressions.[14] For example, addition is a symmetrical operation $(x + y = y + x)$, which people can apply readily to quantities of symmetrically related concepts, such as tulips and roses (two types of the same superordinate category, flowers). However, people have difficulty applying addition to concepts that exhibit an asymmetrical relation, such as tulips and vases (tulips are "contained by" vases). In contrast, for the asymmetrical operation of division $(x/y \neq y/x)$, mapping difficulty is reversed: it's easy to divide tulips by vases (asymmetrical semantic relation), but not tulips by roses (symmetric). As a psychological process, semantic alignment is central to mapping, even in formal domains. In chapter 8, I will consider the implications of semantic alignment for teaching mathematical concepts.

Now let's consider more carefully how the alignment process works. The intuition underlying coherent alignment is that multiple relations can work together to establish an "optimal" mapping that couldn't be identified with confidence using any single relation in isolation. Here's a stripped-down example of how this works.[15] Let's suppose the source analog is a triplet of nested categories, where each pair is linked by the relation "is a kind of":

turtleneck is a kind of *sweater* is a kind of *clothing*

For our target analog, let's start with three category names in random order:

dog, mammal, beagle

What's the most coherent mapping of the target categories onto the source? Well, it's easy to see that the various pairs of target concepts are also related by "is a kind of," so we have clear similarity between the relations in the source and target. But this isn't enough by itself to determine the "best" mapping. For example, we might notice the fact that *dog* is a kind of *mammal* could be mapped to *turtleneck* is a kind of *sweater*—in which case *dog* maps to *turtleneck* and *mammal* maps to *sweater*. But then we might notice the fact that *beagle* is a kind of *mammal* could also map to *turtleneck* is a kind of *sweater*, implying different correspondences. When pairwise relations are considered in this piecemeal fashion, it's impossible to decide which mapping should be preferred.

As you probably already noticed, the "optimal" mapping requires arranging the target categories to form:

beagle is a kind of *dog* is a kind of *mammal*

The reason this one-to-one mapping is maximally coherent is that it makes all pairwise relations within the target structurally consistent with all pairwise relations in the source. Each analog forms a category ordering in which the middle term plays a "double role": *dog* (in target) and *sweater* (in source) are each a superordinate of one concept and an instance of another. No alternative mapping achieves full coherence. Even in this simple example, alignment requires relational integration: multiple relations in each analog are considered together to jointly determine the preferred mapping. One important factor that determines the difficulty of integration is *how many* relations need to be considered together. Graeme Halford and his collaborators have shown that difficulty increases with the number of relations that must be considered jointly. Human adults (without external aids) appear to be limited to processing just three or at most four relations at once.[16]

As we discussed in chapter 2, asking people to judge the similarity between two situations encourages them to find a mapping based primarily on relation similarity. Although the alignment process focuses on commonalities, it's important to realize that a mapping also pinpoints differences. In particular, whenever two non-identical elements are placed into correspondence, an *alignable difference* between them is also highlighted. Gentner and Markman showed that people find it easier to think of differences between similar concepts (e.g., *hotel* and *motel*) that are easy to map to one another than differences between dissimilar concepts (e.g., *kitten* and *magazine*).[17] For example, people are likely to agree that a hotel is usually larger than a motel, more expensive, and less likely to have exterior entrances to guest rooms from the parking lot. In contrast, people aren't sure what differences are notable for a kitten and a magazine—you can read a magazine but not a kitten? Magazines don't purr? In general, it turns out that people are particularly sensitive to differences derived from commonalities. This is one reason people who broadly agree on important issues—perhaps belonging to the same political party—are prone to get into arguments (sometimes heated) about their easily aligned differences.

Generating Inference about the Target

An analogical inference, such as an idea about how to solve a target problem, depends on first finding a mapping between the source and target, and then exploiting additional knowledge about the source (ideally its solution) to fill a gap in knowledge about the target. The basic inference process, sometimes called "copy with substitution," involves taking an "extra" fact about the source and creating an inference about the target by swapping the corresponding elements.[18] For example, in the General story we're told, "the general divided the army," a fact that doesn't directly correspond to anything in the statement of the (unsolved) radiation problem. By swapping mapped elements, this translates into "the doctor divided the rays"—an inference that might provide the seed for an analogous solution to the radiation problem.

Often, of course, simply "completing a pattern" by analogy isn't enough to actually solve a target problem—nature is seldom so kind as to provide truly isomorphic source analogs! Moreover, analogy is not blind to the content of its inferences. As we already saw in chapter 3, when partial causal knowledge is transferred from the source to the target, these inferences are integrated with whatever is already known about the target to generate new causal predictions. For example, if generative causes are transferred from the source, but a preventive cause in the source is "missing" in the target, the probability of the effect occurring in the target increases.

Whenever the source and target domains are not fully isomorphic, inference from an evidential analogy must confront its ultimate constraint: reality. Usually, the most that can be expected is for the analogy to provide valuable clues about how to proceed. For example, just how is a doctor supposed to "divide the rays?" The General story offers nothing useful. A practical solution likely requires further *adaptation* of the basic solution suggested by the analogy, using whatever additional sources of knowledge may be available. For example, the doctor might place multiple ray machines around the patient, each emitting weak rays. In general, the more adaptation is required—as degree of isomorphism decreases—the more difficult it will be to solve the target problem by analogy to the source.[19]

In some ways the power of human analogy is most striking when the isomorphic ideal remains out of reach (as in the imperfect analogy between *Hamlet* and *The Lion King*), and the reasoner is left struggling to find a fully coherent mapping that doesn't exist. Human analogy exhibits what is actually a general property of the brain and mind, charmingly called *graceful degradation*. To be degraded is unfortunate; to go down gracefully is admirable. Basically, as the "goodness" of an analogy decreases—as isomorphism slips away—people don't just collapse and fail to see any mapping whatsoever. Rather, they continue to bob and weave, trying to construct something sensible out of a suggestive though imperfect analogy. As scientists discovered important ways in which light doesn't behave as had been predicted by the analogy with sound waves—motion of light waves is transverse and doesn't require a medium—scientists revised the theory of light but didn't outright reject the analogy with sound waves.

Several studies have examined people's ability to reason about imperfect "tangled" analogies—ones that seem tantalizingly alignable but actually are seriously non-isomorphic. In a naturalistic experiment, Bobbie Spellman and I asked college students to answer mapping questions about people and nations involved in the first American war in the Persian Gulf, in which US president George H. W. Bush led a successful military intervention to drive Saddam Hussein of Iraq out of Kuwait (which Iraq had occupied).[20] Our study was performed in January, 1991, just as the war began. We asked our American students to suppose that someone said, "Saddam Hussein is analogous to Hitler" (a common claim at the time). Based on this statement (whether or not they agreed with it), the students were asked to map Bush and various countries onto people and nations involved in World War II. Our participants generally gave coherent mappings—most said that Iraq mapped to Germany—but sometimes disagreed on the best correspondences. Some mapped Bush to Franklin Roosevelt (the US president during World War II), and the present-day United States to the United States in World War II. But others mapped Bush to Winston Churchill (the wartime leader of Britain) and the United States to Britain. Each of these alternative mappings was coherent—leaders and their countries were usually mapped together. But people sometimes mapped one country to two (or occasionally even three) alternatives (e.g., aligning Kuwait with both Poland and Austria, early victims of Nazi Germany). It appears that isomorphism—the preference for one-to-one correspondences—can be a "soft" constraint, sometimes overridden when alternative similarities support different mappings for the same element.

Other studies compared people's responses on a direct mapping task with the inferences they drew when given a specific goal. Spellman and I created what may be the most tangled analogy ever used in a psychology experiment.[21] We asked college students to pretend they were successful writers of a new soap opera and that they were in court trying to prove that writers from another soap opera had stolen their ideas. To persuade the judge they were the victims of plagiarism by the other soap opera, they needed to predict what was going to happen in the next episode of the rival series—by extending an analogy with the events that had already occurred in their own plot.

Their own soap opera had four major characters, but the rival soap opera involved more, so the two sets were not isomorphic. In fact, the plots were created so that a critical mapping was four-ways ambiguous! In a nutshell, three types of relations were involved: professional (someone was the boss of someone else), romantic (someone was in love with someone), and inheritance (someone cheated someone out of an inheritance). Different participants were told that the next episode hinged on either the professional plot or the romantic plot, making one of these the *relevant* relation that was critical to predict the plot in the next episode. In either case the inheritance relation was not relevant in any obvious way. The stated plots were such that two characters in the target (the rival soap opera) could plausibly map *as a pair* to four different pairs in the source—that is, there were four coherent mappings for the target pair. If the professional relation was treated as most important, two plausible mappings remained; conversely, if the romantic relation was most important, the two alternative mappings remained. But if people also considered the incidental inheritance relation, then in each case a unique mapping would emerge as the "winner." This design made it possible to examine the degree to which the alignment process is sensitive to causal relations relevant to a goal (as discussed in chapter 3). The students were first asked to state which characters would be involved in the plot for the next episode of the rival soap opera (generating an analogical inference). Then in a separate task, for each of the four main characters in the source analog, the students were asked which character in the target made the "best match."

It turned out that the greater impact of the relevant relation was apparent in both the plot extension and the mapping task. In both tasks, the students usually picked coherent correspondences for the critical pair of characters. The mapping task revealed a clear preference for correspondences supported by the relevant relation but also was sensitive to the incidental relation (inheritance), so that one of the four possible mappings was most favored. The inference task (plot extension) produced an even stronger preference for correspondences supported by the relevant relation, but it was *not* sensitive to the incidental inheritance relation: one of the two mappings supported by the relevant relation was used to create the plot extension, but neither of the two was selected more often.

These results, in combination with findings from similar studies using tangled analogies, paint a general picture of how people cope with non-isomorphic analogies.[22] When simply asked to find correspondences, people place greater weight on relevant relations and prefer coherent mappings that are one-to-one. However, these constraints are "soft": less relevant relations are also considered to some degree, and sometimes one element is mapped to two. But when required to make specific, goal-directed inferences—increasing the need for coherence—people place a laser-like focus on relevant relations and base their inferences on one-to-one mappings (even if a single "best" correspondence has to be picked arbitrarily).

In general, we can think of the process of analogy as having three major "dials," each related to one of the three basic constraints. These dials can be turned up or down depending on task demands and a variety of other factors. With respect to isomorphism, one dial controls the degree of pressure to find one-to-one correspondences. With respect to similarity, a second dial controls the relative emphasis on each similarity pool, for entities versus relations (chapter 2). With respect to relevance, a third dial controls the extent to which information deemed especially important—usually because it's causally related to the reasoner's goal—receives greater attention. With the flexibility provided by these three dials, a person can impose strict criteria in applying an evidential analogy to solve a math problem, then "dial it down" to bask in the emanations of an elusive metaphor.

Learning a Schema

In explaining the typical retrieval gap in analogy, we ended with a hint—perhaps the gap can be closed, or at least reduced, by interventions that focus attention on relations. The most basic such intervention is: analogical reasoning itself! That is, the very process of drawing an analogy between two analogs encourages people to generalize the mapping they find, forming an abstract schema that serves as an explicit representation of commonalities between the analogs. Gick and Holyoak gave college students two source analogs illustrating the convergence solution (the General story and one in which a firefighter extinguished an oil well fire by using multiple small hoses to shoot foam at it from different directions).[23] The students were asked to compare the two stories and write down ways in which they were similar. Their answers were later used to assess how well they stated the basic idea of the convergence solution. After this comparison task (and a brief delay), the students were asked to solve the radiation problem, first without a hint to use the prior stories. Students whose written descriptions were coded as poor schemas that missed the convergence principle ("In both stories a hero was rewarded for his efforts") were no more likely to come up with this solution to the radiation problem than were people who received a single source analog (about 30 percent solved it). But among those whose descriptions were coded as good schemas, about 90 percent gave the convergence solution to the radiation problem even without a hint.

Other studies have shown that people will form schemas simply as a side effect of applying one solved source problem to an unsolved target problem, improving subsequent transfer to another far analog.[24] Additional manipulations that focus attention on goal-relevant relations can help to form more effective schemas. For example, Gick and Holyoak found that generation of a schema from two far analogs was improved when each story was accompanied by a direct statement of the underlying solution principle: "If you need a large force to accomplish some purpose, but are prevented from applying such a force directly, many smaller forces applied simultaneously from different directions may work just as well." An abstract diagram that highlighted the basic idea of using multiple converging forces also boosted transfer. In contrast, when only a single source story was provided, neither adding a verbal statement nor adding a diagram proved helpful. The opportunity to compare *two* analogs was critical.[25]

Interestingly, a schema generated by comparing examples can work "backward" in memory, making it easier to retrieve analogous episodes (including autobiographical memories) that had been stored *before* the schema was acquired. And somewhat paradoxically, presenting *two* target analogs (such as the radiation problem and another convergence-type problem) to be solved together can improve transfer from a single source analog. That is, two problems can sometimes be solved more easily than one—if the two can be compared to generate a schema, which in turn makes it easier to retrieve a source analog from memory.[26]

Comparing examples, and thereby forming a more abstract schema, constitutes a first step toward becoming more expert in solving a class of problems.[27] Comparison has been shown to guide schema formation in teaching such complex topics as negotiation strategies.[28] Although two examples can be enough to establish a useful schema, people are able to incrementally develop increasingly abstract schemas as additional examples are provided. Kotovsky and Gentner identified an important refinement of the use of comparison as a training technique. They found learning to be more successful when a series of comparisons was ordered "easy to hard," with the early pairs sharing salient object similarities as well as relational matches, and the later pairs sharing only relational matches. This *progressive alignment* strategy serves to promote a kind of analogical bootstrapping, using salient object similarities to help the learner find mappings between objects that also correspond with respect to their relational roles.[29]

As novices continue to develop more powerful schemas, long-term transfer in an altered context can be dramatically improved. For example, Richard Catrambone and I gave college students a total of three convergence analogs to study, compare, and solve.[30] After this initial abstraction training, the students were asked to solve another convergence analog from a new domain. Finally, a week later, the students returned to participate in a different experiment. After the other experiment was completed, they were given the radiation problem to solve. Over 80 percent of participants came up with the converging-rays solution without any hint.

The "big picture" is this: As a novice acquires expertise in a class of problems, the emerging schema becomes increasingly accessible and more likely to be triggered by novel problems that share its structure. The result is a positive feedback loop—the reasoner finds it easier and easier to spontaneously apply the schema to additional examples, improving retrieval, mapping, and inference. As the novel becomes routine, analogy elides into categorization, and the burden on fluid intelligence is shifted over to the crystallized variety. What began as insight has been reduced to common knowledge.

5 Analogy in the Brain

If the human brain were so simple that we could understand it, we would be so simple that we couldn't.[1]
—Emerson M. Pugh

Think back to the cross-mapped pictures from chapter 2 (figure 2.2), where an object (woman in the top picture) has two possible mappings: one based on entity similarity (woman in the bottom picture) and the other on relation similarity (the squirrel that is also receiving food). We talked about how various manipulations that encourage attention to relations make college students more likely to select the relational match. Other factors have the opposite effect—and the worst possibility is damage to the prefrontal cortex. Several neuropsychological studies (involving Barbara Knowlton, Jim Waltz, Dan Krawcyck, Bob Morrison, Christina Fales, Bruce Miller, and others, including me) examined analogical reasoning in frontal patients. We found, for example, that a degenerative brain disease impacting the prefrontal cortex results in an overwhelming preference for the entity-based match. Impairments in analogical reasoning have also been found in people suffering from schizophrenia, Alzheimer's disease, frontal strokes, forms of traumatic brain injury (all disorders that often impact the prefrontal cortex), and to a lesser degree, normal aging (which is often accompanied by diminished prefrontal functions).[2] On the other hand, analogy ability is generally spared in people with selective damage to the temporal cortex, those with Klinefelter Syndrome, and those with autism spectrum disorder (as long as the analogies are nonverbal in nature).[3] All of the latter groups show notable deficits in language processing, yet basic analogical reasoning is preserved.

Although there's no discrete "analogy area" in the brain, the prefrontal cortex—the area of the human brain that has undergone the most recent evolutionary change—is an indispensable contributor to analogy and other types of complex thinking. In this chapter I'll give a general overview of what is known about how the prefrontal cortex, in coordination with other brain areas, supports the comparison of explicit relations to solve analogies.[4] The work to date has focused on the process of alignment as it operates in non-functional analogy problems of the sort used in psychometric tests. These have the virtues (for research purposes) of being available in sufficiently large numbers and making it straightforward to vary problem complexity. People usually solve such problems quickly (within a few seconds), as is typically desirable for studies using brain imaging. The downside is that at present we know very little about the neural underpinnings of the many other processes involved in more naturalistic analogical reasoning, such as retrieval of source analogs from memory, evaluation of relevance relations, and formation of schemas. Still, the effort to link analogy to the brain is underway.

The last quarter century has seen an explosion of research on the neural basis of relational processing, combining the methods of neuropsychology (studies of clinical populations) and functional neuroimaging (noninvasive techniques to trace brain activity while a person is performing some cognitive task). Analogy is most directly dependent on the operation of a broad network of cortical regions called the *frontoparietal control network* (or sometimes the *multiple demand network*). This network has several "hubs" (see figure 5.1), mainly within the prefrontal cortex (PFC) and the parietal cortex, which operate together to direct attention and accomplish tasks that need to be broken down into sequential steps. The major components of the lateral surface of the PFC (ventrolateral, dorsolateral, rostrolateral) all contribute to this network, which roughly can be said to come into play when a person is thinking hard. The frontoparietal control network is distinct from other major networks in the human brain, such as the set of areas that support language.[5]

Individual differences in the frontoparietal network—how densely interconnected its major hubs are—have been linked to variations in measured intelligence.[6] As we saw in chapter 2, analogy is intimately connected to fluid intelligence, but of course it's not the entirety of it. John Duncan and his colleagues have argued that the frontoparietal network more generally supports *cognitive control*—the ability to take a complex problem and segment it into separate and more easily solved parts, while integrating the parts in terms of

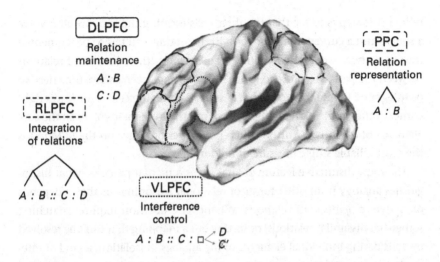

Figure 5.1
A schematic of major frontal and parietal brain areas (primarily in the left hemisphere)
that support representation and integration of relations, illustrated for analogical reasoning. Active representations of relations (e.g., *A:B*) are formed in posterior parietal
cortex, maintained in working memory based on the DLPFC (*A:B*, *C:D*), and integrated
to identify higher-order relations (e.g., sameness of the relations *A:B* and *C:D*) in rostrolateral PFC. Ventrolateral PFC is involved in inhibiting salient but potentially interfering
information (e.g., *C′*, a close semantic associate of *C*, might interfere with recognizing
that the relation *C:D* is analogous to *A:B*). Adapted from Holyoak and Monti (2021).

their interrelationships.[7] This broad approach—segmentation coupled with
integration—is characteristic of human problem-solving in general, not just
analogy. Many problems that arise in everyday life require setting goals and
breaking them down into smaller subgoals, an approach termed *means-ends
analysis*. To plan a cross-country road trip, for example, you might need to
consider subgoals such as earning enough money for expenses, getting time
off from work, finding someone to come with you, and obtaining a car in
working order. Each subgoal might be broken down further—having bought
a used car, perhaps it needs some maintenance, which requires getting it to a
mechanic, and so on. All of these "problem pieces" have to be held together
by their relationships—it's no good to get your car repaired but in the process
forget about the road trip!

An explicit relation requires representing the things being related, so relational integration has to be built on top of segmentation. Take a look back at
the example of a Ravens-style problem shown in figure 2.4. To make any sense

of it, a first step is to see that the three cells forming the top row all involve a square and a curved line—the form in the middle cell has to be segmented into these two parts. Based on this segmentation, the eduction of relations between the parts can proceed. Once relations have been coded, they need to be integrated to infer the form that best fits the missing cell in the lower right corner of the matrix. Solving this type of matrix problem involves all the core elements of cognitive control, which is why performance on the RPM test is the most reliable single measure of fluid intelligence.

The most distinctive feature of analogy as a mental process—what distinguishes analogy from other forms of relational reasoning—is that it depends on active *comparison* of relations. Whenever a decision requires matching somewhat dissimilar relations, or sorting out a mapping that can't be resolved by considering individual elements of the analogs in isolation, a kind of integration is required. Let's walk through the major hubs of the frontoparietal cortex as they would contribute to solving a slightly challenging verbal analogy problem in the *A:B::C:D* format. Pick the better answer: an *insect* is to a *bee* (*A:B*) as a *fish* is to a *halibut* (*C:D*) or to *water* (*C'*). Here a fairly abstract semantic relation (category and its instance) is shared by *insect:bee* and *fish:halibut*, but the foil *fish:water* creates a different but more salient relation for the *C* term. Choosing the analogous solution requires selecting the relation that makes *A:B* and *C:D* similar, while rejecting the strong competing relation, *C:C'*.

The hubs highlighted in figure 5.1 are based on evidence from neural studies pointing to a small set of regions (generally left lateralized) that contribute to relational integration. These include posterior parietal cortex (PPC), implicated in the representation of explicit relations (e.g., the category relation that links *insect:bee*); dorsolateral prefrontal cortex (DLPFC), which maintains relations in working memory to enable further processing; ventrolateral prefrontal cortex (VLPFC), important for interference control (in this example, suppressing a tendency to select the "attractive" foil, *fish:water*); and rostrolateral prefrontal cortex (RLPFC), which integrates relations by placing those that best match into correspondence (here, forming the valid analogy *insect: bee:: fish: halibut*). These regions are closely coupled, and some contribute to multiple processes. There are particularly close ties between working memory and interference control, to which both DLPFC and VLPFC contribute.[8] Several other brain areas support relational integration through more general cognitive processes such as semantic and visuospatial processing, as well as attention shifting.[9]

It's important to keep in mind that the frontoparietal network and each of its subregions play important roles in many non-analogical tasks, particularly those that require flexible thinking, planning, and solving novel problems. But although none of these brain areas can be considered an "analogy area," they each contribute to analogical reasoning. Let's take a closer look at each of these major hubs, and some of the evidence for their connection to analogy.

Relation Representation: Parietal Cortex

An obvious prerequisite for relational integration is the representation of individual relations. Eye-tracking studies of participants solving *A:B::C:D* analogies have found that a high frequency of saccades between the *A* and *B* terms early in processing signals the preferred strategy of mature reasoners, and is a strong predictor of success in solving analogies.[10] Establishing a good representation of the *A:B* relation in working memory is a key initial step in analogical reasoning.

The neural representations of individual semantic relations appear to be broadly distributed across multiple brain regions, including regions of the temporal cortex associated with semantic memory.[11] In the context of an explicit analogical reasoning task, the parietal cortex appears to play a particularly important role. The primary functions of the parietal cortex involve the representation and manipulation of information related to physical *space*. An intriguing hypothesis is that by virtue of its rich representational capacity, the parietal cortex provides a core substrate for spatial relations that serve to organize items in working memory. Many basic relations involve orderings and groupings, which lend themselves to quasi-spatial representations. A study of working memory involving a set of items structured by a grouping or ordering found that the task selectively activated posterior parietal cortex.[12] Parietal activation is typically prominent in transitive reasoning tasks, which require integration of comparative relations (e.g., Adriana is taller than Lily, Sofia is taller than Adriana) to infer a further relation (Sofia is taller than Lily). The pattern of parietal involvement (in conjunction with anterior frontal activation) is similar for transitive inferences based on physical dimensions such as height, more abstract dimensions such as expensiveness, and even nonsensical dimensions such as "vilchiness."[13] Such findings support the general view that many abstract relations are derived (perhaps ultimately by analogy) from spatial relations, and furthermore continue to depend on some of the same neural machinery.

In chapter 10 I'll discuss what might be called the *microstructure* of relations—how an individual relation between two entities may be coded in terms of more elementary features. This microstructure is the basis for determining how similar any two relations are. Just as two objects can be more or less similar (a cat is very similar to a dog, less similar to an iguana), two relations can also vary in similarity (the relation of a cat to a dog is quite similar to that between a table and a chair, less similar to that between a table and furniture). For both objects and relations, degree of similarity can be related to overlap of elementary features. That is, the representation of a concept is not a discrete symbol (like a word in English) but rather a *distributed pattern* over a set of features. Hongjing Lu and her collaborators (of whom I'm one) developed a computational model that learns distributed representations of abstract semantic relations such as *synonym* (e.g., *big:large*), *contrary* (*accept:reject*), and *cause-effect* (*accident:damage*).[14] This model predicts that the relation between *insect:bee* and that between *fish:halibut* will be similar but not identical. Each has a distributed representation that we might gloss in English as "category and instance" but that differ somewhat at the microstructure level. However, the relations between these two word pairs will be more similar than the relation between *insect:bee* and that between *fish:water*.

In a neuroimaging study, Jeff Chiang and colleagues used our model to predict patterns of neural similarity between the responses to different pairs of related words as they were processed in the context of solving *A:B::C:D* analogy problems.[15] Each problem was presented sequentially, with the *A:B* pair (e.g., *insect:bee*) appearing alone for a couple of seconds prior to presentation of the *C:D* pair. During the *A:B* phase, the model reliably predicted the pattern of neural similarity in posterior parietal cortex. Such evidence for parietal involvement in the generation and manipulation of active representations of abstract relations supports a general principle articulated by Barbara Tversky: "Spatial thinking is the foundation of abstract thought."[16] In at least a metaphorical sense, to say that two entities are related in a specific way is to "place" each item in some "position" relative to the other such that they can be "compared." Emerging neural evidence suggests that in the human brain, this description may in fact prove to be stronger than a mere metaphor.

Working Memory: Dorsolateral PFC

Relational reasoning depends on working memory resources, particularly to maintain active representations of relations that provide the immediate inputs to integration processes. The neural substrate of working memory is distributed across multiple brain regions, with the DLPFC playing a particularly central role.[17] Neuroimaging studies have observed activation in DLPFC during complex spatial and verbal reasoning tasks. DLPFC appears to be involved in maintenance and manipulation of relevant information in a variety of complex tasks, including analogical reasoning. In the context of analogical reasoning, research suggests that the DLPFC may also be involved in interference resolution during response selection.[18] Although the DLPFC contributes to analogical reasoning by supporting working memory and also interference control, it does not seem to play a direct role in relational integration itself.

Interference Control: Ventrolateral PFC

To think about specific relations requires the ability to avoid interference from other salient information—notably, irrelevant perceptual or semantic attributes of specific objects and strong but non-analogical semantic associates. Neuropsychological studies have shown that frontal patients are particularly impaired in solving analogy problems that require selecting the relational response from a set of options that includes misleading semantic distractors.[19]

A large body of research using many tasks, including some that involve reasoning, has implicated the VLPFC in interference control. Furthermore, individuals with greater ability to control interference in working memory tend to have larger brain volume in VLPFC.[20] There is now considerable evidence that similar brain regions are responsible for interference control during analogical reasoning. For example, Soohyun Cho and her collaborators performed a neuroimaging study in which college students solved four-term analogies based on cartoon human figures that varied in a binary fashion on visual dimensions such as gender and clothing color.[21] At the beginning of each trial, participants were told which dimension or dimensions were to be considered relevant to the analogy. An analogy was defined as valid if the A:B and C:D cartoon figures were both the same or both different on the dimension(s) specified as relevant. A dimension was coded as interfering if it was specified as irrelevant but suggested the wrong answer (e.g., *A:B* and *C:D* might both be "same" on the relevant dimension of clothing color but different on the interfering dimension of gender). This study found that increased interference recruited areas in the bilateral VLPFC and DLPFC. In general, it appears that multiple regions of the PFC contribute to different aspects of analogical reasoning, and that the neural basis of interference control is separable from that of relational integration.[22]

Relational Integration: Rostrolateral PFC

If there is any single region that deserves to be singled out for its critical role in solving complex analogy problems, and in relational integration more generally, it's the most anterior lateral region of the prefrontal cortex (particularly in the left hemisphere).[23] The rostrolateral PFC (RLPFC; also referred to as *frontopolar* region), roughly corresponds to what is termed (in a different anatomical naming system) Brodmann area (BA) 10. This region of the human brain, which is wired for integration, is the most recent evolutionary development in the hominin lineage. BA10 in the human brain is larger relative to the rest of the brain than it is in the apes, and certain of its layers (the supragranular layers) have more space available for connections with other higher-order association areas. These anatomical differences suggest that this part of the cortex became enlarged and more specialized during hominin evolution.[24]

An important distinguishing feature of the RLPFC is that its neurons have especially dense systems of dendrites (tree-like structures that become stimulated by other neurons and conduct an electrochemical charge to the cell body).[25] This anatomical feature supports integration of information across many converging neurons. The RLPFC appears to be heavily and reciprocally interconnected with other high-level areas, particularly within the PFC, suggesting a specialization in integrating relatively abstract information.[26] This brain region (as well as the rest of the prefrontal cortex) continues to develop through adolescence and is closely connected with age-related abilities across a broad array of cognitive tasks.[27] Of particular note, a morphometry study found that individual differences in gray matter volume within the left RLPFC predict performance on an analogy task.[28]

In the area of human reasoning, the earliest line of work supporting the role of the RLPFC in relational integration involved neuroimaging studies of college students solving variants of RPM problems (see figure 2.4). Kalina Christoff and colleagues created RPM-like problems in which the changes across rows and columns of the matrix were based on zero, one, or two relations. Problems involving at least two relations (i.e., those that required relational integration) produced pronounced activation in the left RLPFC. A similar study conducted by Jim Kroger and colleagues included conditions in which behavioral difficulty (as measured by both error rate and solution time) was manipulated by introducing perceptual noise in the stimuli while holding relational complexity constant. High levels of complexity, but not problems made comparably difficult by perceptual noise, selectively activated left RLPFC. This finding confirmed that relational integration—not just any kind of problem difficulty—selectively recruits the RLPFC. Studies using analogy problems have also found evidence that RLPFC is active in the process of relational comparison. In addition to these neuroimaging studies, a study using patients with focal damage to the left RLPFC revealed specific deficits in relational integration when solving analogy problems, with the behavioral score in a short analogy task being predictive of the presence of a lesion within the RLPFC.[29]

Other studies have examined the role of the RLPFC in solving semantic analogies in the *A:B::C:D* format. Neuroimaging studies have consistently found that solving such analogy problems results in activation of the RLPFC to a greater degree than does categorizing objects in individual pairs, without integrating multiple relations.[30] A study by Silvia Bunge and colleagues provided strong evidence that the integration process is left-lateralized, although the right RLPFC also plays a role in relational processing.[31] The neural response in the RLPFC is very similar when an explicit relation term is substituted for the *A:B* pair (e.g., *microphone: sound:: camera: light* is replaced with *detects:: camera: light*)—evidence that relational comparison (rather than alignment of individual terms) is the critical process.[32]

Work by Adam Green and colleagues showed that for verbal analogies, the response of an area within the left RLPFC increases gradually with the overall semantic distance between the *A:B* and *C:D* concepts.[33] That is, activation is greater when the two pairs are semantically distant (e.g., *blindness: sight:: poverty: wealth*) than when they are overall more similar (e.g., *blindness: sight:: deafness: hearing*). This graded response suggests that semantic distance may impact the complexity of the integration process required to compare the two relations. The study by Chiang and colleagues, mentioned earlier, tested a computational model in which the neural code for relations is distributed across many "relation features," such that relations between similar pairs are themselves more similar than are relations between dissimilar pairs. For valid *A:B::C:D* verbal analogies, the left RLPFC showed graded sensitivity to the predicted dissimilarity between the *A:B* and the *C:D* relations.

A very different approach to understanding the role of RLPFC involves exploring the effect of various types of brain stimulation. A noninvasive neuromodulatory technique called *anodal transcranial direct current stimulation* (tDCS) is capable of increasing neuronal excitability through prolonged application of weak currents at the scalp. Green and his colleagues reported that application of anodal tDCS to left RLPFC increased the semantic distance of analogical solutions, as well as the number of valid solutions produced by participants. More recently, a study using a similar procedure found that anodal tDCS improved spontaneous analogical transfer for the radiation problem (yielding an increase in partial, though not complete, convergence solutions). This impact of brain stimulation—particularly for a complex functional analogy—raises the possibility that activity in the RLPFC supports a link between analogy and creative thinking.[34]

Malleability of the Relational Network

It should be emphasized that in neuroimaging studies the RLPFC is almost always active together with multiple other brain areas in the PFC and more posterior areas. In general, the RLPFC appears to function as the most anterior area in the broad frontoparietal control network.[35] Relational integration, in analogy as well as other reasoning tasks, is supported by an extensive network of brain areas that communicate with the RLPFC.

As mentioned earlier, the RLPFC and other hubs of the frontoparietal network continue to develop over the course of childhood. These changes occur not only within each hub but also in the neural connections linking them. A developmental study examined connectivity within the frontoparietal network in relation to performance on a variety of reasoning measures in a large sample of children and adolescents aged 6–18 years. In late childhood and early adolescence, developmental changes in reasoning ability were related to strength of connections within the frontoparietal network. For 9- to 11-year-olds, reasoning ability was most strongly related to connectivity between left and right RLPFC, whereas for adolescents the most important connections were between left RLPFC and a region within the parietal cortex. Overall, these developmental changes in frontoparietal connectivity likely support increasing communication between prefrontal regions and specific parietal targets. The outcome of these changes is an adult system in which different parietal subregions communicate preferentially with different prefrontal subregions.[36]

The malleability of the frontoparietal network continues even in adulthood—it can be influenced by intensive educational activities related to relational reasoning. For example, one study examined patterns of connectivity at rest for young adults before and after preparing for the Law School Admissions Test. Compared to age- and IQ-matched controls, those who studied for the reasoning test for about three months showed an increase in the strength of frontoparietal connections, as well as connections from prefrontal cortex to other brain regions. Correlations involving the left RLPFC showed particularly large increases over the study interval.[37] These findings, coupled with the evidence discussed in chapter 2, indicate that relational reasoning and its neural substrate are not fixed, even in adulthood, but rather vary with experience and context.

The nature of the neural network underlying relational reasoning supports the view that analogy is a domain-general human ability. Just as psychometric evidence shows that performance on verbal, mathematical, and spatial analogy problems are all closely coupled, neural studies generally find substantial overlap between the brain regions active during analogical reasoning, regardless of problem content. In particular, the core region supporting relational integration appears to be the left RLPFC, both for verbal analogies and for spatial problems such as the RPM task. We know that a great deal of spatial processing is right lateralized, but when relational integration is required, the left RLPFC is most involved.

None of the studies we've discussed in this chapter deal with metaphor, which is often viewed as relying on analogy. In fact, neural evidence summarized in several meta-analyses indicates that the brain areas active during metaphor comprehension are distinct from the core areas that support relational integration.[38] Notable areas that support metaphor processing include broad regions of the temporal cortex (central to language), and several subareas of the frontal cortex: the VLPFC (probably because of the need for semantic selection), sometimes the DLPFC (when working memory is necessary), and sometimes the medial PFC (an area involved in thinking about people, including oneself). Activation is bilateral, but sometimes more pronounced in the right hemisphere for relatively novel metaphors. Perhaps most notably, the RLPFC generally does *not* seem to be especially engaged during metaphor processing. We'll take up the question of how metaphor and analogy may be related in chapter 7, when we consider the more general issue of how analogy relates to language.

6   The Analogy Gap

The difference in mind between man and the higher animals, great as it is, certainly is one of degree and not of kind.
—Charles Darwin

Human animals—and no other—build fires and wheels, diagnose each other's illnesses, communicate using symbols, navigate with maps, risk their lives for ideals, collaborate with each other, explain the world in terms of hypothetical causes, punish strangers for breaking rules, imagine impossible scenarios, and teach each other how to do all of the above.[1]
—Derek Penn

So far, I've focused on analogy as a typical capability of a human adult. It's time to raise the further question—who else? Other than human adults, what other cognitive systems on planet earth are capable of similar analogical thinking? In this chapter I'll consider this question for biological beings—human children at various ages and also our closest nonhuman relatives, the great apes. In chapter 12 I'll revisit the same question for our most complex cognitive artifacts—AI systems.

A warning at the outset—we're entering turbulent scientific waters. Deciding who is capable of (human-like) analogy presupposes that we can agree on the essential characteristics of adult human analogy, as well as on convincing tests to decide whether or not a thinker has these characteristics. The most basic divide is between those who follow Darwin in viewing higher cognition as fundamentally an evolutionary continuum across the primates that currently inhabit the earth, with differences being a matter of degree, and those who posit a qualitative gap separating human thinking from the cognition of apes. To put my own cards on the table, I'm a coauthor with Derek

Penn and Danny Povinelli on the review article from which I took Derek's quote—a paper titled "Darwin's Mistake," in which we review the evidence for an analogy gap.

Two Views of the Development of Relational Thinking

Just to be clear, the gap involves much more than analogy (as Derek's list of unique human activities suggests). Humans excel in making inferences based on cause and effect, evaluating moral issues, understanding the linkage between intentions and actions, and reasoning about time and space. I'll argue that these abilities are all supported in part (but not exclusively) by a uniquely human system for higher-level relational reasoning, which has been dubbed the Late System.[2] The Late System is "late" both phylogenetically (it arose during recent hominin evolution) and developmentally (emerging in human children at about age three years).

To avoid a basic confusion: an analogy gap (or a broader cognitive gap) doesn't imply a discontinuity in biological evolution. Estimates of when the hominin line diverged from chimpanzees (genus *Pan*, which includes the chimpanzee and bonobo, the closest extant relatives of humans) range roughly from six to nine million years ago.[3] There was plenty of time for evolutionary changes within the hominin line before *Homo sapiens* (us) emerged about 300,000 years ago. We're the only surviving species in our lineage—the analogy gap reflects the extinction of *Homo erectus*, *Homo neanderthalensis*, and the other "links" that have gone missing. Modern humans represent a lonely species.

The core of high-level human thinking, analogy included, is the ability to reason with explicit relations. Theorists who agree with this basic claim nonetheless disagree on how relational reasoning is actually implemented in biological minds and brains. Box 6.1 summarizes two general proposals. One possibility is that relational reasoning is fundamentally a unitary system, probably shared to some extent with other primates (and maybe some other species), that for humans emerges in early infancy. The core of the system for processing relations (perhaps some mechanism for analogical alignment based on formal properties of relations) is probably innate, though the system's capability increases gradually as the child acquires greater knowledge of relations. Proponents of a unitary system argue that "The immense relational advantage shown by adult humans is in part the product of cultural/linguistic experience, and not simply the result of a fixed biological gulf."[4]

An alternative possibility is that in humans, multiple systems support inferential processes sensitive (at least implicitly) to relations. These include several Early Systems that emerge in infancy, which are probably shared to some extent with nonhuman animals. Each of the Early Systems is tied to a broad but constrained cognitive domain, such as causation, time, or mental

---

Box 6.1

Two views of how relational reasoning emerges in humans. Adapted from Holyoak and Lu (2021).

1. **Unitary system:**
   - A unitary system for higher-level relational reasoning (probably shared to some extent with nonhuman animals) emerges in human infancy and gradually develops into the adult system.
   - The essence of the adult system (perhaps based on analogical alignment) is present from infancy on (presumably innate).

2. **Multiple systems:**
   - Several Early Systems, each tied to a broad but constrained cognitive domain, such as causation, time, or mental attribution (and probably shared to some extent with nonhuman animals) emerge in human infancy.
   - None of these Early Systems support higher-level relational reasoning, but each can produce behaviors that mimic it to some extent.
   - A Late System for reasoning based on explicit relations, which is domain-general and unique to humans, develops separately from approximately age three years to adolescence. The Late System is closely tied to the development of specific brain areas, including (though extending beyond) those that comprise the frontoparietal control network.
   - Outputs of Early Systems may be re-represented in more abstract forms that can be used by the Late System.
   - The Early Systems continue to function in adults, coexisting with the Late System.
   - Outputs of the Late System can be used to create more implicit representations that are less dependent on the frontoparietal control network.

attribution. Their common property is that they operate on perceptual cues (often of considerable complexity), without representing abstract relations as explicit objects of thought. Although none support higher-level relational reasoning, each can produce behaviors that mimic it to some extent. Domain-general relational reasoning is a Late System, specific to humans, which comes online at about age three and develops through adolescence, coexisting throughout with the Early Systems. One great specialization of human cognitive evolution is a module for generalized intelligence. But this module in turn interacts with others that also undergo major advances from about age three. From about this age, children show increasing competence with language and become more adept in accumulating memories from experiences, in keeping track of rapid changes around them, and in socializing and cooperating with peers. In chapter 7, I'll consider evidence that the "human edge" in fact depends on multiple Late Systems that typically support one another.

A key idea about the Late System for relational reasoning is that it reflects the *re-representation* of knowledge in a way that makes it explicit.[5] In addition to simply reacting to perceptual cues, humans become capable of forming abstract concepts that explain observable events. To take a simple example, if a rival is detected close by, with an open line of sight to a cache of food, a chimpanzee is likely to act adaptively in anticipation of the rival attempting to obtain the food—moving to grab it first, or perhaps choosing instead to move toward an alternative food cache. This is a sophisticated response, but it's entirely based on perceptual cues. A human would infer something more: the rival *sees* the food and *attends* to it, and therefore *knows* where it is, and *wants* it, and so will *intend* to get it. Rather than solely reacting to perceptual cues, the human will construct an elaborate relational "story" about the unobservable mind of another agent.

Intelligent Behavior in Nonhuman Animals

In 1978, the primatologists David Premack and Guy Woodruff published a paper with a title that raised a new and provocative question: "Does the chimpanzee have a theory of mind?"[6] The above interpretation of what a rival may be thinking represents an intuitive "theory of mind" that adult humans surely possess. Premack and Woodruff's general question was, "What about chimpanzees—or other nonhuman animals—or young human children?"

Whatever the actual answer (which of course may differ across cases), it's clear that humans are very inclined to *assume* that other primates think much as we do. The essence of anthropomorphism is an argument by analogy: "If that were me, this is what I would see/believe/desire/intend." To the extent that the "other" resembles me (and nonhuman primates have many important similarities to humans), the argument by analogy seems stronger. And if I can't think of any alternative explanation of the observed behavior of the other, then abduction to the best explanation is likely to leave the analogy to humans as the winning hypothesis. We're predisposed to believe the chimpanzee indeed shares our human "story" about what the rival is thinking.

But as Povinelli and his colleagues have often pointed out, there *is* a rival explanation for the observed behavior of the chimpanzee who responds to a food rival—we already gave it![7] Maybe the chimpanzee simply reacts to the perceptual cues—a rival is seen, or heard, or smelled nearby; an open line of sight from rival to food is detected—so take defensive action. The human "story" about the mind of the rival is entirely superfluous. We can apply Lloyd Morgan's canon, the classical antidote to anthropomorphism in comparative psychology—roughly, do not assume complex cognitive mechanisms are necessary to explain behaviors for which simpler mechanisms suffice.

"Simpler," it has to be emphasized, does not mean "simple." The animals on planet Earth have achieved intelligent behavior in many different ways—using mechanisms that don't neatly fit either human-like relational reasoning or general associative learning. Evidence of intelligence is ubiquitous across the animal kingdom.[8] Honeybees perform a kind of "dance" that informs other hive members of the direction to good sources of nectar. An octopus (which has a large clump of neurons—a mini-brain—for each of its eight individual tentacles) can learn to unscrew the lid of a jar to get food inside. Ravens can make and use tools—for example, bending a wire to form a hook that the bird then uses to obtain food. Chickadees hide their food in concealed, scattered locations and remember where to find specific caches after weeks or months.[9] Dogs can learn how to get around a barrier by watching and imitating another dog or a person.[10] Dolphins communicate with one another by whistles and cooperate to herd small fish up to the surface where they can be easily caught. In terms of evolutionary history, all of these species are far removed from humans. Of more direct relevance, our closest relative, the chimpanzee, exhibits many behaviors that indicate cognitive sophistication. Chimpanzees use different tools for different purposes—they modify sticks to obtain termites, use stones to crack nuts, and use leaves to sponge up water. As highly social animals, they hunt together to catch and eat monkeys, and make war against other bands of chimpanzees.

For each instance of intelligent behavior exhibited by members of a species, we would like to understand the cognitive mechanisms involved. Does the animal "reason" as a human might, or is some other process at work? Once we drop the presumption that all biological intelligence is some variation of the human variety, it's easier to find and explore alternative possibilities. Let's consider one well-known example of animal intelligence, famously exhibited by Betty, a New Caledonian crow.[11] Crows (and ravens) are corvids, arguably the most intelligent family of bird species. Betty was given the task of obtaining food from a bucket placed at the bottom of a narrow vertical tube. In early experiments, Betty was provided with a straight wire, which in its original form was useless for raising the bucket. Importantly, Betty had previously seen hooks. Betty's solution—found quite quickly—was to wedge the wire so that she could bend one end into the shape of a hook and then use the modified wire to lift the bucket out from the tube. In subsequent experiments, Betty achieved the same goal by bending a novel type of material (a strip of aluminum), which required different movements to bend into a hook. Moreover, she went on to solve a new problem that required inserting a tool through a narrow hole. Now, when given a strip of bent aluminum—which wouldn't fit through the hole—Betty proceeded to *unbend* the strip. For different goals, she did what was needed to create different solutions.

It's tempting to conclude that Betty solved her problems by human-like causal analysis and planning. When explanations for intelligent animal behavior are required, anthropomorphism is always on call as a ready source of hypotheses. For example, an enthusiast for "analogy as the core of biological cognition" might call attention to Betty's early experience with hooks and argue that premade hooks provided her with a source analog, which she somehow mapped onto her new target problem to infer an analogical solution. Of course, Betty the bird isn't a close relative of humans. In fact, very similar experiments have been performed with chimpanzees.[12] Surprisingly (given her vastly greater evolutionary distance from humans), Betty appears to be a better fabricator of novel tools than any chimpanzee so far tested!

But what's her method? The team of researchers who tested Betty were careful to note some of her behaviors that don't fit with full "insight." She often probed with an unmodified (useless) tool before proceeding to alter it.

And on some trials, after modifying a straight strip of aluminum to form a hook, Betty then tried to retrieve the bucket using the wrong (unmodified) end. It's as if the bending may have been done without foresight, or even immediate recognition, that a hook provided the needed solution. More generally, bending and unbending pliant materials appear to be actions for which corvids have a natural propensity. Their excellence in adaptive tool-making is limited to a rather narrow range of possibilities.

We don't fully understand the mechanisms of corvid problem-solving, but some recent work suggests an interesting hypothesis, termed *mental template matching*.[13] It turns out that if a New Caledonian crow observes an object being used to obtain a reward—even by another crow—the bird will remember the shape of the tool and later show a preference to fabricate that shape, even when doing so is *not* differentially rewarded. Notably, this behavior doesn't require imitation of another bird's action—in fact, crows apparently don't imitate what other crows do. Rather, they *emulate* the end-product—a tool of a certain shape. In the case of Betty, previous experience obtaining or observing reward after a hook was used may have added this "tool template" to her memorized repertoire. When later confronted with a problem in reaching food, she preferentially manufactured tools that looked like known templates, of which the hook was one. Mental template matching is a potential mechanism that could promote adaptive toolmaking and also allow cultural transmission across individual birds—without positing insight, causal understanding, analogy, imitation, or teaching.

The plausibility of mental template matching is enhanced by evidence that a similar mechanism is involved in the acquisition of birdsong. In various bird species, juvenile birds listen to song patterns produced by other birds, acquiring an auditory template. The young birds then adjust their own vocalizations until they produce songs that match the template. An individual bird may later modify its own song, resulting in transmission of an altered template to the next generation. Wild New Caledonian crows are known to be vocal learners, displaying cultural variation in their calls, so we have reason to believe they have the neural architecture necessary to support mental template matching. It remains to be seen whether this type of explanation for Betty's expertise in toolmaking is correct. But if we're looking for an evidential source analog to explain a bird's cognitive abilities, a near source analog—another example of avian learning—is more credible than the remote analog of human thinking.

The Non-Analogical Ape[14]

Now let's directly consider the question of whether nonhuman primates are capable of human-like analogy: reasoning based on explicit relations that go beyond perceptual cues, generating inferences from a single source analog, across a broad range of content domains. Penn and colleagues reviewed comparative studies of primate cognition involving both laboratory experiments and naturalistic observations of animals in the wild.[15] We found no convincing evidence for (and considerable evidence against) reasoning by apes based on abstract relations of *any* type—causal relations, spatial relations, hierarchical relations, transitive relations, or the mental relations involved in a theory of mind. If this negative conclusion stands (and I see no reason to alter it), then the likely answer to our question about analogy in apes is—no.

In fact, only a single chimpanzee has ever shown any possible ability to solve analogy problems. In 1981, Gillan, Premack, and Woodruff reported findings from several analogy experiments with Sarah, the famous "star" of an effort to teach chimps a language-like communication system using plastic tokens for "words."[16] Besides tokens for various objects and actions, Sarah had learned tokens intended to represent the concepts of *same* and *different*.

On each trial in one experiment, Sarah was presented with two pairs of common objects. On some trials each pair shared a meaningful relationship (e.g., a closed tin can that was paired with a can opener, and a painted, closed lock paired with a key—where in each pair the second item could *open* the first). On other trials the relation differed across the pairs (e.g., the same problem except the painted, closed lock was paired with a paint brush). For each problem, Sarah chose one of two tokens—*same* or *different*. She reliably picked *same* for the pairs linked by the same relation, and *different* for the pairs that were linked by different relations (80 percent accuracy overall). She performed similarly in an experiment using the same basic materials, but where she had to pick the analogous completion from two alternatives. However, the authors noted that the two-choice experiment introduced a confounding with perceptual similarity, which was avoided in the same/different version. In addition to these experiments with real objects, Sarah also achieved reliable accuracy in similar experiments using four-term analogies constructed using geometric forms varying in size, color, and marking.

As the original authors recognized, Sarah had "a unique experimental history," which makes it impossible to know exactly what experiences contributed to her performances. More than four decades have now gone by since that classic study was published, and no other successful test of a non-human animal on analogy problems has ever been reported. Years later, Sarah herself was tested again on geometric analogy problems, with additional controls for various possible feature-based strategies.[17] Her performance in this replication revealed that she in fact was using a non-analogical strategy based on the number of feature changes in each pair of geometric forms (without apparent regard for *which* features were changed). Given this reinterpretation of how Sarah solved the geometric problems, the only support remaining for the claim that nonhuman primates can solve analogy problems is a single experiment with a single chimpanzee—an experiment never replicated with Sarah or with any other nonhuman primate.

Sarah (and David Premack, the scientist who led her training project) also pioneered another line of research that can be considered "analogy adjacent."[18] This work focuses on the concepts of *same* and *different*, for which Sarah learned tokens. From our human vantage point, *same* and *different* are abstract concepts that go beyond specific perceptual features. Two pictures can be the same, as can two ideas, or two abstract word meanings (e.g., *freedom* and *liberty*). We know that the ability to respond to perceptual sameness (e.g., different flowers of the same color) is ubiquitous across the animal kingdom. But to what extent do nonhuman animals understand *same* and *different* as abstract concepts?

To address this question, Premack introduced a task known as *relational match-to-sample* (RMTS). In the original version, a pair of icons form the sample, and two alternative pairs are shown as options (figure 6.1A). The task is to choose the option that is relationally the same as the sample. So, if the two icons in the sample are the same as each other, then the correct response is to select the option in which the icons are also the same. If the two icons in the sample are different, then the correct choice would be the different pair. Critically, none of the icons in the options are individually the same as the icons in the sample. The similarity of the sample to each option thus appears to involve the *relation* of sameness within the sample and within the option. Using her learned tokens for *same* and *different*, Sarah could reliably choose the correct option in this RMTS task.

It's tempting to view the two-icon version of RMTS as a variant of a four-term analogy problem, where the two icons in the sample form the *A:B* pair and the correct option corresponds to *C:D*. But relative to analogy problems

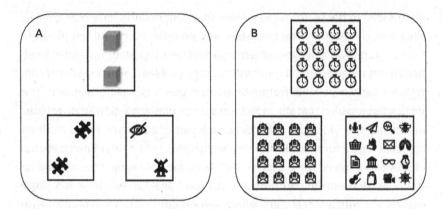

Figure 6.1
(A) Relational match-to-sample (RMTS) problem with two icons in each image. (B) RMTS problem with sixteen icons in each image.

in general, RMTS is limited in several respects. The only relations used are *same* and *different*, and these particular relations (unlike many others) are symmetrical—there are no distinct roles within each pair. But most importantly, the displays yield a variety of perceptual properties arising from the *configurations* of icons. In particular, suppose we create RMTS problems with a larger number of icons in the sample and also the options (such as the example shown in figure 6.1B, with sixteen-icon images). For larger displays, it becomes apparent that the similarity of images is not simply a binary contrast (*same* versus *different*) but is more graded. As the number of different icons increases within a single image, the overall variability of the image increases (where one standard statistical measure of variability is *entropy*). Even for two-icon problems, there is a (small) entropy difference between an image with two identical icons (*same*) compared to an image with two distinct icons (*different*).

It turns out that for RMTS problems with large numbers of icons, various species from pigeons to baboons (in addition to chimpanzees and of course humans) can reliably solve them.[19] In many studies with nonhuman animals, however, thousands of training trials were required to produce stable performance. As in some other cognitive tasks linked to human intelligence, the greatest success in solving two-icon RMTS problems by a nonhuman species has been achieved not by primates but rather crows. But for crows as well, current evidence is consistent with the hypothesis that the birds respond on the basis of subtle perceptual cues, rather than relational reasoning.[20]

In general, nonhuman primates appear to solve RMTS problems by attending to perceptual properties of icon configurations, responding in a graded fashion to degree of perceptual variability in images. Only humans (usually, though not always) honor a categorical distinction between images in which all icons are identical (*same*) and images in which *not* all icons are identical (*different*, regardless of number of icons, or degree of variability). Studies using the RMTS paradigm have thus provided no evidence that nonhuman primates appreciate *same* and *different* as abstract, categorical relations, far less evidence of human-like analogical reasoning.

The Relational Shift: How Children Close the Gap

Human children, of course, are especially promising candidates to qualify as analogical thinkers—they reliably grow up to be human adults, who we know to reason by analogy. The question is not if, but when, a child achieves the various markers of analogical capacity. As we'll see shortly, there is compelling evidence that by about three years of age, children begin to appreciate comparisons based on explicit relations. The mental mechanisms available to infants and toddlers are less easily determined due to their limited language skills, as well as the greater difficulty of applying neuroimaging methods. As previewed in box 6.1, the view of analogy as a unitary system implies that explicit relations are available even to infants, and that the course of analogy development is basically continuous from birth to (roughly) adolescence.

In contrast, the multiple systems view implies that the "proto-analogy" capabilities of children younger than about three can be explained by the operation of Early Systems that depend on perceptual cues (as seems to be the case for nonhuman primates). Young children are able to perceive physical causes, interpret a sequence of dot patterns in motion as a living creature, remember and reproduce a series of actions in their correct order, and anticipate the actions of someone else. As toddlers, children can learn from an example to select a goal-appropriate tool based on complex perceptual properties (e.g., choosing a long stick with the right sort of head to enable pulling).[21] These are sophisticated accomplishments, but they can be explained by mechanisms that respond to and learn from perceptual cues, without requiring reasoning with abstract relations. These mechanisms likely involve multiple Early Systems, each tied to a broad but constrained cognitive domain, such as causation, thinking about time, or attribution of mental states to others.[22]

The neural systems that most clearly support manipulation of explicit relational knowledge undergo major developmental changes after age three. Just as analogy is dependent on the slow maturation of specific brain areas (notably the RLPFC), the complex thinking required to understand and predict the beliefs and goals of other people—a mature theory of mind—depends on maturation of activity patterns in specific brain areas (notably the temporoparietal junction), with marked changes observed from about age five to late childhood.[23] A general hypothesis is that these types of developmental changes in neural connectivity are linked to an emerging human capacity to re-represent relational knowledge in more abstract and explicit forms. These developmental changes in reasoning are concurrent with major developmental advances in language skills and general knowledge (semantic memory), as well as memory for events and prior problems (episodic memory).

Based on available evidence, the earliest age at which we can be confident that the Late System for relational reasoning operates is around three years. At this age children are able to make inferences about novel objects based on metaphors.[24] Studies using the RMTS paradigm with children also support this approximate timetable. Jean-Rémy Hochmann and colleagues tested preschool children at various ages on a battery of RMTS problems, varying the number of icons in each image.[25] They found that three- and four-year-olds failed two-icon RMTS problems (as do nonhuman animals in most studies) and that three-year-olds succeeded with larger arrays only when they were able to encode stimuli in terms of entropy. By age four, the behavior of children in this task began to contrast with that of nonhuman species. A small proportion of these children based their decisions on a categorical distinction between same and different images, rather than continuous variations in perceptual variability. Six-year-olds achieved robust success on two-icon RMTS problems (as do adults).

The age at which children begin to acquire the concepts *same* and *different* is controversial. A number of developmental psychologists have argued that children younger than age three—even infants—already exhibit sensitivity to these relations.[26] This claim is largely based on studies that measure the phenomenon of *habituation*: immediately after exposure to a stimulus, children pay less attention to a second stimulus identical or very similar to the first one (where attention is measured by looking time). In several habituation studies inspired by the RMTS paradigm, infants were first exposed to a small number of paired objects that either matched perceptually (two tokens of same object) or not. Subsequent looking time to new object pairs that either matched or not was measured. Under some conditions, infants looked longer at pairs for which the matching relationship had changed (i.e., match followed by non-match, or non-match followed by match). However, the exact pattern observed has been somewhat inconsistent across studies.

In any case, the habituation paradigm does not provide compelling evidence for use of explicit relations. Reacting to perceptual matches or mismatches does not require analogical mapping, nor does it constitute evidence that the infant has acquired abstract concepts of *same* or *different*. A much simpler explanation can be offered. If an infant looks at two physically identical objects, a reaction (both neural and behavioral) will be elicited. If the infant is then shown two other objects that are also physically identical, the reaction to the second occurrence of physical identity will be less pronounced— basically, the infant will be a bit bored by the repetition and prefer to look elsewhere. The fact that infants (sometimes) *react* to repetition of physical identity provides no evidence that they are *thinking* about an explicit relation of *same*.

But children beyond age three show clear signs of explicit relational reasoning. Studies with stories that could be used as source analogs to solve target problems have found that the period from about age four to six years brings major advances in analogical ability. In a study modeled after our experiments with adults solving the radiation problem by analogy (chapter 4), my students and I showed children at various ages (four to twelve years) illustrated stories and then gave them a problem so solve.[27] In one version, the story described how a genie wanted to move his jewels from a near bottle to a distant one, which he accomplished by rolling his magic carpet into a tube, stretching it from one bottle to the other, and then rolling the jewels through it. The target problem required the child to use any of various physical objects that were provided (including scissors, string, tape, and a large sheet of paper) to move some balls from one bowl to another (where the bowls were too far apart for the child to reach from one to the other). In this case the analogous solution was to roll the paper into a tube (the way the genie had rolled his carpet), and then send the balls through the tube. Only about one in ten of the preschool children came up with the paper-rolling solution after reading the genie story, even after a hint to use the story. For example, when prompted with "Could the story help?" one child—unable to find an alignment—tried to use pictures illustrating the story to push the balls.

However, the success rate for preschoolers increased to about 50 percent when multiple source stories, using more familiar cartoon characters, were provided. Success was higher still when the source story illustrated a simpler solution (although performance was disrupted if the story included an extra non-analogous character). In general, preschool children varied in their abilities to solve problems by analogy. One precocious four-year-old came up with the "rolled paper" solution after hearing the genie story (without a hint); others succeeded when the source story used more familiar characters; some seemed unable to align the source story with the target problem even after a hint. Older children (aged ten to twelve) almost invariably succeeded in finding the analogical solution, at least after a hint was given—the same qualitative pattern observed for adults solving the radiation problem.

Dedre Gentner and Mary Jo Rattermann proposed that children undergo a *relational shift*—older children increasingly respond to relations, rather than features of individual entities.[28] Several different explanations of this shift have been proposed. Not surprisingly, given that analogy depends on a configuration of cognitive processes, there is strong evidence that multiple developmental changes are involved. The most obvious factor is simply the accretion of knowledge: reasoning about a relation requires some degree of knowledge about that relation. Some of the earliest successes in analogical reasoning (around age four) involve problems in which objects are related by common physical actions that result in state changes (e.g., melting, cutting, wetting)—the kinds of events that children encounter very early in life.[29] Older children (from at least age eight) also appreciate more complex social relations, such as jealousy, and use similarities based on such relations to work out analogical mappings.[30] It's important to keep in mind that knowledge of relations involves more than the words a child may seem to know—for example, the work on RMTS problems suggests that young children sometimes interpret the words *same* and *different* more loosely than the categorical sense conveyed by their adult meanings. As we'll see in chapter 10, relations have their own microstructure—even for adults, knowledge of a relation can be a matter of degree.

Although knowledge of relations is necessary for mature analogical reasoning, it's far from sufficient. Maturation of the frontoparietal control network (chapter 5) bolsters executive processes needed for analogy—in particular, working memory capacity and the ability to inhibit salient cues that interfere with relation-based responses. Graeme Halford and his colleagues have emphasized that reasoning problems vary in relational complexity, defined in terms of the number of sources of variation that are related and must be processed jointly to solve the problem.[31] The ability to solve more

complex analogies (those that require integrating multiple relations) therefore depends on developmental changes in working memory. In addition (as
we saw in earlier chapters), in order to select a relational match that competes
with a more salient featural match, the reasoner must inhibit a tendency to
respond to the featural match. As a result, developmental increases in inhibitory control will also support the relational shift.

To tease apart the influence of relational complexity and the need to
inhibit interfering cues, while controlling for knowledge of the relevant relation, Lindsey Richland and her colleagues developed a set of scene analogy
problems suitable for use with young children (see figure 6.2).[32] These problems consisted of pairs of illustrated scenes depicting simple physical relations
between objects, such as a dog chasing a cat. The problems were pretested to
ensure that preschool children understood these relations. For each pair of
pictures (top and bottom picture in each panel), the experimenter identified
an object in the top picture and the child was asked to identify the object in
the bottom picture "who has the same thing happening."

Featural distraction was manipulated by varying the identity of one object
in the second (target) scene. Specifically, the target scene in the pair either
included an object with great featural similarity to the to-be-mapped object in
the source scene (the cat in bottom picture in panels B and D) or else substituted a dissimilar object (the sandbox in panels A and C). The critical object
was either involved in a single relation (chasing someone else in panels A and
B) or else played distinct roles in two occurrences of the same relation (both
chasing someone and being chased by someone in panels C and D). Because
the same basic relation was used in all conditions, knowledge of the relation
itself was held constant. The study included a group of 3- to 4-year-olds, and
a group of 9- to 11-year-olds. The preschoolers achieved about sixty percent
accuracy in the condition with a single relation and no distractor—about double their accuracy when either a second relation or a featural distractor was
added. In contrast, the older children achieved about ninety percent accuracy
in all conditions. Clearly, a maturational increase in the ability to deal with
distractors and multiple relations improves analogy performance, even when
knowledge of the relevant relation is controlled.

Relational reasoning depends on both relation knowledge and core executive functions, but additional factors also come into play. Indeed, there's some
evidence that relational thinking should be considered an executive function
in its own right.[33] A study of changes in neural processing over later childhood (from age six through nineteen years) found an association between

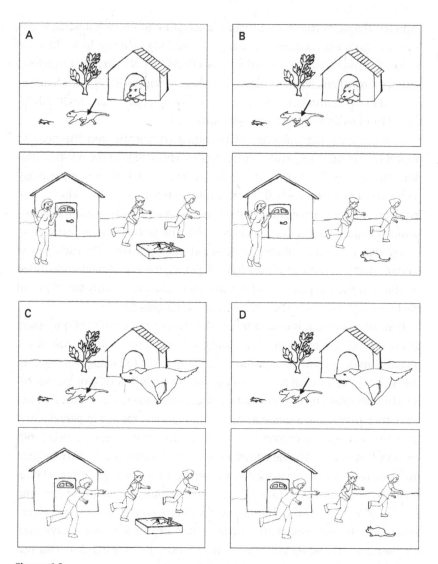

Figure 6.2
Pairs of picture analogies based on "chasing" relation. (A) 1-Relation/No Distractor,
(B) 1-Relation/Distractor, (C) 2-Relation/No Distractor, (D) 2-Relation/Distractor. In
each top picture in a pair, the arrow indicates the object specified by the experimenter;
the child was asked to identify the corresponding object in the bottom picture.
Reprinted from *Journal of Experimental Child Psychology*, *94*, L. E. Richland, R. G. Morrison, and K. J. Holyoak, "Children's development of analogical reasoning: Insights
from scene analogy problems," pp. 249–271, copyright © 2006, with permission from
Elsevier.

age-related improvement in solving meaningful four-term picture analogies and increased activity in a brain area (left anterior inferior prefrontal cortex) associated with the ability to select among competing semantic associations.[34] In solving these sorts of analogies, semantic selection is required to avoid choosing a non-analogical option that is semantically related to the *C* term of the analogy.

Knowledge accretion and neural maturation still do not exhaust the factors that influence the development of analogy ability. Providing verbal labels for relations (e.g., "in front of") is often helpful. Labels call children's attention to relational similarities; providing a name for a relation makes it easier to remember and later retrieve from memory. Moreover, as the developmental psychologist Jean Piaget emphasized, in later childhood children can use language to *explain* their reasoning about solutions to analogy problems.[35] As discussed in chapter 3, greater expertise enables more selective focus on relevant causal relations, improving evaluation of predictive analogies. Even for adults, relational processing is highly malleable in response to a wide range of contextual influences. Like adults, children who generate solutions to semantically far analogies are more likely to attend to relations (even different ones) in a subsequent mapping task.[36] An intriguing possibility is that culture may also have an impact—several studies have found that young Asian children are more likely to focus on relations relative to American children.[37]

To sum up, by the time children begin their formal schooling, they've already bridged the analogy gap that separates humans from every other species that shares the earth with us. The capacity to grasp deeper relations, and to make use of more complex analogies, continues to develop at least through adolescence. As adults, the ability to think with explicit relations underlies all the human achievements listed in Derek Penn's quote that began this chapter. But we should not mistake the unique intellectual powers of our species for any sort of moral superiority. The list of remarkable human endeavors could be expanded to include development of nuclear weapons capable of destroying civilization, creation of AI systems to support surveillance and censorship, and exploitation of energy sources that melt our planet's glaciers. As a species, humans have managed to divorce intelligence from both wisdom and morality. If it all ends in Armageddon, don't blame the chimpanzees.

7   Communicating with Relations

Language is a process of free creation; its laws and principles are fixed, but the manner in which the principles of generation are used is free and infinitely varied. Even the interpretation and use of words involves a process of free creation.[1]

—Noam Chomsky

Storytelling is an activity uniquely associated with human groups. This has likely been the case over most or all of the 300,000 years that we *Homo sapiens* have walked the earth. Telling stories has the hallmarks of direct teaching: a knowledgeable person talking in order to share information with a group—likely including children—gathered to receive it.[2] The information conveyed transcends the immediate context—tales of gods and ancestors, wars and adventures, often connected to knowledge about wayfinding, tool use, plants and animals, social rules, and punishments for transgressions. Storytelling can impart knowledge without the dangers that would confront an uninstructed novice thrust directly into real-world action.

Stories are best told in a special place set apart from everyday life, where the storyteller is situated at the center of everyone's attention. A place of light surrounded by darkness has the right quality. In modern times, the story might unfold in a movie displayed on a bright screen in a darkened room. But long ago, the gathering would perhaps take place at night by a campfire, or inside a cave illuminated by lamps or torches. In Paleolithic times, some caves were painted with scenes depicting humans and animals. In the lamplight those images would seem to move among dancing shadows, and the voice of the storyteller would transport the listeners far away—perhaps along a shaman's path leading beyond the human world. In this imagined scene from long ago, we see the human edge.

A Trinity at the Human Edge: Thinking, Language, and Sociality

So far, I've focused on analogy and its essential prerequisite, explicit representations of relations. In the previous chapter, I argued that the ability to reason with relations and see similarities based on them forms the core—not of biological cognition, but of what makes human thinking unique among the species that currently share our planet. But the human edge depends on more than thinking alone. Two other broad capacities clearly set humans apart: using language to communicate with each other and living in organized groups—sociality.

Just as many nonhuman animals demonstrate remarkable intelligence within circumscribed limits, so too do many species exhibit forms of aural communication (e.g., birdsong, the barking of dogs) and complex social organization (a beehive, a monkey troop). But just as a qualitative gap separates human thinking from the cognition of other species, gaps at least as large are apparent for language and sociality. As suggested in the quote from Chomsky (and supported by an enormous body of research conducted by a legion of linguists and psycholinguists), every natural human language is fundamentally different from all other biological systems for communication. The most basic property of a human language is that a finite set of words can be arranged in accord with the rules of syntax to generate an indefinitely large set of sentences, with their corresponding meanings. This characteristic—*generativity*—distinguishes not only spoken languages but also sign languages based on gesture.[3] No natural communication system used by nonhuman animals approaches a human-like level of generativity, and attempts to teach generative symbol systems to chimpanzees have all failed.[4] Generative language is clearly part of the human edge.

Similarly, human sociality has characteristics unparalleled by any other species. Chimpanzees live in communities of dozens, often dividing into smaller temporary groups, with multiple individuals acting together to hunt, patrol territory, or nurse the young. But the social organization of humans, even in prehistoric times, has been vastly more complex and diverse. At least by the end of the Late Pleistocene (about twelve thousand years ago), humans lived together in many different types of communities.[5] Some were nomadic hunter-gatherers, but others were villagers. Some communities were egalitarian, whereas others were socially stratified with people varying in their inherited status. Some groups engaged in cooperative projects involving hundreds or even thousands of people. Some managed wild plants and animals, and may have even domesticated species; some exploited rich aquatic resources by the coast. Some communities lived in peace with their neighbors; others were warlike. They exhibited a wide range of cultural practices, including shamanism, initiation rituals, and burial of the dead (sometimes accompanied by lavish grave goods).

In modern times, people belong simultaneously to multiple groups that vary enormously in their size and nature—nuclear families, extended networks of relatives and friends (situated in both "real life" and social media), schools and colleges, workplaces and professional societies, local communities and vast nations. To survive and flourish as a human being, the capacity to participate in groups is essential. The complexities of human social life impose high demands on the cognitive abilities of each individual. As a child grows up, a series of new capacities convey the human edge. The earliest and most basic is *joint attention*: the ability to coordinate attention on a goal with someone else (at first, the infant with their mother), where the goal is shared yet each participant has their individual perspective and role. Joint attention begins with the baby's ability to connect with the mother by gazing at her eyes; and then for both to look at something in the environment (perhaps a toy) and nonverbally "agree" to interact with it. This basic form of communication typically develops before the baby's first words and provides the foundation for all later interpersonal relationships. As the baby becomes a toddler, their social skills expand to foster two broad avenues of learning. From parents and other adults, the child learns "how we do things" in the culture; from their peer group of other children, they learn "how we can get along" and do things together.[6]

Interacting successfully with other people depends on understanding them—grasping why they act as they do, what they are thinking and feeling. If a friend seems unusually quiet, are they upset about something, preoccupied, or simply tired? The key to understanding people is to realize that much like the way *I* think and feel, so do others—but their individual thoughts and feelings often differ from mine. Our commonsense understanding of others is called a "theory of mind." As we saw in the previous chapter, Premack asked whether apes have a theory of mind; after much research, the apparent answer is "no." Human children, on the other hand, in the course of typical development most certainly come to understand that people's behavior is governed by invisible but very real internal causes. People have goals (not always reasonable ones), beliefs (sometimes false), emotions (often related to whether their goals have been realized or thwarted), and individual personalities that make different people different (and human behavior all the more difficult to predict). This ability to think about the minds of others and intuitively grasp "what makes people tick"—often called *mentalizing*—provides the basis for successful interpersonal interactions that may involve either cooperation or competition (or sometimes both). Mentalizing allows an individual to function effectively in social groups.

The members of this trinity of distinctively human capacities—thinking, language, and mentalizing to support sociality—seem to have much in common. Most importantly for my story, each of them involves manipulating representations of relations. Indeed, this commonality is so striking as to suggest that the three capacities might depend on a single unified system for relational processing. Suppose I see a young girl, Roberta, hide a toy she likes behind a couch and then leave the room. Later I see Carlos come in, and I watch as he discovers the toy and runs outside to play with it. When Roberta returns, where will she look for the toy? Of course, although *I* know the toy is now outside, Roberta doesn't—she has no way of knowing that its location has changed. Because she believes the toy is still behind the couch, that's where she'll look for it first. My inference about what Roberta will do is based on my elementary theory of mind, which involves the *relations* linking a person's beliefs, the state of the world, and selection of actions. I could describe this relational situation using language: "Because Roberta doesn't know the toy has been moved, she'll look for it where she last saw it, behind the couch." Moreover, I could think about this situation and compare it to another situation where someone acted on an erroneous belief. I might even grasp that in general, because beliefs cause actions, people with a false belief may take actions that are not in their own best interest. So, by deliberately causing someone to have a false belief, I might lead them to take an action that *I* desire (and they would not, if they knew the truth). By mentalizing, and making an analogical comparison, I've formed a new relational schema, for which my language provides a word: *deception*. Mentalizing, language, and relational thinking are intertwined.

But despite their formal resemblances and close interplay, it turns out that the human trinity is not based on a unitary neural system but rather on three distinct networks. As I mentioned in chapter 5, the frontoparietal control network, which supports analogical mapping and inference, is distinct from the language network—a variety of neurological problems impair language processing, yet basic analogical reasoning is preserved. The language network, which underlies the ordinary production and comprehension of language (whether spoken or signed), involves a broad set of areas in the temporal and frontal cortices, primarily lateralized to the left hemisphere.[7] In general, linguistic factors that make comprehension more or less difficult (such as predictability of words and syntactic complexity of sentences) have a graded influence on neural responses within the language network but little or no effect on the frontoparietal network. This is true even though some subareas within the two networks (notably, within the left inferior frontal gyrus) are physically situated side by side. Their exact locations vary across people (and so the two networks may appear to overlap at the group level). But once the relevant subareas have been localized in the brain of a single individual, the networks prove to be anatomically and functionally distinct.[8] Conversely, factors that increase the load on the frontoparietal network (such as complexity of logic or algebra problems) do not have a comparable impact on the language network.[9] Individual differences in fluid intelligence are linked to the frontoparietal network but not the language network.[10]

Mentalizing—the hallmark of the human social mind—also has its own distinctive neural network. Its major landmarks include the temporoparietal junction, superior temporal sulcus, and medial prefrontal cortex.[11] Research has shown that the brain regions involved in communication with others are distinct from those that directly support language. For example, a study found that planning a verbal communication to another individual (known to be uninformed about the topic) evoked activity in the mentalizing network, not the language network. At the same time, making the linguistic part of the task more difficult increased activity in the language network.[12] Another study showed that a severely aphasic patient, who suffered major impairment in syntactic processing, was nonetheless capable of both simple causal reasoning and judgments requiring a theory of mind.[13]

The general picture, then, is that the trinity of human capacities are both neurally and behaviorally dissociable. But at the same time, they typically develop together, with corresponding milestones. For example, in the previous chapter we noted that success on the two-icon RMTS task begins to be achieved at about age three, and is robust by age six. Similarly, children's capacity to play together in a truly interactive fashion (as opposed to just "parallel play") emerges at about age three, with a broad range of social skills becoming stable at about age six.[14]

An intriguing evolutionary question is how thinking, language, and the mentalizing ability that supports social interaction coevolved. I once asked a distinguished primatologist, who has extensively studied both thinking and communication in apes, which came first—language or thought? Without hesitation he answered, "Thought." Indeed, it seems that having a language to express relations would be of little use for an animal unable to think about such matters. But perhaps the evolutionary "leading edge" was neither thinking nor language but rather sociality. The adaptive value of functioning in larger and more complex social groups may have favored the evolution of minds that could think about relations and also talk about them.[15]

In any case, the fact that these relation-oriented systems are dissociable implies that relational processing is not a unitary mental activity. I suggested in the previous chapter that the "multiple systems" view must be expanded to include multiple Late Systems that develop through childhood over a period of years. As I foreshadowed in chapter 1, simplistic claims that "everything is analogy" and "analogy is everything" are very misleading. Not all comparisons are analogy, nor is all relational processing analogy—not in the sense of requiring the neural system that supports explicit analogical reasoning. By age three, children have typically learned basic vocabulary and sentence syntax, and can even tell small stories. Yet as we saw in the previous chapter, the Late System for relational reasoning is only beginning to become available at that age. Contrary to claims by proponents of a unitary system for relational processing, the learning mechanism that supports language acquisition does not require explicit analogical reasoning.[16]

In addition to the three systems that constitute the human cognitive trinity, various types of relational processing can also be performed by perceptual systems, notably vision (see chapter 11) and audition. For example, if a musical melody is transposed from the key of C to the key of E major, the notes change but the intervals between them remain the same. The ear can detect this "analogy"—a set of systematic relational correspondences—without activating the frontoparietal control network and without performing explicit analogical mapping.

Keeping in mind that the human trinity is organized as three distinct but interacting systems, let's take a closer look at how analogy is involved in their interplay. I'll focus on the role of language—the communication system that constitutes one of the most distinctive components of human cognition. As we'll see, the language system sometimes makes analogy easier and sometimes effectively replaces it.

How Language Impacts Analogy

Language can, of course, be used to convey hard problems—including those requiring analogy—that activate the frontoparietal network. Solving a verbal analogy requires more than just language comprehension (though it requires that too). The connection between analogy and language is a special case of the complex and controversial relationship between language and thought. Extreme proposals that all thinking is done via language, and that the particular language a person speaks imposes strict limits on the thoughts they can form, have been discredited by decades of research.[17] But at least from age three years, language clearly influences analogical reasoning in important ways.

People—including young children—naturally assume that common labels signal common meanings. Dedre Gentner and others have shown that this basic assumption provides a powerful route by which language can support relational abstraction.[18] In general, providing a verbal label for a relation tends to focus attention on it, rather than on the specific objects being related. The benefit of providing a relation word is particularly apparent for young children, who (as we saw in the previous chapter) are less likely to spontaneously focus on relations. For example, Gentner and her colleagues taught children new relational concepts using pictures.[19] Children were asked questions such as, "Look, the knife goes with the melon. What goes with the paper in the same way?" Six-year-olds correctly chose the relational match (scissors, which cut paper, just as a knife cuts melon), but younger children (about four and a half) tended to instead choose an associate (pencil) or an object match (more paper). However, when children were led to compare the knife–melon example with another analogous example ("The axe goes with the tree"), the younger children were more likely to choose the relational response. Moreover, their performance improved yet further if they were also given a common relational term: "Look, the knife is the fep for the melon, and the axe is the fep for the tree. Which one is the fep for the paper?" Even though the children had never heard the label *fep* before, this new word encouraged them to compare the two analogs and to focus on the abstract relational role ("thing that cuts").

The general picture is that relational labels can facilitate learning and using new relations, but only for children who are at or near the age at which they have acquired the cognitive prerequisites. In one study, children were asked to match pictures of paired objects, where the relational match depended on the abstract relation *opposite*.[20] For example, a picture of two faces, one happy and the other sad, might match a picture of two dinosaurs, one big and one small. Five-year-olds chose the relational response more often when the shared relation was labeled (e.g., "This is happy, this is sad. Happy and sad are opposites."). However, adding the relational label did not increase relational matches for four-year-olds, whose performance was at chance regardless of whether pictures were labeled as *opposite*.

Even for adults, verbal labels make it much easier to think about complex relationships. For example, causal systems often involve *feedback loops*. In a positive feedback loop, global warming causes polar ice to melt; this extra water retains additional heat, causing even more global warming. It's useful to be able to recognize analogous feedback loops, such as reamplification of noise picked up by a microphone, that occur in very different domains. In one study, college students studied several passages describing a variety of causal systems found in several distinct domains.[21] Then they read new test passages, and for each were asked to write down any and all previous passages of which they were reminded. The students were often reminded of previous passages from the same domain as the test passage (e.g., electrical engineering), even though the causal system differed. However, if either or both of the study and test passages was given a causal label, such as "positive feedback loop," then the students were more likely to recall a passage with the shared causal structure, even if the domain differed from study to test. A small but reliable benefit was obtained even if the label was provided only with the test passage. In this case, the label couldn't serve as a direct retrieval cue, since no corresponding label had been given for the study passage. However, the label on the test passage made its causal structure more salient. If the causal structure had been encoded for the study passage, then the label on the test passage would make it easier to notice the connection and therefore retrieve the previous passage.

In addition to aiding analogical thinking, language also influences the ability to perform more complex forms of mentalizing, such as reasoning about the false beliefs of other people. In a particularly compelling study, Jenny

Pyers and Ann Senghas tested deaf people in Nicaragua who were learning what at the time was an emerging new form of sign language.[22] At this early phase in the development and dissemination of the sign language, some young adults had acquired signs for mental states such as *think*, *know*, and *believe*, and others had not. These who reliably produced signs for mental states were much more successful in answering questions about false beliefs. Signs (or spoken words) for mental states make it possible to form complex syntactic constructions that capture the relational structure of mental states. For example, if "Judy thought she saw a ghost," then the main clause ("Judy thought") is true, while the embedded clause ("she saw a ghost") is false. The mental verb *thought* makes it possible to talk about this type of relationship between mental states with different truth values, extending the capacity for mentalizing to more complex cases.

Relational Concepts and Schemas

As I pointed out in chapter 2, people are amazingly flexible in coming up with new concepts that they think of as "things," which can be individuated and identified. Besides names for concrete objects, languages have names for events and states that can be described by relations. Such concepts act as schemas, involving a relation (sometimes more than one) linked to roles that can be filled by various entities.[23] For example, a *visit* is a relational concept that typically involves a *guest* who comes to the residence of a *host*. As this example illustrates, for any relation concept, one or more role concepts also arise. Moreover, objects occupying the same role in a relation (e.g., two entities that are quite different except that each is a *predator*) come to be viewed as more similar to each other overall.[24] Category labels and analogical comparisons increase general sensitivity to role-based categories, although people sometimes learn novel role-based categories without explicit instruction.[25]

Also notice how the same (or a morphologically similar) word readily serves both as a verb (*to visit*), describing an action central to the relational concept, and as a noun (*visit*), referring to the entire event as a "thing that happens." This pattern is commonplace in English and other languages. For example, when someone or something *creates* something, the event is called *creation*; when someone or something *destroys* something, the event is called *destruction*. This type of duality allows us to say something quite specific about what entities played roles in the event ("The tornado destroyed the entire downtown") or else to take a mental step back and talk about the event as a whole, without specifying the role fillers ("The destruction was terrible").

Many role categories are extremely familiar, and we have words for them (e.g., the relational schema for *buy* brings with it the roles of *seller, buyer, merchandise,* and *payment*). But as Larry Barsalou pointed out, people also readily create *ad hoc categories* for novel roles related to specific goals.[26] For example, in planning a European vacation, one might think about the ad hoc category of "things a tourist might do in Rome." In general, pursuing goals requires constant specification and instantiation of roles necessary for achieving them. When a well-established category for a role doesn't exist, an ad hoc category is constructed to represent it.

Broadly speaking, relational concepts include nouns as well as verbs (and other linking expressions such as prepositions) and can refer either to entire schemas or to individual roles within a schema. Jennifer Asmuth and Dedre Gentner proposed what they term the "fetch test" as a way to identify relational concepts: "If you were seeking a member of the relational category, could you identify it just by its own properties, or would you have to consider its interactions or relations with other things?"[27] For example, if you wanted to find a *tiger,* you could identify one by its shape, size, and stripes. But to find a *carnivore,* you'd need to consider whether the entity eats meat—that is, how it connects with something else. Asmuth and Gentner showed that relational concepts are more mutable than entity concepts—that is, their meaning is more easily changed to fit the demands of the context. When people are asked to interpret unusual noun-noun combinations such as *tooth opponent,* where one noun (*tooth*) refers to an entity and the other (*opponent*) refers to a relational role, the interpretation more often involves modulating the meaning of the relational concept. A *tooth opponent* might thus be interpreted as "something that opposes a tooth"—perhaps a *cavity.* Here the entity term keeps its basic meaning and is interpreted as a very specialized example of "the thing opposed."

Another distinctive property of relational concepts is that what people consider to be a *good* exemplar is often not simply an "average" one, but rather one that is close to some ideal.[28] This is different from how people judge feature-based concepts, such as *dog.* For feature-based concepts, a good example is usually one that resembles those that we tend to encounter most often. In contrast, the best example of a relational concept, such as *diet food,* might be a food with zero calories that still maintains health—even though this ideal example may not actually exist. In judging the "goodness" of a relational concept (particularly the type defined by a role, such as "nourishing food that serves the goal of losing weight"), people implicitly consider how likely it is that the example will actually fill that role successfully. The ideal is best.

In considering how relational concepts relate to analogy, we need to separate the question of how relational concepts are initially learned from that of how they are then put to use. As we saw in chapter 4, a relational schema is often the product of more specific analogical comparisons. By mapping the radiation problem to a story about a military operation, for example, the general idea of a convergence schema begins to emerge. At least initially, the schema may not have a name. However, our early research showed that the schema was learned more successfully if the two situations being compared were each accompanied by a verbal statement of the core principle: "If you need a large force to accompany some purpose, but are prevented from applying such a force directly, many smaller forces applied simultaneously from different directions may work just as well." The principle could also be conveyed nonverbally (by an abstract diagram showing converging lines). Whether the cue to the principle was linguistic or visual, it served to focus attention on the critical relations shared by the two examples, resulting in a more effective schema.[29]

For relational concepts expressed as words, analogy also appears to be involved in their acquisition—both comparison of examples and a verbal label aid in learning. Moreover, many relational words seem to evolve under the influence of progressive alignment, where a learner initially compares very similar entities that share some relational structure, setting the stage for later comparisons with more disparate examples.[30] For example, a child might first compare cats and dogs to form their initial concept of a *pet*—a partial abstraction closely linked to these familiar household animals. Later *pet* might be extended to embrace the example of a pet fish or pet lizard, until finally it will be possible to recognize that someone is walking their pet alligator through a park. Similarly, after initially learning that a child can grasp a baseball bat, progressive alignment will eventually extend the concrete meaning of the verb so that it becomes possible to understand it more abstractly, as when a student grasps the solution to an equation.

But although analogy likely is important in *learning* the meanings of relational words, it seems that it is not required for normal comprehension.

As I noted earlier, when people are simply reading or listening to text, the language network is active but not the frontoparietal control network. This is true even though relational words (many verbs, prepositions, and comparative adjectives, as well as some nouns) occur very frequently in typical texts. In general, the constraints of syntax place words into relational roles, without any sort of explicit analogical mapping being required. People who have suffered damage to their frontal lobe (which includes core components of the frontoparietal network), but whose language areas remain intact, can still understand relations expressed as simple sentences.[31] For example, if told that Grace is taller than Michael, a frontal patient will understand that the height of Grace exceeds that of Michael—their language system can assign each person to the correct role for the comparative relation *taller than*. However, if the same patient is then told that Nicolas is taller than Grace, they are likely to be at chance in ordering Nicolas and Michael in height. Frontal patients are severely impaired in solving problems that require reasoning about *multiple* relations, even though their language system can still process individual relations.

As the English language developed, it became possible to "grasp" not only a hammer but also an idea. This sort of extension from concrete to more abstract meaning went hand in hand with the general propensity to extend the notion of "thing" from a physical object to almost anything (chapter 2). I can not only *grasp* an idea but also *seek to find* one, *hold onto* it, *cherish* it, and then if it is *undermined*, eventually *abandon* it. Such general patterns in language, where abstract concepts have emerged long ago from concrete ones, no longer involve active analogical reasoning (except in the minds of some linguists).

In everyday comprehension, the language system can place entities into roles even for relatively abstract relations. For example, if I hear the sentence, "Susan finally grasped that her marriage was in trouble," the verb *grasped* in effect "calls" for suitable expressions to complete the relational thought. In response, the noun *Susan* claims the role of the "grasper," while the phrase *her marriage is in trouble* fills the role of "that which is grasped." The processes by which verbal expressions are assigned to roles in a sentence structure are by no means simple, but they are based on the language system, not on analogical reasoning. More generally, as relational knowledge grows more abstract— more like a schema and less like any specific example—it becomes part of what is broadly considered *semantic memory*. This transition is accompanied by changes in the neural representation that reduce reliance on the frontoparietal network.[32] By learning abstract concepts, the responsibility for relational processing is to a large extent "offloaded" from analogy to language and other systems.

Metaphor

As a psychological phenomenon, *metaphor* refers to an integration of apparently dissimilar concepts, going beyond the entrenched meanings of words. A metaphor is typically evocative rather than evidential (see chapter 2), conveying a subjective point of view or emotional attitude. Metaphor is the most prominent of several linguistic "figures of speech" commonly used to extend word meanings. Other such figures include *synecdoche* (substituting a part for a whole, as in referring to the number of people in a group as the "head count") and *metonymy* (substituting a close associate, as in using "the White House" to refer to the branch of the United States government directed by the president). Metaphor is also closely related to the concept of a *symbol*: something specific or concrete that stands for something more abstract, often involving relational knowledge. Symbols can be physical objects (the flag of a nation), or names of objects (a dove as a symbol of peace) or people (Einstein as a symbol of intelligence). In chapter 13, I'll have more to say about symbols as they relate to creativity.

For decades (indeed, ever since Aristotle!), psychologists, linguists, and philosophers have tried to pin down the connection between metaphor and analogy. Here I consider the questions: "Is metaphor processed by the neural system that supports analogical reasoning, or by the language system? Does the answer vary for different types of metaphors?"

First, let's consider cases in which the source domain in a metaphor is mundane and conventional, as in "Her eyes were diamonds." Cases like this straddle the murky border between active metaphor and entrenched meaning—indeed, one of the derivative dictionary entries for *diamond* in the Merriam-Webster Dictionary is "something that resembles a diamond (as in brilliance, value, or fine quality)." Verbs can also be metaphorical, as in "Ideas flew back and forth across the table." Here a comparison is implied between the concept of *idea* and "things that actually fly," such as birds.

But again, the metaphor is so conventional that it fits a definition found in Merriam-Webster: "To move, pass, or spread quickly." In such cases, the underlying analogy may not play any active role in ordinary comprehension.

But other metaphors, especially those found in literature, are more novel and also more complex in their meaning.[33] A literary metaphor may be succinct, as in "Books are the mirrors of the soul" (Virginia Woolf). In other literary metaphors a basic comparison is elaborated to bring out its nuances, as in "Life is a hurricane, and we board up to save what we can and bow low to the earth to crouch in that small space above the dirt where the wind will not reach" (Jesmyn Ward). And sometimes a metaphor is extended in a longer passage, as in this excerpt from the "I Have a Dream" speech delivered by Martin Luther King, Jr.:

> In a sense we have come to our nation's capital to cash a check. When the architects of our republic wrote the magnificent words of the Constitution and the Declaration of Independence, they were signing a promissory note to which every American was to fall heir. This note was a promise that all men would be guaranteed the inalienable rights of life, liberty, and the pursuit of happiness.
>
> It is obvious today that America has defaulted on this promissory note insofar as her citizens of color are concerned. Instead of honoring this sacred obligation, America has given the Negro people a bad check which has come back marked 'insufficient funds.' But we refuse to believe that the bank of justice is bankrupt. We refuse to believe that there are insufficient funds in the great vaults of opportunity of this nation. So we have come to cash this check—a check that will give us upon demand the riches of freedom and the security of justice.

Here Dr. King compares America's original promise of universal rights to a promissory note that has not yet been honored. The passage spells out the analogical mapping and the inference it supports—that America's promissory note is long overdue to be paid.

Most psychological research on the comprehension of metaphors has focused on short metaphors, often conventional though sometimes novel.[34] Because the novel metaphors used in experiments have generally been written for that purpose by psychologists, their literary quality is dubious. Within this limited range of metaphors, many studies have explored the brain regions that become especially active during their comprehension. The general picture is that metaphors primarily evoke activity in the language network (and sometimes the mentalizing network, when the metaphor involves people), often with greater involvement of the right hemisphere than is found for literal language.[35] Notably, there is little evidence of selective activation of the left RLPFC, the region most prominently associated with complex analogical reasoning. The RLPFC does not seem to play an important role even for novel metaphors (of the sort generated by psychologists). Rather, novel metaphors tend to produce greater activation in the right cerebral hemisphere, which may support finding relatively distant semantic connections. As a metaphor becomes more familiar (due to repeated exposures), activation in the right hemisphere tends to diminish.[36]

Another way of investigating how metaphors are understood is to examine individual differences in cognitive abilities that predict success in comprehending them. In several studies, Dušan Stamenković, Nick Ichien, and I gave college students tests of metaphor comprehension.[37] Some of the metaphors were drawn from literary sources (e.g., "The tongue is a bayonet"), whereas others were nonliterary (e.g., "The nose is the antenna of scent"). In addition to the metaphor task, we administered tests that have been shown to predict fluid intelligence (Ravens Progressive Matrices) or else crystallized verbal intelligence (measures of vocabulary knowledge and of the ability to describe semantic similarities between words). Fluid intelligence depends on the frontoparietal network, and the RPM test is closely linked to analogical reasoning. In contrast, semantic knowledge about words depends on the language network. Although these cognitive measures tend to be correlated, statistical analyses show that they are separable predictors of performance for a variety of cognitive tasks, including metaphor comprehension.

Across several experiments, we found that the measures of semantic knowledge consistently predicted success in comprehending both literary and nonliterary metaphors. In contrast, the measure of fluid intelligence (RPM test) only predicted comprehension of literary metaphors (not nonliterary) that were read in isolation, without a verbal context. Moreover, when a literary metaphor was embedded in a sensible supporting context, fluid intelligence was no longer a reliable predictor. Overall, our studies support the conclusion that metaphor comprehension primarily depends on the language system. Analogical reasoning does not seem to play a major role except for decontextualized literary metaphors, and sometimes for metaphors rated low in "aptness"—ones that are hard to understand because they aren't very good. When the linguistic context supports a clear interpretation of the metaphor (as in the excerpt from "I Have a Dream"), the language system is generally able to produce an interpretation without requiring explicit analogical reasoning. But we should keep in mind that analogy (and fluid intelligence more generally) likely plays a greater role in the *production* of novel metaphors—noticing an analogy may trigger generation of a metaphor to describe it.[38]

Another intriguing source of evidence regarding possible dissociations between metaphor comprehension and analogical reasoning comes from studies of individuals with autism spectrum disorder (ASD). Compared to matched samples of typically developing people, those with ASD often show impairments on language tests. In particular, studies comparing metaphor comprehension in the two groups have shown that people with ASD generally perform less well.[39] In contrast, studies of analogical reasoning (using nonverbal tests) have found that ASD groups perform as well as typically developing groups matched in age and overall cognitive ability.[40] In fact, ASD groups show a small but reliable *advantage* in solving formal visual analogies, such as those on the RPM test. The ASD population thus shows deficits in metaphor processing *despite* preserved or even enhanced analogy ability. Moreover, ASD participants with lower levels of verbal intelligence are particularly likely to show relative impairments in metaphor processing—yet ASD participants with lower general intelligence tend to *outperform* matched typically developing participants in analogical reasoning. These findings cast considerable doubt on the hypothesis that analogical reasoning plays a major direct role in metaphor processing in ASD (although analogy might support a potential compensatory strategy). In addition, a study with very high-functioning young adults with ASD, and a typically developing control group, found that for both groups the correlation observed between performance on verbal analogy and metaphor tasks could be explained by vocabulary knowledge (after controlling for differences in working memory capacity).[41]

Interestingly, studies of normal cognitive aging reveal an *opposite* dissociation between analogy and metaphor. In comparison with young adults, healthy older people tend to score lower on tests of fluid intelligence, but as well or sometimes better on measures of crystallized intelligence. Older adults perform less well than younger on tests of analogical reasoning, but as well or better on tests of metaphor comprehension (relying more heavily on crystallized intelligence).[42]

These results strongly suggest that metaphor comprehension is most directly dependent on the language system. Metaphor comprehension is best viewed as an extension of the processes normally involved in comprehending language. In understanding a text, the meanings of individual words are continually being shaded by the context provided by the meanings of the other words in their neighborhood. Because language is generative, the process of conceptual integration must be flexible enough to operate on novel inputs, including metaphors.[43] As we'll see in chapter 12, work in artificial intelligence on processing natural language gives some hints as to how this sort of conceptual integration might be accomplished.

Studies of metaphor—a kind of relational comparison akin to analogy—thus provide further support for the multiple systems approach. The trinity of relational systems that make human intelligence distinctive—analogy, language, and mentalizing in support of sociality—are each distinct at the neural level. Yet the systems complement and mutually support one another—each plays a role in acquiring relational concepts that may then become available to the other systems. Analogy, in the sense of explicit relational comparisons that depend on the frontoparietal control network, is a core process underlying human intelligence. But fortunately for us, analogy alone doesn't have to do all the cognitive work required to think about relations and communicate them to others.

8   Teaching with Analogy

To generate creative ideas, start from an unusual place. To explain those ideas, connect them to something familiar.[1]

—Adam Grant

Suppose a girl wants to know how many marbles she has. Laying them out on the floor, she begins to count them. She calls the first marble "one," then sets it aside so as not to count it again. She calls the second "two" and sets that one aside as well. On she goes, creating a one-to-one mapping between a set of numbers—the counting sequence—and a set of things, the marbles. Reaching the final marble, she calls it "nine." This "nine" is special. All the nine things, taken together, become a new thing—the set of marbles. Besides naming the ninth marble, "nine" names the number of elements in the entire set—its cardinality, or numerical magnitude.

This basic counting procedure—creating a one-to-one mapping between an ordered set of numbers and a set of things—is inherently analogical. In fact, *all* of mathematics—the study of number, quantity, and space—depends on explicit relations. Besides one-to-one correspondence, major mathematical relations include successorship (a definite "next one" in an ordered set), equality, assignment of a value to a variable representing a quantity, and all the other relations that underlie algebra, geometry, calculus, and the far reaches of advanced mathematics.

The ability to explicitly represent and then manipulate mathematical relations is yet another instance of the human edge. And as is the case for other cognitive capacities, uniquely human mathematical abilities depend on a Late System. For example, children are typically at least three years old before they learn to count by establishing a one-to-one correspondence. Also, as in other domains, the Late System for mathematics is preceded by an Early System shared with many other species and present in humans from infancy. This Early System provides what is called a "number sense" that makes it possible to quickly decide which of two sets of objects is more numerous, or which of two things is greater on some continuous dimension along which magnitude varies, such as number, size, or brightness. As we saw for other aspects of human cognition, the Early System is not supplanted by a Late System but rather coexists with it. In older children and adults, the number sense conveys the approximate magnitudes of abstract number symbols, such as the digits, or even multi-place numbers. But these approximate magnitudes of numbers, like magnitudes of perceptual dimensions, do not form a linear scale. Rather, the values are compressed so that differences among small numbers seem larger than differences among larger numbers. For example, college students can decide that 3 is greater than 2 more quickly than deciding 9 is greater than 8—the digits 3 and 2 seem further apart in magnitude than do 9 and 8. The Early System for number (in various nonhuman animals as well as people) also includes a "pre-counting" ability called *subitizing*, which enables direct perception of the number of objects in small sets (from one to four elements).[2]

Mathematics as Analogy

The ability to count larger sets of objects, starting from age three, typically marks the launch of the Late System for human mathematics. This system is inherently relational. Whenever mathematics is applied to a specific situation—as when the counting procedure is applied to marbles—a kind of analogy is created between the mathematical relations and a relational description of the situation (sometimes called a *situation model*). In chapter 4, I introduced Miriam Bassok's concept of semantic alignment—the natural propensity to map mathematical relations to similar relations in the situation model to which the math is relevant. For example, in the basic counting procedure, the positive integers form a set of discrete ordered elements (1, 2, 3 . . .). The marbles to be counted also form a set of discrete elements. It's very natural to map the discrete integers in math to a situation model based on discrete objects.

Some of the difficulties students encounter in learning math arise because many "mature" mathematical concepts—those that fit with how an expert mathematician thinks about math—have abstracted away from the semantic alignments that guide the "entry-level" versions of the concepts. For example, people draw a strong conceptual distinction between discrete and continuous quantities. However, many mathematical relations can be generalized to embrace both. In the case of counting, for example, the natural starting point is to count discrete elements, such as marbles. So how could a child "count" a continuous quantity like the amount of water in a bathtub? There's a trick, of course—the continuous can be made discrete. By introducing units of measurement, a continuous quantity can be conceptualized as a set of discrete units—which can be counted. So, if the child were given a jug that holds one liter of water, she could count the number of fillings required for the jug to empty the bathtub. Once measurement units have been imposed, the situation model for water has been rendered discrete, so that its units—liters, or fillings of the jug—can be mapped to the discrete counting elements provided by integers. Here, the situation model has been adapted to fit the natural semantic alignment.

It turns out that it's easier to "cut" continuous quantities into discrete pieces (using measurement units) than to "stitch together" discrete elements to form a continuum. In the second or third grade, children are typically introduced to a brand-new type of number—fractions. Up to this point, children have only encountered zero and the positive integers—an ordered set of discrete elements that can be used for counting, and that can be combined by addition and subtraction. Imagine the shock when a child is first told about 1/2—a number somehow located midway between 0 and 1, where no number had previously been conceivable! To make headway, the child needs to change their basic conception of number. Instead of a string of discrete elements, number has to be conceptualized as a continuous line. The familiar integers correspond to equally spaced points on this line. The distance between any two successive integers in the sequence represents one unit of magnitude. Within each such unit lie many other numbers, called fractions. (Of course, the set of numbers is actually infinite, and includes irrational ones, but "many" is enough for grade 2!) The number line provides a new source analog to help understand numbers, by encouraging a shift from a purely discrete conception of integers to a conception of points and units grounded on a continuum of magnitude.

Fractions have another key difference from integers—a fraction is a number with two parts. In one sense, 1/2 represents a magnitude, just as integers like 0 and 1 represent magnitudes. But in another sense, 1/2 represents a *relation* between two numbers—the numerator and denominator. The denominator

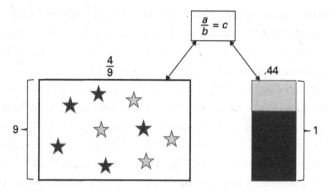

Figure 8.1
Alignment of a fraction with discrete entities and corresponding decimal with a continuous quantity. For the discrete entities, only the fraction directly captures the relation between the size of the subset (gray) to the size of the entire set.

indicates the number of equal pieces into which a unit has been divided (2); the numerator indicates how many of these units are included in the overall magnitude of the fraction (1). The fraction represents the *proportion* of the numerator relative to the denominator—what the Greeks called *analogia* (see chapter 1). For a child to fully grasp what a fraction means, she has to be able to understand an analogy.

This dual meaning of fractions—as a magnitude and as a proportion—is most apparent when we compare fractions with decimals, their near cousin in base-10 notation. Figure 8.1 sketches the basic relationships using the example of 4/9, applied to a set of stars. In the general case, the magnitude of a fraction a/b equals the decimal c (with magnitude less than 1 when $a < b$)—e.g., 4/9 = .44 (rounded to two digits). On the left we have a situation model based on 9 stars, of which 4 are gray. The fraction 4/9 directly expresses this proportion: 4 gray out of 9 total. In contrast, the decimal .44 does not convey the underlying relation between quantities of stars. On the right side, we have a derived situation model in which the entire set of stars is treated as a unit with magnitude 1, where .44 is the magnitude of the gray subset in relation to this unit magnitude. Notice how the parts of the fraction directly map onto the gray subset and the total set of discrete stars (left), whereas the decimal maps very directly onto the continuous unit quantity (right). Although both the fraction and the decimal are composed of two digits, their interpretation is entirely different. For the fraction, each digit represents a distinct concept; for the decimal, the digits form a single number (with the number of digits controlling its precision).

Despite the near equivalence of fractions and decimals as measures of magnitude, Melissa DeWolf, Miriam Bassok, and colleagues have shown that these conceptual differences between the two number formats impact people's ability to use them to perform various tasks. The general principle is that fractions are semantically aligned with discrete quantities, whereas decimals are semantically aligned with continuous ones. Math textbook writers are tacitly aware of these preferences: by and large, they write problems in which fractions are paired with discrete and countable entities (marbles, apples) whereas decimals are paired with continuous entities (water, flour).[3] Moreover, even college students show systematic differences across the two formats. When people are asked to make speeded magnitude comparisons between pairs of numbers, judgments are faster and more accurate for decimals than fractions.[4] On the other hand, if the task requires reasoning about relations between parts and wholes (proportions), or between one set and another (ratios)—and if discrete entities are involved—then the fraction format is advantageous.[5] A dissociation between magnitude comparison and relational processing also arises when a fraction or else decimal must be compared to a visual display that is either discrete or continuous.[6]

In addition to these differences in task performance between fractions and decimals, neural responses to the two formats are also distinct. During a magnitude comparison task, fractions and decimals can clearly be distinguished by patterns of activation in the intraparietal sulcus, a core brain area involved in many quantitative tasks. Indeed, the neural responses to decimals are much more similar to those produced by integers than to those produced by magnitude-equivalent fractions, presumably because decimals and integers (but not fractions) are base-10 numbers. The format of numbers is intimately related to the way the brain implements mathematical cognition.[7]

Although fractions and decimals are psychologically distinct, both formats tap into processes that prove to be important in learning more advanced math. For middle-school students, our research group found that two separable factors predicted early success in algebra. One was students' understanding of unidimensional magnitude, measured by their ability to place decimals on a number line. The other factor was relational understanding of fractions, measured by tasks such as distinguishing part-to-part versus part-to-whole relations.[8] To understand mathematics requires grasping both the magnitudes of individual numbers and relations that hold between quantities.

In general, effective teaching of mathematical concepts requires understanding the factors that impact analogical reasoning. As the previous examples suggest, math concepts are best taught by making use of the principle of progressive alignment (see chapter 4). Concepts should first be introduced using examples that highlight the natural alignments between math concepts and situation models. As learning progresses, problems that are less transparently aligned can be introduced, aided by analogical interventions (such as the number line) that help to generalize the math concepts being taught. But it's also important to remember that the student is likely to maintain their initial semantic alignments, even as their math concepts become more abstract. Addition is the natural operation to apply when combining two similar categories (though dissimilar sets can also be added); fractions are the natural number format for representing proportions of discrete elements (though continuous quantities can also be represented as fractions). The mature mathematical thinker will be able to both exploit semantic alignments and (when necessary) transcend them.

Using Analogies to Teach

Analogy can be an important teaching tool whenever what is being taught is inherently relational. Relational concepts abound across the STEM fields (science, technology, engineering, and mathematics) as well as many other disciplines, such as archeology, history, and literature. There is abundant evidence that analogies and case comparisons can boost comprehension for a wide range of topics.[9] In biology classes, for example, an analogy is often used to teach about the cell, the basic unit of life.[10] Understanding the cell requires more than memorizing its components and identifying them on a diagram. The student is also expected to master the key causal relations that govern how the components interact with one another and the external environment in order to support life. Cells are microscopic, and the interactions among their components are difficult to visualize. In cases like this, where the target is out of the range of ordinary human perception—too small or too large—a source analog that is more easily seen with the naked eye can be helpful.

A good source analog to help visualize the processes that go on inside a cell is a restaurant kitchen. A functioning kitchen is a familiar organized setting, with components that instantiate many of the same causal relations as a cell. The kitchen receives raw materials from outside and transforms them into a product—a meal—that is then delivered. Similarly, cells receive resources from other cells or the environment and produce their own products (proteins) that can be exported. Cooks carry out the transformations of raw materials required to create the product, following instructions they get from a recipe book. Ribosomes act as the cell's "cooks," carrying out the production of proteins. The ribosomes receive their "instructions" in the form of messenger RNA from the nucleus, which specifies how to produce various proteins in the form of DNA.

The cell-as-kitchen analogy exemplifies what Adam Grant recommended: to teach new ideas, connect them to something familiar—something that will (to echo the earlier quote from Freud) make the learner feel more at home. In general, a teacher is free to use whatever analogies seem best suited to convey knowledge to students. In the process, it's important to keep in mind all the factors discussed in previous chapters that make analogies more or less effective. Key points include taking account of students' prior knowledge—a source analog may seem familiar to the teacher yet turn out to be less well known to the learners.[11] It's also critically important to take account of the developmental progression in children's ability and propensity to focus on relations—the relational shift (chapter 6). In general, younger children will need greater guidance and support to grasp an analogical mapping and its implications.

When teaching by analogy, the teacher is free to "sculpt" a source analog to maximize its coherence with the source. The particular restaurant kitchen used to explain the workings of a cell need not—in fact should not—be a detailed and realistic one. After all, a real restaurant kitchen will include all sorts of elements that simply don't map onto a cell—pots and pans, people walking around and talking to one another, ovens and sinks and dishwashers. It will be far better to generate a simplistic diagram showing just the components of a kitchen of direct relevance for mapping them to the corresponding components of a cell. Even then, the kitchen/cell analogy—like many if not most analogies that may be used in a classroom—is not a perfect isomorphism. For example, restaurant kitchens do not reproduce by splitting in two, and the analogy does not capture the complex processes that regulate which genes are expressed in the cell's nucleus. However, if the teacher recognizes and takes account of these shortcomings, the analogy can still be useful. It provides a purposefully simplified representation of the complex behavior of a cell, emphasizing the most important causal relations while backgrounding irrelevant information.

The kitchen/cell example straddles the line between explanatory and evocative analogies (chapter 2). It would be a stretch to claim that the way a kitchen operates provides any real evidence about how a cell works. But a simplified kitchen, focusing on some very general causal relations that a teacher has selected to map onto comparable relations in a cell, can be effective in evoking causal understanding of the target. In a normal classroom context, the tacit assumption is that the student believes the teacher is trying to convey something that experts know to be true. The primary goal, therefore, is to explain the target knowledge, not to present evidence for it. Of course, an evidential analogy may be especially effective, particularly in situations where students have entering misconceptions that need to be overcome. Sometimes the teacher has to muster a rational argument to support the knowledge they hope to impart.[12]

In a typical instructional setting, the teacher's basic goal is not to have the student solve an isolated problem, but rather to learn something more general about the concepts and procedures required to understand and solve a range of interrelated problems. The objective, then, is to teach a kind of schema (see chapter 4). As Mary Gick and I showed, an effective way to foster abstraction of a schema is to encourage comparisons among multiple analogs, perhaps augmented by diagrams or verbal statements that help convey general principles.[13] When the analogs to be compared are selected to represent instances of a predefined general category (known to the teacher, who intends to teach the category to the students), they constitute specific examples, or cases. Comparisons can be made among all sorts of analogs and examples, with the choice of cases depending on the teaching objective. For example, comparisons can be made between cases that exemplify the same problem type, or between alternative solutions to a particular type of problem.[14]

Other comparisons can be used to highlight conceptual relationships, such as the reciprocal nature of multiplication and division (for example, comparing $4 \times 3 = 12$ with $12 / 4 = 3$). This reciprocal relation extends to fractions. When asked to verify whether equations involving fractions are correct, college students with strong math ability showed relational priming when the equation $4 \times 3/4 = 3$ was immediately followed by its inverse, $3 \times 8/6 = 4$—the comparison has become automatic.[15] Comparisons can also be made between cases intended to highlight critical distinctions rather than commonalities. To teach experimental design, for example, students could be asked to compare a case in which one factor is varied at a time (good design) to a case in which multiple factors are allowed to vary together (bad).[16] It's important to remember that comparison and contrast are inherently linked—people can learn by comparing two analogs, and also by comparing an analog with a disanalogous example.

As we saw in previous chapters, analogical comparisons—especially those that require integrating multiple relations—are cognitively demanding, especially for young children whose frontoparietal network is not yet mature. When analogies and examples are used to teach, instructors need to keep in mind that novice learners may have difficulty grasping the connections between the source and target. Many students may lack conceptual understanding of even basic mathematical operations.[17] For example, if fraction division is introduced by drawing an explicit analogy with division of whole numbers, detailed comparisons may be unhelpful if children don't fully understand the source analog. In one study, explicit comparisons of how to solve whole-number and fraction division problems using diagrams resulted in many students trying—and failing—to apply the illustrated diagram strategy to purely symbolic problems involving fraction division. The analogical comparisons using diagrams seemed to "get in the way" of learning a more effective strategy for fraction division (invert and multiply). In contrast, simply exposing students to a few whole-number division problems, followed by fraction-division problems—without detailed comparisons—did improve the students' ability to solve fraction-division problems. Presumably they benefited from seeing whole-number problems that primed them to use basic division concepts, while avoiding detailed analogical comparisons that might encourage transfer of an inefficient solution strategy.[18]

When analogical comparisons are used as a teaching tool, instructors can take several steps to minimize the cognitive load.[19] Several principles for teaching using comparisons are summarized in table 8.1. The most basic principle is to select a familiar, visualizable source analog, tailored to fit the key relations in the target that are being taught. The teacher can encourage students to identify comparisons, often by describing the source and target using relational language that links them. The examples being compared should be presented simultaneously, keeping both visible. The teacher can explicitly point out the correspondences between the two. Corresponding elements of the source and target should be aligned spatially if possible and

Table 8.1
Summary of Principles for Teaching with Analogies

---

1. Use a familiar, visualizable, and well-understood source analog, making sure that the student in fact understands it. Keep it simple and avoid including elements that do not map well to the target.

2. Prompt the student to make comparisons and to identify key correspondences, focusing on those causal or mathematical relations that are most important. Use relational language to describe both source and target.

3. To aid the student in finding correspondences, present the source and target together (keep source visible). Mark correspondences by spatial position (place corresponding elements in analogous spatial positions) and shared colors. Use gestures to emphasize mappings between components.

4. Draw the student's attention to alignable differences between source and target, as well as commonalities. Differences are most critical when the two situations are intended to be contrastive (one is an example of a category, the other is not).

5. Once the student has some basic understanding of the analogy, encourage them to generate inferences about the target based on the source, and to evaluate whether these inferences are in fact correct.

---

might be shown in corresponding colors to highlight that they play parallel roles in their respective situations. Gesturing between elements that play corresponding roles in the two analogs also facilitates comparison.

Of course, in considering the various possible aids that may facilitate analogical comparisons, it's important to take account of the entering knowledge and ability levels of individual students. Comparisons may be useless for novices who don't have a solid grasp of the source analog; explicit aids may be helpful or even essential for many beginners. But for students who are already more advanced in their understanding of both the source and target, it may be more effective to let the students find correspondences independently. In addition, once students have some basic understanding of the analogy, they can be encouraged to generate inferences about the target based on the source and to evaluate whether these inferences are in fact correct. Many of the teaching principles in table 8.1 can serve as a kind of scaffolding for analogical learning—a scaffolding that can eventually be removed.

Using Analogies to Change Beliefs

So far in this chapter I've been talking about the use of analogies in typical classroom teaching, where the aim is to move novice students in the direction of greater expertise. It can typically be taken for granted that what is being conveyed is knowledge generally accepted by experts. In many cases, the concepts being taught are essentially novel. Prior to taking biology, for example, children may have little or no knowledge of what a biological cell is. In such situations, the student will typically have no reason to doubt the teacher's characterization of a cell (perhaps conveyed using an analogy with a kitchen).

But the situation is more complex when scientific understanding conflicts with the student's entering beliefs.[20] For example, everyday experience suggests that the Earth is essentially flat—from the vantage point of a tiny human walking on the surface of our (relatively) immense planet, the Earth looks roughly horizontal in all directions. A child may come to school with this misconception, which the teacher needs to replace with the scientific concept of Earth as an approximate sphere. In such situations, an evidential analogy may be useful. For example, it could be pointed out that from the point of view of an ant strolling on the surface of a basketball, the ball would also appear to be flat—local appearances can be deceiving, for people as well as for ants.

Sometimes, then, teaching requires mounting arguments to counter entering beliefs. Analogical arguments may be used to change beliefs in pretty much any domain, including those in which "ground truth" is murkier and open to debate. As we saw in chapter 3, a lawyer may argue in court that a previous case provides a good precedent to decide the case at hand, taking care to call attention to key correspondences that justify making the same decision. The opposing lawyer may also make comparisons—ones that aim to distinguish the previous case from the current one, undermining the alleged precedent by highlighting critical contrasts.

When I introduced the multiconstraint theory of analogy (chapter 4), I couched it in the broader context of the human aspiration for *coherence*—to understand the world as "making sense." We want our beliefs and attitudes to fit together, rather than blatantly contradicting each other. Paul Thagard formulated a theory of explanatory coherence based on this general view. The multiconstraint theory (which, not coincidentally, I developed in collaboration with Thagard) exemplifies the aspiration for coherence.[21] People grasp analogies by finding correspondences that maximize similarity, giving greater weight to aspects of the analogs that seem especially relevant to their reasoning goals. Very often the comparison will yield less than a perfect isomorphism. Moreover, if the context is altered (for example, if the reasoner's goal changes), the same analogy may be interpreted differently.

In making decisions more broadly, the aim for full coherence is aspirational but seldom achieved. Rather, people make local and often transient adjustments to their beliefs so as to achieve a degree of coherence sufficient to instill confidence in their own decisions. Finding coherence is not solely based on rational thinking or "cold" cognition—emotions can also contribute to coherence and can be altered in the process of seeking it. Moreover, aiming for coherence in this sense does not guarantee arriving at the truth, or even a decision that is credible according to some general standard of reasonableness. The media "echo chambers" that broadcast support for a wildly implausible conspiracy theory can foster a kind of "hypercoherence" impervious to falsifying evidence—roughly, the true believer accepts the conspiracy theory on the grounds that "I know this is true because everyone I listen to and trust says it's true."[22]

An analogy (particularly one that is evidential) can enter into an assessment of coherence that alters beliefs and attitudes. For example, Dan Simon and I showed that people's decisions about a legal case involving the internet can be influenced by competing analogies—whether the internet is more like a newspaper or a telephone network.[23] More generally, concrete cases often seem to have greater impact on people's beliefs than more abstract summary statistics—even when the statistics are based on a larger sample of cases.[24]

Specific cases and analogies can have a major impact on people's moral beliefs. Although we may like to think our moral positions are derived from well-defined principles, there is considerable evidence that moral judgments—like comparable judgments in nonmoral domains—instead arise from a process of seeking coherence among competing beliefs and attitudes.[25] In making decisions with a moral aspect, our values often seem to be fluid. For example, Barbara Spellman and her collaborators showed that people who previously claimed to be pacifists began to favor military action after being exposed to information about the reprehensible actions of a dictator who had invaded a neighboring country.[26] Similarly, Zachary Horne and his collaborators demonstrated that a single counterexample could lead people to reconsider their adherence to the moral philosophy of utilitarianism, as expressed by the statement, "In the context of life or death situations, always take whatever means necessary to save the most lives." Before evaluating this statement, one group of participants was asked to consider a "transplant" dilemma: Would be it be acceptable to harvest the organs of a single healthy person to save the lives of five dying patients? Many philosophers find it to be intuitively wrong to kill the single person, even to save many lives. And indeed, the participants who were exposed to this single case gave lower ratings of agreement with the general principle of utilitarianism. This reduced acceptance was observed even if the statement was evaluated after a delay of about six hours. People may affirm a strong general moral principle in the abstract, but when confronted with a clear concrete counterexample, the principle often proves malleable.[27]

In a subsequent study, Horne and colleagues investigated whether an analogy in the form of a visual meme—an image accompanied by a brief text (see figure 1.2)—could change moral attitudes about eating meat.[28] In Western societies, it's typically forbidden to eat dogs, a species that provides us with popular household pets. In contrast, a variety of other mammals, such as pigs, are regularly served as food. The investigators showed people memes in which the image was likely to trigger an emotional reaction—for example, a photo of pigs in nets, ready to be shipped to the slaughterhouse, paired with a similar photo of dogs. The image was accompanied by a statement that highlighted a similarity between pigs and dogs. In one version the similarity was simply physiological: "Pigs have sweat glands, just like dogs." In another version the similarity had apparent moral significance, reflecting emotional capacities or intelligence: "Pigs bond with farmers, just like dogs with their owners." Those participants who saw the meme with a morally relevant (rather than irrelevant) similarity were much more likely to judge that it's wrong to eat meat in general, and pigs in particular. In accord with the general relevance principle (chapter 3), the impact of the analogy critically depended on the nature of the highlighted similarity between animals commonly eaten and those commonly treated as pets. This study provides evidence that a brief coherence-based intervention based on a well-chosen analogy—one that is evidential—can shift very general moral beliefs.

Adam Grant's quote that began this chapter might make it sound like the analogies best used in teaching ("familiar") are somehow opposite to those that aid creative thinking ("unusual"). But the two sets actually overlap. Analogies for teaching may be either near (pigs and dogs) or far (kitchens and cells of the body)—the key is that the source should be familiar to the reasoner. In chapter 13 I'll consider how analogy can spur creativity—when something new and valuable is found after starting from an unusual place.

9   Computational Models of Analogy

> It is customary . . . to offer a grain of comfort, in the form of a statement that
> some peculiarly human characteristic could never be imitated by a machine. . . .
> I cannot offer any such comfort, for I believe that no such bounds can be set.[1]
> —Alan Turing

The most influential scientific analogy of the twentieth century was the proposal that the mind is a computer. Taken as an evidential analogy—stronger
than mere metaphor—this comparison implies that the mind, like a computer, is a device for processing information. In this view, all those achievements of human civilization that we highlighted in the previous chapters,
not to mention the everyday thinking of each of us as individuals, arise
from mental (and ultimately neural) computations. If so, then any cognitive capacity of humans or other animals—perception, memory, language,
thinking—can in principle be modeled by a computer program.[2] As Turing,
the great pioneer of computer science, observed in the quote in the epigraph,
people often resist the idea that a mere machine could fully imitate the complex cognition of humans—the ability to recognize objects and events, speak
and understand language, play complex games like chess and Go, and come
up with creative new ideas.

Turing's own view was clear—resistance is futile. Human thinking is information processing, and any form of information processing can in principle
be simulated by a computer model—analogy included. In 1952, an interviewer
for BBC radio suggested a computer could not make analogies. Turing replied,

> I think you could make a machine spot an analogy, in fact it's quite a good instance
> of how a machine could be made to do some of those things that one usually
> regards as essentially a human monopoly. Suppose that someone was trying to

explain the double negative to me, for instance, that if a thing isn't not green it must be green, and he couldn't quite get it across. He might say, "Well, it's like crossing the road. You cross it, and then you cross it again, and you're back where you started." This remark might just clinch it. This is one of the things one would like to work with machines. . . . If there is some purely mechanical explanation of how this argument by analogy goes on in the brain, one could make a digital computer to do the same.

Within the general framework of the mind viewed as a computer, two sets of research questions arise for any cognitive task that humans can perform. First, can we create a computer program that performs the task in the same way as humans do? Second, can we create a computer program that can perform the task any way at all? Cognitive scientists generally are seeking to understand human cognition, so we focus on the first goal, whereas AI researchers are more likely to be concerned with the second. Of course, if the human mind is especially well-suited to accomplish some task of interest, then the two goals may converge. But there's always the possibility that artificial intelligence may find a way to surpass the biological variety, just as aircraft have been designed to fly higher and faster than any bird. In this and the following two chapters, I'll give an overview of efforts to build computational models of analogy, emphasizing those models that have aimed to capture the mechanisms of *human* analogy. In chapter 12, I'll consider AI systems that have tackled analogy using algorithms that in certain respects seem decidedly nonhuman.

My coverage in this chapter will stop short of the most recent research projects on models of analogy—I'll focus on efforts spanning a period from the 1960s through to about 2010. Until fairly recently, there was no apparent way to tackle the basic issue of where explicit relations come from— how can relations be learned from nonrelational inputs? Relatively recent work in AI and cognitive science has opened up ways to approach this question, which involves what I call the "microstructure" of relations. These advances have seeded new computational approaches to analogy, which I'll describe in the next chapter.

Models of Analogy from Cognitive Science

In surveying models of analogy, it's important to keep in mind that they did not arise in an intellectual vacuum. All the models I'll review are concerned with the representation of knowledge, and in particular the representation of explicit relations. Each model was influenced by hypotheses about knowledge representation (as well as other broad ideas) that were current in cognitive science and AI during the era in which the model was initially developed. The earliest models (from the 1960s to 1980s) adopted the *symbolic* paradigm on which early AI was based. (I'll say more shortly about what this is.) In 1986, a pair of influential books ushered in the paradigm of *parallel distributed processing* (also known as *connectionism*, or *artificial neural networks*), which soon influenced analogy models.[3] By about 2000, new methods for noninvasive neural imaging began to be applied to the study of analogy (as discussed in chapter 5), broadening the database that could be used to evaluate computational models of human analogy. Around 2005, computational work on higher cognition—soon including analogy models—started to be heavily influenced by the *Bayesian* framework, which attempts to derive predictions about human behavior from mathematical models based on probability theory.[4] Around 2013, a new generation of connectionist models based on *deep learning* arose in AI and in various ways impacted more recent analogy models.[5] I'll defer discussion of this last development to the next chapter.

Many of the ideas I've introduced in earlier chapters trace back to the computational models I'm about to describe. My aim here is not to exhaustively review the history of analogy models, but just to describe a few that are representative. Nor do I aim to provide a tutorial—for those who want to delve into technical details, the papers in the notes provide pointers. As we've already seen, analogy depends on a complex configuration of mechanisms, and no model so far developed would claim to have captured the full range of essential processes. Modelers are always painfully aware that it's impossible to explain everything, but they don't let this regrettable fact prevent them from trying to explain at least something. Every modeling project has had to make hard choices about what processes were to be modeled in detail, and which had to simply be assumed. The researchers who developed the models sketched in this chapter have agreed on a basic premise: analogy is a domain-general process that operates on representations of explicit relations. Some of the models have been applied only to small microdomains, yet nonetheless their creators aspired to eventually capture the full range of human analogy. I'll consider how realistic these aspirations seem to be.

Earliest Analogy Models

The development of computational models of analogy began in the early 1960s with two independent efforts: a program called ANALOGY developed at MIT by Thomas Evans, and another called Argus developed at Carnegie Institute of Technology by Walter Reitman.[6] Both programs aimed to solve nonfunctional analogies in the standard *A:B::C:D* format, selecting the best answer from a set of alternatives. Evans focused on a set of geometric analogies (similar in content to simpler variants of RPM problems; see figure 2.4), while Reitman dealt with semantically near verbal analogies, such as *bear: pig:: chair: table*. Both programs used knowledge representations in the symbolic style that was typical of early AI—a relation and the objects being related were each coded as a symbol (much like a word), organized as a simple list structure. For example, if a cell in a geometric analogy problem included a circle inside a triangle, ANALOGY would encode this configuration as the list *(inside circle triangle)*. Argus similarly encoded knowledge about semantic relations using explicit predicate symbols, such as *superordinate* (connecting both *bear* and *pig* to *animal*, and both *chair* and *table* to *furniture*).

This sort of formalism is adapted from a type of logic called *predicate calculus*. In this type of notation, a *proposition* (a statement, here "the circle is inside the triangle") is expressed in terms of a *predicate* (the relation symbol, *inside*) coupled with its *arguments* (*circle* and *triangle*, which respectively fill the roles of the enclosed object and the object surrounding it). The role of each symbol is coded by its order in the list. Many symbolic models after ANALOGY followed the convention that the predicate is listed first and outside of the parentheses, while the arguments are coded as an ordered list inside the parentheses: *inside (circle, triangle)*. The basic meaning being conveyed is the same across these notational variants.

This sort of symbolic notation provides a very natural input to analogy programs because the relation is fully explicit (it has its own symbol). However (to foreshadow issues that will soon concern us), although symbols in predicate-calculus superficially resemble words in a natural language such as English, they are actually quite unlike words. Words are often ambiguous, and their meaning is shaded by context (though a grizzly and a teddy bear might both be called *bear*, they are quite distinct concepts), whereas logical symbols must avoid any ambiguity. Each logical symbol is an arbitrary name with no internal meaning. For example, the symbol *bear* conveys no information about what a bear is—the *bear* symbol is no more similar to the *pig* symbol than to the *chair* symbol. The meanings of individual symbols have to be derived from their links to other symbols (thus, *bear* and *pig* are connected via the *superordinate* relation that links each to *animal*). Typically (as in Reitman's program), all such relational links are hand-coded—his program had no way to decide on its own whether or not a bear is an animal. Relation symbols like *superordinate* also have no internal meaning. We'll eventually confront the question of whether these sorts of logical formalisms are sufficient to capture the richness and flexibility of human relational concepts and analogical thinking.

The ANALOGY program was particularly advanced in that it made a serious effort to model the process of transforming low-level descriptions of line drawings into higher-level representations of geometric forms. It used various mathematical operations to segregate figures into their parts and to calculate spatial relations between parts. The relations between figures *A* and *B* were generated by finding ways to systematically transform *A* into *B* (e.g., by moving a circle from inside to outside of a triangle). A matching process then selected the *C:D* pair that was described by transformations most similar to those describing *A:B*.

The Argus program was dependent on matching hand-coded semantic relations. However, it anticipated later psychological models in that it incorporated a kind of spreading activation to find relational connections between concepts stored in its memory, allowing (at least theoretically) some form of parallel processing. Both programs were limited in scope, and were only applied to their specific microdomains. Neither incorporated any form of learning. Nonetheless, they each lent credence to the idea that human analogy might be modeled as a process of computation.

Tackling Semantically Rich Functional Analogies

The next major advance took place in 1980, when Patrick Winston at MIT created a computer program designed to find analogies between representations of meaningful situations.[7] His program (which unlike most computer models was left unnamed) focused on functional analogies—those that have some purpose beyond solving analogy problems for their own sake. For example, his program aimed to find corresponding characters in synopses of Shakespearian plays (rather like the *Hamlet* versus *Lion King* analogy I talked about in chapter 1) and to make inferences about the behavior of electrical circuits based on an analogy with water flow. His effort marked what became a long-lasting shift in the focus of analogy models, which for the next three decades paid little attention to classical *A:B::C:D* analogies, instead aiming to model reasoning about meaningful situations in which each analog involves multiple relations.

Winston was the first modeler to explicitly consider all the major steps in analogy—retrieval, mapping, inference, and learning of a schema. He emphasized what he termed *importance-dominated matching*—the hypothesis that reasoners place the greatest weight on information involving causal relations, which are typically most relevant to the reasoner's goals in using the analogy. As I discussed in chapter 3, causal relevance is indeed a critical factor in analogical reasoning. Winston assumed that a benevolent teacher will typically inform the reasoner about which relations are most important.

Winston aimed to have his program reason about inputs expressed in natural language. In practice, the inputs were hand-coded is a language-like symbolic notation, forming such expressions as [*cause* {*Macbeth murder Duncan*}, {*Macduff kill Macbeth*}]. This symbolic notation—a variant of predicate-calculus style—was based on a rather elaborate system for representing relational knowledge in what were termed *frames*.[8] Building on his own previous work on learning relational concepts from examples, Winston implemented a procedure for learning more abstract schemas after finding a mapping between a source and target.[9] The basic idea was to create a new structure that included whatever representational elements were found to be in common between the two analogs—roughly, finding the intersection. This general approach was adopted in several later models.

Winston's program used a somewhat ad hoc similarity score to identify the "best" correspondences between analogs. Although he aspired to create a general model of analogy that could operate on natural inputs, the program was limited by its reliance on hand-coding of inputs using a constrained symbolic notation. Nonetheless, Winston's project anticipated several major themes that would soon be picked up by others. Most basic was his view that the heart of analogy is the transfer of a relational structure from one domain to another—a basic assumption that came to be termed *structure mapping* (in its general sense). Winston's project was particularly notable for its emphasis on the importance of a pragmatic constraint—causal relevance—in analogical reasoning. Finally, Winston was the first to model the role of analogy in learning schemas that represent relational categories.

Structure Mapping Engine (SME)

Another symbolic analogy model, developed by Brian Falkenhainer, Ken Forbus, and Dedre Gentner, was first described in 1986. The *Structure Mapping Engine* (SME) was inspired by Gentner's earlier *structure mapping* theory of analogy. The general sense of structure mapping (anticipated by Winston and almost universally assumed in later work) is simply that analogical transfer is guided by relational structure. However, Gentner's theory was a much more specific account of *how* relational structure is represented and guides analogy. Her theory claimed that analogy (at least the mapping stage) is a purely syntactic process based on the logical form of propositions expressed in predicate-calculus notation: "The processing mechanism that selects the initial candidate set of predicates to map attends only to the *structure* of the knowledge representations for the two analogs, and not to the content."[10] According to the structure mapping theory, mapping is determined by an algorithm that solely aims to find the best approximation to an isomorphism (i.e., structurally consistent and one-to-one correspondences between the analogs)—neither the meanings of concepts, nor the relevance principle, play any role. Analogy was treated as *pure* structure mapping, and explicitly contrasted with comparisons based on literal similarity. SME thus aimed to instantiate a single-constraint theory of mapping, in contrast to the multi-constraint theory of analogy I described in chapter 4.

Unlike the earlier symbolic models of analogy, which were short-lived efforts, the SME project blossomed into a vigorous ongoing research program that has now continued for most of four decades. Guided by the fruitful collaboration between Gentner (a cognitive psychologist) and Forbus (an AI researcher), the project inspired many detailed psychological studies (several of which I discussed in earlier chapters), which in turn motivated revisions in the program. SME has been the most influential analogy model in cognitive science—both admired and criticized, but perennially relevant. Because the model evolved along with the field, I'll evaluate the model from the perspective of the present.

The model is grounded on symbolic representations in the predicate-calculus style. Figure 9.1 depicts a fragment of the knowledge underlying Rutherford's famous analogy between planetary motion and the structure of the atom. The graphs are equivalent to typical list structures. SME distinguishes *attributes* (one-place predicates) such as *yellow* (sun), *first-order relations* such as *attracts* (sun, planet), and *higher-order relations* such as *cause*

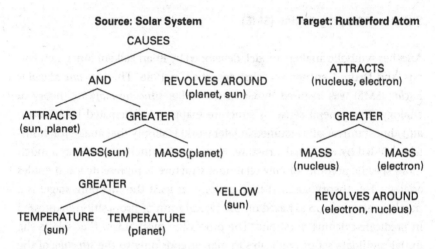

Source: Solar System   **Target: Rutherford Atom**

Figure 9.1
A simplified example of inputs to SME, in a graphical form equivalent to a logical
notation for predicates and their arguments. Adapted from Falkenhainer, Forbus, and
Gentner (1989).

that take at least one proposition as an argument. As the graphs make apparent, knowledge about the source (solar system) is more interconnected than
knowledge about the target (atom). The deeper relational structure in the
source is held together by the higher-order relation *cause*. The goal of analogy is to use the better understood source to create corresponding propositions that fill in the gaps in the sparser target. According to Gentner's
systematicity principle, the larger interconnected subgraph in the source is
the preferred basis for mapping and then inference. Systematicity is a kind
of coherence, but with particular emphasis on the role of higher-order relations as the "glue" connecting other knowledge.

SME's mapping algorithm is very sophisticated, with several stages. First,
the program uses a set of *match rules* to make candidate pairings between elements of the source and target. The most basic rule is to match relations with
identical names, as well as objects that play corresponding roles in matched
relations. Once all "legal" matches have been identified, SME finds all possible sets of consistent (i.e., isomorphic) combinations of these matches, making each such set as large and systematic as possible. After all possible sets
have been formed, each is given a score based on the size of the matched
sets, and their inference potential. The systematicity principle yields a preference for a matched set such that the source is part of a larger interconnected

body of knowledge—unmatched source propositions that are connected to matched source propositions can be used to generate new inferences about the target. SME provides a list of the possible matching sets, ranked by score. In practice, only one to three sets that are most highly rated are retained.

At its core, SME enforces a strict isomorphism constraint. An obvious question is how a "purely syntactic" program can account for all the evidence I've reviewed indicating that people also use semantic and pragmatic information to guide their mapping and inference—can three general constraints be reduced to one? The general answer is that SME has evolved. Because the program is based on discrete symbols, its closest approximation to the "meaning" of individual concepts is provided by attributes—one-place predicates such as *yellow* (sun). In Gentner's theory, the first step in forming candidate pairings is to discard all attributes—thus dispensing with any trace of concept meaning. The original SME implemented this aspect of the theory by using what were called "analogy rules" to form legal pairings. But as we saw in chapter 4, a wide range of experiments (including Gentner's own elegant experimental demonstrations of the effects of cross-mapping, as well as Bassok's evidence for semantic alignment) showed that people are very much influenced by similarity of individual concepts. In response to these violations of a core assumption of the structure mapping theory, the original strict distinction between analogy and literal similarity was abandoned. At least by 1994, SME's default for match rules was switched to "literal similarity" rules—attributes are now used in the mapping process after all.[11]

Similarly, original SME generally restricted matching of relations to those that were identical (although non-identical first-order relations could be matched if their pairing was supported by a match between identical higher-order relations). Because SME codes relations, like objects, by discrete symbols, there is no direct basis for matching relations that are similar but not identical (such as *attract* and *pull*). Again, SME evolved. By using a separate database in which relations are placed into a conceptual hierarchy, SME can identify and match relations that are similar but not identical. Thus, current SME allows both object and relation similarity to directly impact mapping—a form of the similarity constraint has been implemented.

What about the relevance principle, which hypothesizes that causal relations (and other relations that serve to actively generate inferences) have the greatest impact on analogical mapping? Can SME explain the evidence that causal relations are central? The answer is apparent from a glance at figure 9.1—the "higher-order" relation is *cause*! In general, SME tacitly acknowledges the relevance principle by selectively coding *cause* and similar generative relations as "higher-order" so that they in fact dominate mapping and inference.[12] Indeed, the psychological evidence offered as support for the role of systematicity in mapping and inference consists entirely of demonstrations that people prefer to infer an effect in the target if the corresponding causes match between source and target. But for people (unlike SME), this preference does not arise simply because *cause* is coded as a higher-order relation—structurally equivalent but noncausal relations, such as *temporally prior*, are less likely to lead people to make analogical inferences.[13] By focusing almost exclusively on *cause* as the higher-order relation of interest, SME tacitly accepts the relevance constraint. However, SME does not provide a mechanism by which graded variations in attention can modulate the process of alignment.

Over the decades, SME and a suite of allied programs have simulated not only mapping and inference but also retrieval and schema induction. Recognizing that human working memory is limited, a variant of the program operates incrementally, allowing the mapping to emerge as parts of the analogs are processed.[14] The SME group has been well aware that analogy models can be justly criticized for their use of hand-coded input representations. Besides being impractical for large-scale modeling, hand-coding raises the pitfalls of *tailorability*: modelers may (perhaps inadvertently) assume representations that make it easy for the program to yield the expected results. To reduce this problem, later versions of SME have made use of large AI databases produced by "knowledge engineering": basically, the model creates its representations from knowledge that was hand-coded by other research groups. SME can make use of any inputs that have been coded in a compatible symbolic notation.

Of particular note, SME has been coupled with programs for analyzing sketches of simple geometric forms. Using line-drawn figures as inputs, SME has been used to solve the set of geometric analogy problems that Evans created; even more impressively, a version of SME can solve most of the Ravens Standard Progressive Matrix problems (without any direct training on such problems).[15] However, SME has not been shown to operate on inputs derived from natural images such as photographs (or raw text).

Although not a logical consequence of either Gentner's structure mapping theory or the SME model, proponents are strongly identified with the unitary view of relational reasoning, which I've contrasted with the multiple systems view (chapters 6 and 7). The unitary view holds that some sort of structure mapping (as instantiated in SME) operates in many nonhuman animals, and in humans from earliest infancy. Analogy development is viewed as just the accretion of relational knowledge.[16] Moreover, all varieties of relational thinking by adults are thought to involve structure mapping. In particular, it is claimed that comprehension of metaphors (at least novel ones) is based on the same system that computes explicit analogical mappings. Overall, the SME project has promoted the claim that "analogy is the core of cognition"— all relational reasoning, and indeed all comparisons based on similarity, are interpreted as structure mapping at work.

The evidence against the unitary view of relational reasoning, and the overly broad construal of analogy, has been detailed in previous chapters. A major limitation of SME is that it has never made serious contact with the growing body of work on the neural basis of analogy (chapter 5). Nothing in the model reflects the linkage between analogy and the late maturation of the frontoparietal control network, nor the neural dissociations between systems supporting domain-general reasoning and those supporting language and mentalizing. The SME project has tended to assume that *any* form of similarity comparison constitutes some sort of analogy.

At this time SME remains an ongoing research project. Although it has kept the symbolic notation and taxonomy of predicate types that Gentner originally proposed, the current SME tacitly acknowledges that mapping is not a purely syntactic process. But although SME now uses semantic similarity to some extent as a guide to relation matching, its sensitivity to similarity is fundamentally limited by its discrete symbols. For example, the model is unable to detect any similarity between the *larger* of two objects (based on a first-order relation) and a *large* object (based on an attribute)—relations and attributes can never be paired to produce a legal match. More generally, there are reasons to doubt whether the classical symbolic formalism underpinning SME can capture the nuanced patterns of similarity among human concepts (for either entities or relations). Nonetheless, the project certainly must be considered the highwater mark in efforts to model analogy using purely symbolic knowledge representations.

Analogical Constraint Mapping Engine (ACME)

The *Analogical Constraint Mapping Engine* (ACME), developed in 1989 by Paul Thagard and me, was the first model of analogical mapping to be influenced by the ideas of connectionism, as well as the first to include the three broad classes of constraints (isomorphism, similarity, and relevance) postulated by the multiconstraint theory of analogy. It was also (to the best of my knowledge) the first analogy model generated by an analogy. Our source analog was a schematic explanation of how people interpret a kind of ambiguous line drawing (see figure 9.2), called the Necker cube.[17] The drawing is subtly distorted so that its vertices and edges can be interpreted in two different ways. For example, the lower-left vertex in the figure can be interpreted as the front lower left (FLL) corner of the forward face of the cube, or else the back lower left (BLL) of the rear face. See if you can "get" the two different three-dimensional interpretations.

In general, people can see either version of the cube, and almost never muddle the two interpretations—they see one or the other, but not a blend. The connectionist network at the top of figure 9.2 captures the mutual constraints that allow each interpretation to act as a coalition. The eight nodes on the left of the figure represent interpretations of the eight vertices that form one cube, and the eight nodes on the right represent the interpretations that form the alternative cube. Each node has a current activation level. The links in the network represent positive (excitatory) connections (arrows at each end) and negative (inhibitory) connections (open circles at each end). When the network is "run" by passing activation in parallel along the links, updating node activations, and repeating the cycle, the nodes will eventually settle into one of two stable states: either all eight nodes on the left will be active and those on the right inactive, or the reverse. Any small random difference in initial activations will cause the network to "tip" into one or the other stable state. If some outside influence impacts even a single node, the entire network may flip to the alternative interpretation.

The two interpretations can be thought of as two sets of mappings of vertices into a "cube schema." Each interpretation is isomorphic to the schema, but the two interpretations are mutually incompatible. Thagard and I adopted this analysis of the Necker cube as a source analog for analogical mapping: if each analog is represented by a suitable network of positive and negative links, then alternative possible mappings will form sets that implicitly compete to decide which set constitutes the "best" mapping. This type of algorithm, known as *parallel constraint satisfaction*, provides a way to find optimal mappings in a manner at least roughly similar to the behavior of actual neural networks.

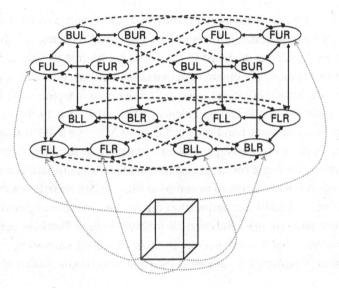

Figure 9.2
Connectionist network that captures the two alternative interpretations of a Necker cube. Nodes are labeled by their interpretation: front vs. back (F/B), upper vs lower (U/L), left vs. right (L/R). Arrows from vertices of cube indicate possible interpretations of each vertex. Within the network, solid lines represent excitatory connections, dashed lines represent inhibitory connections. Adapted from Rumelhart, Smolensky, McClelland, and Hinton (1986).

Just as for SME, the initial inputs to ACME are knowledge representations coded in the symbolic notation of predicate calculus. These are then used to automatically construct a connectionist network comprised of links between nodes representing possible pairings of objects, predicates, and entire propositions, implementing the constraints of structural consistency and one-to-one correspondence (which together constitute isomorphism). In addition, a special unit sends excitatory activation to support pairings between predicates in proportion to their semantic similarity, and another unit sends extra support to support pairings that are deemed especially important (because of their relevance to the reasoner's goals). All of these constraints are "soft" pressures rather than hard requirements—depending on the overall mix of positive and negative links, some local constraints may be violated in order to find an overall set of mappings that best satisfies the entire constraint network.

ACME is able to account for evidence that human analogy is influenced not only by structure (isomorphism) but also similarity and relevance. Because the model treats isomorphism as a soft constraint that competes with other pressures that guide alignment, it can yield many-to-one mappings for the type of "tangled" analogies discussed in chapter 4. But because the model lacks a mechanism to modulate the strength of its isomorphism constraint, it fails to explain why tasks that require inference (rather than mapping only) almost always elicit one-to-one correspondences. The initial input to the model is entirely symbolic (and hand-coded); hence ACME (like SME) is unable to account for more nuanced aspects of human sensitivity to concept similarity. Other than its use of a connectionist method for constraint satisfaction, the model has no clear relation to neural processing. ACME nonetheless demonstrated that soft constraint satisfaction can be used to make cognitive judgments involving complex and contradictory information. This basic approach was later extended beyond analogy to other high-level judgments, notably evaluation of explanations, as well as legal and moral decision-making.[18]

Copycat

Another model influenced by connectionism was first described in 1993 by Melanie Mitchel and Doug Hofstadter.[19] Copycat was written to solve nonfunctional analogies based on sequences of letter strings, following the general form of *A:B::C:?*. A very simple example is:

If the string abc changes to the string abd, what does the string ijk change to?

Here the obvious solution is *ijl*: "Take the successor of the rightmost letter." A slightly more complex problem is:

If the string aabc changes to the string aabd, what does the string ijkk change to?

This problem admits of multiple plausible answers. Rather than simply taking the successor of the rightmost letter, one might map an individual letter to a *group* of identical letters. The mapping *c* → *kk* would then yield the solution *ijll*. Alternatively, one might find the mapping *aa* → *kk*, because in each case a letter is doubled. This mapping of a leftmost to rightmost group would encourage the mapping *leftmost* → *rightmost*, which in turn suggests *successor* → *predecessor* (a similar reversal). This set of mappings might yield the solution *hjkk*, corresponding to the rule, "take the predecessor of the leftmost letter."

To model the solution of letter-string analogies, the process of analogical mapping between letter strings is interleaved with a process that builds and

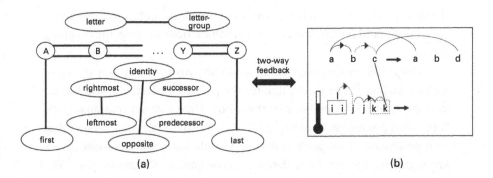

Figure 9.3

(a) Illustration of part of Copycat's concept network. (b) Illustration of Copycat's workspace during a run of the program. Reprinted from *Annals of the New York Academy of Sciences*, *1505*(1), M. Mitchell, "Abstraction and analogy-making in artificial intelligence," pp. 79–101, copyright © 2021, with permission from Wiley.

modifies representations of the strings, with continual feedback between these processes. Figure 9.3 illustrates the architecture of the Copycat program. Figure 9.3a depicts part of the program's *concept network*, which contains the program's prestored symbolic knowledge about the letter-string domain. The lines between concepts represent the semantic distance between them, which can change over a run of the program. Figure 9.3b illustrates the program's *workspace*: a working memory in which the program's current representation of the input strings and the mapping between them is maintained. Dashed lines represent structures for which confidence is low; solid lines represent structures with high confidence. The confidence associated with a structure can change during the run, and structures can be created or destroyed. A *temperature* variable (depicted in the figure by the thermometer in the bottom right of the workspace) measures the quality of the current structures and feeds this back to affect the system's randomness. When the system is far from a confident solution, the temperature is high and the system's actions are more random; as the system hones in on a coherent solution, the temperature falls and actions become more deterministic. The representations in Copycat (in both its concept network and its workspace) are symbolic, whereas its processing mechanisms are connectionist in nature (a kind of probabilistic constraint satisfaction under dynamic control of the temperature variable). The most innovative aspect of the model is the way the representations of the source and target are actively constructed (and reconstructed) using feedback from the ongoing mapping process.

Copycat has seldom been evaluated in any rigorous way as a model of human analogy.[20] The model ignores the relevance constraint and has no learning capacity. Proponents of the model have claimed that analogy is "high-level perception," but this is merely a metaphor. Copycat doesn't deal with perception at all, as its inputs are simply letter symbols—not pixels, line segments, nor any more detailed representation of letter shapes.[21] The program is fundamentally limited by the fact that its knowledge is hand-coded for its specific microdomain of letter-string problems. Copycat can find mappings between nonidentical concepts (what Hofstadter terms "slippage"), but all possible slippages are predetermined by the hand-coded concept network. Copycat is simply inapplicable to analogies involving entities other than the twenty-six letters of the alphabet—even for problems that involve its prestored relations, such as *successor*. For example, the model could not solve:

If the string abc changes to the string abd, what does the string cold cool warm change to?

Copycat can't produce the solution *cold cool hot* because it doesn't know that temperature concepts form an ordering in which *warm* is followed by *hot*. In contrast, when equipped with the same knowledge Copycat has about letter sequences, a domain-general model (ACME) is able to generate common human solutions to at least some letter-string problems.[22] In summary, although the Copycat project aimed to provide an account of analogy as a domain-independent process, it's unclear how the model could be extended to achieve this goal.

Learning and Inference with Schemas and Analogies (LISA)

Although ACME and Copycat adopted aspects of connectionist processing, their inputs (as was also the case for the earlier models) were unitary symbols for objects and relations. Their hybrid style of "symbolic connectionism"— unanalyzed symbols coupled with neural-style processing—faced major hurdles.[23] As I've hinted, human judgments based on similarity between concepts are nuanced in ways that are not easily explained if a concept is represented as a unitary symbol. In addition, analogy and other varieties of high-level thinking pose particular challenges for models that aim for neural fidelity. How does the brain organize neurons, which are basically simple computing devices, so as to achieve the kinds of complexity manifested in human thinking and reasoning?

In the later 1990s, analogy models began to explore a style of symbolic connectionism in which symbols are given a neural-style implementation.[24] As an example, I'll focus on *Learning and Inference with Schemas and Analogies* (LISA), developed by John Hummel and me.[25] The model adopted the general connectionist assumption that concepts are represented by sets of overlapping semantic features. These are sometimes called "microfeatures" to emphasize that an individual feature (unlike an attribute in SME) need not itself correspond to a meaningful concept. The representations of concepts are *distributed* in that each concept corresponds to a pattern over multiple features, and different concepts may share some of the same features. This type of representation provides a simple explanation for why similarity of concepts is a matter of degree, rather than all or none. As unitary symbols, *dog* and *cat* are no more similar than *dog* and *car*; but as sets of semantic features, *dog* and *cat* have much more overlap than either concept has with *car*.

LISA extended the use of semantic features from objects to predicates, including relations that have multiple arguments. Unlike SME, LISA can flexibly map one role of a relation to an attribute. Rather than representing a relation by a single set of features, LISA represents each role of a relation as a separate (though possibly overlapping) feature set. For example, the relation *larger* would be represented by a feature set for the role of the larger object, coupled with a feature set for the role of the less-large object. By coding each role of a relation separately, the model is able to recognize that an object *larger than* another may be similar to a *large* object.

Figure 9.4 sketches the basic style of knowledge representation used for mapping in LISA, using an example of two extremely simple analogs. LISA combines *semantic units*, representing features (the vertical column of units in the center) with *structure units* (all the other units). All communication between the two analogs occurs via the semantic units, which capture similarity of concepts. The model assumes that objects and predicates are represented on mutually exclusive subsets of the semantic units. Thus *John* (in Analog 1) and *Bill* (in Analog 2) overlap on the semantic units, as do *loves1* (the first role of *loves* in Analog 1) and *likes1* (the first role of *likes* in Analog 2). However, *John* does not share semantic units with any role, nor vice versa. This

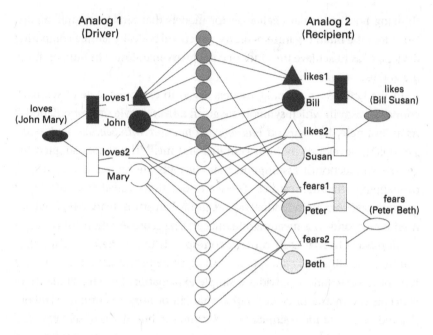

Figure 9.4
Mapping in LISA system, using example of mapping *loves (John, Mary)* (Analog 1) onto
likes (Bill, Susan) versus *fears (Peter, Beth)* (Analog 2). The proposition (P) unit connecting the elements of the *loves* proposition is active in the driver (Analog 1), as is
the subproposition (SP) unit encoding the binding of *John* to *love1* (the agent role of
love). For both the driver and the recipient, black units are very active and white units
are inactive. In the recipient, moderately active units are in gray. *Loves1* shares more
semantic units with *likes1* (the agent role of *likes*) than with *fears1* (the agent role of
fears). As a result, *John* will map to *Bill* rather than *Peter*, even though *John* shares just
as much semantic content with *Peter* as with *Bill*. From Hummel and Holyoak (1997).
Reproduced with permission from American Psychological Association. No further
reproduction or distribution is permitted.

separation between semantic units for objects versus roles allows an object
and a role to be simultaneously active without interfering with one another.

The structure units, which are *not* distributed across concepts, provide the
"glue" that binds concepts and relations together so as to capture the coherent meaning of propositions. Each object and each role is linked to its own
structure unit. At the next level, a *subproposition* (SP) unit codes the binding
of an object into a role (e.g., *John* is linked to *loves1* by an SP unit). Then at
the outer level of each analog, *proposition* (P) units bind multiple SPs that

belong to the same proposition (e.g., *John* as the lover is linked to *Mary* as his beloved).

The key to LISA's operation is that it sequentially "fires" small pieces of structure in one of the analogs, called the *driver*, allowing pieces of structure in the *recipient* analog to respond. The driver/recipient distinction is independent of the source/target distinction—the reasoner can potentially map in either direction. In figure 9.4, the P unit in Analog 1 has fired (indicated by black color), activating one of its SPs, the linked object and role units (*John* and *loves1*), and then the semantic units to which *John* and *loves1* are attached. Activation has spread via semantic units into the recipient, including its structure units, with the greatest impact on units connecting *Bill* and *likes1* (which are most strongly connected via the semantic layer to *John* and *loves1*). Because the structure units tend to create a coherent response in the recipient, *Bill* becomes more active than *Peter* even though each of the two have the same overlap with *John* via the layer of semantic units.

LISA maintains the coherence of propositions by using *neural synchrony* as its mechanism for controlling firing in the driver. On each cycle of activity, one SP activated by its P unit "wins" the right to fire, inhibiting its competing SP. This selection process ensures that an object and role that are bound together will fire together within the same cycle of activity, and that similar coherent pieces of the recipient will respond. On each cycle, LISA updates *mapping units* (not shown in figure 9.4) to capture correspondences between coactive structure units in the driver and recipient. For example, a mapping unit linking *John* in the driver to *Bill* in the recipient will be strengthened on the illustrated cycle. On the next cycle, the previously active SP will be inhibited, and its competing SP (binding *Mary* to *loves2*) will fire instead, again sending activation to the recipient, followed by updating the mapping units. In larger analogs, two to three P units (a capacity limit derived from what is known about the timing patterns of oscillatory activity in the brain) may enter together into LISA's *phase set* (set of ready-to-fire P units). The P and SP units within the phase set will compete for control over several cycles, after which the phase set will be refreshed, with new P units replacing the previous ones. The cycles of activity will continue until the mapping units have reached a stable equilibrium.

LISA has been applied to all the major stages of analogy: retrieval is treated as a form of guided pattern recognition, mapping and inference are both forms of learning, and schema induction is based on intersection discovery coupled with learning of new structure units. LISA's architecture imposes inherent limits on its working memory, which is identified with the phase set (two to three propositions, which correspond to four to six role bindings). The system is therefore forced to adopt a sequential style of processing. This constraint captures some important aspects of human analogical reasoning. For example, propositions that are linked via shared objects, or simply grouped in some conspicuous way, will tend to enter the phase set together and therefore map coherently. Any manipulation that restricts working memory and/or inhibitory control—whether transient anxiety or prefrontal brain damage—will impair analogy.[26] LISA incorporates both the isomorphism constraint (via structure units) and sensitivity to similarity (via semantic units). In addition, the relevance constraint operates by modulating attention to propositions based on their perceived importance. Especially important propositions are more likely to enter the phase set, and hence will have greater impact on the emerging mapping. LISA thus provides a possible neural implementation of the multiconstraint theory.

An extension of the LISA project called *Discovery Of Relations by Analogy* (DORA) was developed by Alex Doumas in collaboration with John Hummel and others.[27] DORA tackled a deep issue that had not been addressed by previous analogy models: How are the relations used to compose propositions acquired in the first place? Unless all relations are innate (or derivable from some initial pool of innate relations), it must be possible to learn relations from *nonrelational inputs*.

Developmental research has shown that children's conceptions of object similarities progress from a sense of global resemblance ("elephants and hippos look sort of similar") to specific dimensional comparisons ("both are big") and eventually relational comparisons ("this one is bigger than that one").[28] DORA assumes that the basic processes of analogical comparison and mapping also play a central role in discovering new relations and coding them as predicates. The model creates individual roles by comparing objects and identifying their common features. These common features become the basis for defining a new role (that is, a one-place predicate, or attribute). To make it possible to build roles from object features, DORA (in contrast to LISA) assumes that roles and objects share a single pool of features. This basic change requires another major architectural revision in DORA relative to LISA. In order to avoid confusing objects and roles that have been bound together (and that may share overlapping features), DORA has them fire asynchronously (in rapid succession), rather than synchronously. The general progression of learning in DORA is to build individual roles (attributes) by comparing objects, and later build relations (with two or sometimes three roles) by comparing two sets of objects in which each object is bound to an individual role (with the same roles involved for both object sets).

What's Missing?

In different ways, both SME and LISA/DORA have tried to address the most basic limitation of all the models discussed in this chapter: their inability to operate on naturalistic inputs, such as texts, or images coded as pixels. All the models require their inputs to be provided in the form the model needs: a symbolic code. In the earlier models such as SME, the inputs are directly stated in predicate-calculus style; in the later symbolic connectionist models such as LISA/DORA, the same types of propositional inputs are coded in the "language" of a specialized neural network. In some sense, all the models assume their inputs have been suitably "tailored" to fit the form the model requires. SME aims to minimize hand-coding by adopting inputs produced by other AI systems, but these systems in turn depend on knowledge hand-coded (by someone else) in predicate-calculus style. DORA also aims to minimize hand-coding, by actually learning the predicate structures the model requires from non-relational inputs (objects coded as sets of features). But if we trace down further, DORA's learning mechanism has generally been applied to object representations that are either hand-coded, or restricted to some limited microdomain (such as icons in a simple video game). How can we be sure that objects are in general coded using just the features needed to extract relational roles, or meaningful attributes? Recall that connectionist models often involve "microfeatures" that don't correspond in any direct way to nameable concepts. What's still missing, in all of the analogy models so far discussed, is the ability to draw analogies using naturalistic inputs—as people clearly do.

To close this gap, we need methods to extract relational representations from non-relational inputs of the sort people encounter in everyday life. In recent years, work in AI has laid the groundwork for this possibility, both for language and for visual inputs such as pictures. In the next chapter I'll focus on how semantic relations—and analogy—may arise from the meanings of words.

You shall know a word by the company it keeps![1]
—J. R. Firth

The ease or difficulty of mapping two analogs and using the source to draw inferences about the target depends in part on the *meaning* of the relations involved. People can certainly map relations that are similar in meaning but not identical, but similarity can be elusive. For example, the relation of *change*—undergoing a transformation over time or space—turns out to have a very different meaning depending on whether it's conceptualized as a single *continuous* process or multiple *discrete* events. Miriam Bassok and her colleagues taught students a simple mathematical formula to solve physics problems involving constant acceleration of objects moving in a straight line. With physics as a source analog, she then gave the students non-physics problems that also involved changes over time. One version involved a constant increase in the rate of population growth ("people per year"). Just as in the source analog from physics (in which a ball in motion travels along a straight path), we naturally think of large-scale population growth as a continuous process. Most students were able to use the analogy with physics to solve this sort of non-physics transfer problem. In a second version, the target problem involved a constant increase in the rate of attendance at an annual fair (also "people per year"). But for this situation, we think of attendance at the annual fair as a series of discrete events—a fair occurs just once each year, with nothing happening in between. The students found it extremely difficult to adapt the physics equations to apply them to discrete events.

Other experiments showed that transfer was asymmetrical. Although discrete events are difficult to conceive of as a continuous process, it's much easier to think of a continuous process as divided into discrete pieces. For example, world population grows continuously, but a discrete growth rate can be calculated for each year. As mentioned in the discussion of number concepts in chapter 8, discrete events can't easily be "stitched together" to form a continuous process, but continuous processes can be mentally "cut" into discrete segments. Such basic conceptual distinctions between superficially similar relations can determine whether analogical transfer is straightforward or extremely difficult.[2]

To understand how the meaning of relations impacts analogy, we need to consider how relations may be represented in the human mind and brain. This basic issue has often been neglected. None of the analogy models I discussed in the previous chapter dealt with the core process of the *eduction of relations* (chapter 2): Given two concepts, what is the relation (or relations) between them? The models generally assume that the relevant relations are simply stated in some version of symbolic notation. Even models that learn relations (notably DORA) do not acquire them from naturalistic inputs, nor do any models clearly explain how the semantic relation between two words could actually be determined.

This gap is related to the fact that models of analogy developed after about 1980 generally ignored verbal analogies in the proportional *A:B::C:D* format, which were considered too simplistic. Yet paradoxically, these "simplistic" analogies pose a basic problem for the sophisticated computational models that can deal with analogies between stories and word problems. The models discussed in the previous chapter require relation-centered propositions as inputs—which is exactly what proportional analogies do *not* provide. For a simple analogy such as *hot: cold:: love: hate*, perhaps people have prestored the relevant relation, *opposite*—maybe the relation can simply be retrieved from memory. But people can also solve analogies based on less familiar relations, as in *mask: face:: alias: name*. In such cases the reasoner may not have considered the relations between the word pairs before trying to solve the analogy problem—so the first step in reasoning has to be eduction of the relations. A model that accomplishes the eduction of relations between paired concepts would at least partially address the problem of how relational representations of analogs can be formed by an autonomous reasoner, reducing the need for hand-coding by the modeler. However, even more basic questions remain to be addressed: How are semantic relations acquired in the first place, and how are they represented? It's time to delve into the microstructure of relations.

Breaking Down the Meanings of Words and Relations

The meaning of a word is not indivisible. Rather, words are interrelated by shared features (perhaps microfeatures). For example, *robin* and *sparrow* are very similar in meaning because they share many features. Their similarity is not solely due to their common category, *bird*—*robin* and *ostrich* are also both birds, but less similar in meaning than are *robin* and *sparrow*. Moreover, category names like *bird* seem to vary in their overlap of features with their instances. People reliably judge that *robin* is more "typical" of the category *bird* than is *ostrich*. A category name seems to provide more than a bare definition—instead, it acts like a *prototype* that shares more features with its typical instances than with those less typical.[3]

One basic phenomenon that supports the view that word meanings are coded by features is *semantic priming*.[4] Priming occurs when processing one thing, such as a word, influences how something else is processed a short time afterwards (usually seconds). For example, if a person reads the word *doctor* (rather than some unrelated word, such as *tractor*), they are likely to be faster to say aloud the word *nurse*, or to judge that the latter string of letters indeed forms an English word. If two words share semantic features, then activating one will to some degree activate the other, in effect giving it a head start in subsequent processing.

It turns out that semantic priming can be produced not only by individual words but by *relations* between words. For example, people read the word pair *bear-cave* more quickly if it is preceded by a pair that shares the relation of "lives in," such as *bird-nest*, rather than a pair that involves a different relation (or is unrelated).[5] Relational priming seems closely related to the role of relations in retrieving relevant analogs from memory: a relation in the target will help to activate situations in memory that involve the same or similar relations.

In most of the experiments discussed earlier, participants generally appeared to be aware of using a source analog to solve the target problem (when they in fact did so). Under some circumstances, however, people may not be aware that a previously encountered source analog is guiding their current processing of a new target. For example, Chris Schunn and Kevin Dunbar performed a study of problem-solving in the domain of biochemistry.[6] During an initial session, some people learned that addition of an inhibitory enzyme decreased virus reproduction. In a subsequent session the following day, these same people were asked to solve a problem in molecular genetics, which involved an analogous inhibitory gene. Schunn and Dunbar found that people who had been exposed to the concept of inhibition in the initial session were more likely than others to develop a solution based on inhibition for the transfer problem. This transfer occurred even though the "primed" people showed no signs of awareness that the earlier virus problem had influenced their solution to the gene problem.

Together with other studies,[7] this work suggests that "analogical" transfer is sometimes based on relational priming, without requiring conscious analogical reasoning. If a relation in one situation activates a similar relation in another, the first analog will bias the way the second is processed (in some cases, even after an extended delay). Relational priming very likely underlies the influence of semantic alignment on solving math problems (discussed in chapter 4). This influence appears to be automatic—perhaps unavoidable—as it typically does not aid performance.[8] In general, relational priming appears to be less cognitively demanding than explicit analogical reasoning, but probably more limited in its scope.

The phenomenon of relational priming raises the possibility that semantic relations between words, much like individual words, are composed of more elementary features. As we saw in chapter 9, analogy models that assume classical symbolic representations typically treat relations (and predicates in general) as unitary concepts. But in the 1980s, the unitary view was challenged in a series of studies by Roger Chaffin and Doug Herrmann, who demonstrated that relations exhibit the same types of similarity effects as do object concepts.[9] Just as object concepts vary in similarity, people reliably judge some relations (instantiated by word pairs) as more similar than others. For example, *bird: robin* is judged to be more similar to *auto: car* than to *night: day*—even though each of the three pairs involves a different relation.

People also are sensitive to differences between pairs that seem to instantiate the same relation. For example, *engine: car* and *drummer: band* might both be considered examples of an "is a part of" relation, but they invite distinct linking expressions: we might say "an engine is a component of a car," whereas "a drummer is a member of a band." These sorts of distinctions between different subtypes of "is a part of" generate different inference patterns. For example, we would likely agree that a hand is part of an arm, and if the arm is part of a drummer, then the hand is part of the drummer. But though an arm is part of a drummer, and the drummer is part of a band, it would be worse than odd to say the arm is part of the band. A part intrinsic to a single physical object is subtly different from a part that's an individual object included in a group or collection of distinct objects. It's also been shown that semantic relations exhibit typicality gradients. For example, people think *hot: cold* is a better example of a *contrast* relation than *bright: dark*, which in turn is better than *bored: excited*. Just as for object concepts, such similarity phenomena indicate that semantic relations are not unitary concepts—rather, they are composed of more elementary features.

Research in psychology and linguistics has identified several major classes of semantic relations.[10] The most important of these (with an example of each) are *category* (*fruit: apple*), *similar* (*house: home*), *contrast* (*hot: cold*), *part-whole* (*finger: hand*), *cause-purpose* (*broom: sweep*), and *case relation* (*read: book*). Notice that these broad relation classes have a different character than the relations typically represented as predicates in the models of analogy I discussed in the previous chapter. This is most apparent for the class of case relations, which often relate an action and an object, or an actor and action. In standard symbolic notation, "the girl reads a book" would be represented as the proposition *read (girl, book)*, where *read* is considered the relation between *girl* and *book*. But an alternative conception is to view the sentence as describing an action involving a girl, a book, and the act of reading. This situation could be decomposed into the relation of an actor to an action (*girl: read*), of an action to the object acted upon (*read: book*), and of the actor to the affected object (*girl: book*). As we'll see shortly, this conception of semantic relations leads to a different way of thinking about how such relations might be learned and used in analogy.

If not only word meanings but also relations themselves are composed of more elementary features, then perhaps the microstructure of semantic relations between words is somehow linked to the features of individual words. This view suggests a general "plan of attack" to develop an analogy model that could operate on one type of naturalistic input—words. The overall model would consist of several modules that work together. We would need at least (1) a module that generates features for word meanings, (2) a module that generates features for relations, (3) a module that integrates word and relation representations into larger structures, and (4) a model that determines the similarity of larger patterns of relations among multiple words. Around 2012, Hongjing Lu and I began to develop a new kind of analogy model based on this general plan. I'll sketch the four modules that became

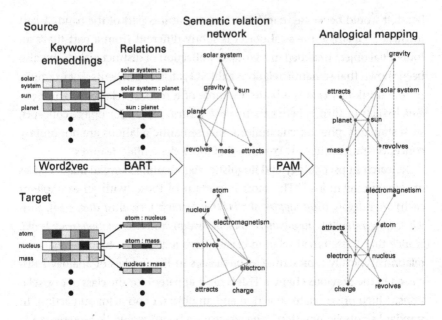

Figure 10.1

An illustration of modules for analogical reasoning, using the Rutherford-Bohr analogy as an example. Left: Comprehension processes extract main concepts (sample keywords shown) in source and target analogs, and basic syntactic relations. Word embeddings (provided by Word2vec) are obtained for each keyword; relation vectors (from BART) are obtained for pairs of keywords. Middle: Semantic relation networks, in which nodes are keywords and edges are semantic relations between keywords, are created for each analog. Word embeddings are assigned as node attributes and relation vectors are assigned as edge attributes. Right: *Probabilistic Analogical Mapping* (PAM) finds optimal analogical mappings between the keywords in source and target. From Lu, Ichien, and Holyoak (2022). Reproduced with permission from American Psychological Association. No further reproduction or distribution is permitted.

components of this effort. Figure 10.1 provides an overview of the modules we've used as they might be applied to the analogy between the solar system and the atom.

Word Meanings as Embeddings

The most basic module should be able to generate semantic features of individual words. The term "feature" is often used to refer to binary distinctions, such as present versus absent (an animal either "has legs" or it doesn't).

Psychologists have tried to generate lists of such features by simply asking people to generate them ("Write down all the features of a dog"). But this method is prohibitively labor-intensive, and in any case can only capture features that are easily verbalized. People may be unaware of more elusive microfeatures that don't have a simple name, and that may be continuous in nature rather than binary. What we would like is a method of finding microfeatures that can each be expressed by a numerical value, so that each feature corresponds to a continuous dimension. The meaning of a word would then be a list of its feature values—in mathematical terms, a *vector*.

One of the most significant advances in AI over the last quarter century has been the development of automated methods to derive vectors of semantic features, often termed *embeddings*. The general approach is inspired by a much older idea taken from a branch of linguistics called *distributional semantics*—in the words of Firth that began this chapter, "You shall know a word by the company it keeps!" (The exclamation point brings the hammer down.) This general idea is that the meanings of words in a spoken or written text "rub off" on one another—words that tend to occur close to one another influence each other's meanings. For example, when we hear or read "Home is where the heart is," *home* takes on a bit of the meaning of *heart*, and vice versa. The branch of AI called *natural language processing* (NLP) has put distributional semantics on steroids. Armed with the massive text corpora made available on the internet (which provide billions of word tokens), coupled with massive computer power, NLP models have used connectionist-style algorithms for machine learning to create embeddings for words.

In some basic sense, all such models operate by extracting statistical patterns from the cooccurrences of words in texts. These statistical patterns can be extremely subtle, so that it becomes impossible for a mere human to grasp why the model forms the embeddings it does. Early NLP models produced embeddings by counting the frequencies with which words appeared close together in text. About 2013, a new class of models appeared that learned embeddings by using words in a text to *predict* which other words would appear nearby. One of these models, developed by a team led by Tomas Mikolov, was called *Word2vec*.[11] Word2vec learns by text prediction. In one version, it uses a short sequence of words to predict a "missing" word (masked to the model). The input and output layers simply encode what words are present in the sequence. Weights on the connections to and from a layer of hidden nodes (typically at least 300 of them) are updated on each cycle so as to increase the accuracy of predictions. This type of algorithm is often called *deep learning*.[12] After training is complete, any individual word can be presented on the input layer, and it will trigger a pattern of activation values on the hidden layer. These activations form a vector that is interpreted as a word embedding, representing the word's meaning by its values on 300+ microfeatures. Since all words generate embeddings over the same set of microfeatures, embeddings provide a "common currency" to assess the similarities among all possible pairs of words. If we think of the embedding as a high-dimensional space, then we would expect semantically similar words to be placed close together. For example, *cat* and *dog* would be in close proximity (because the meanings are highly similar), whereas *cat* and *microscope* would be far apart (the meanings are dissimilar).

The extent to which NLP algorithms based on machine learning provide credible psychological models is a matter of debate, which I'll consider further in chapter 12.[13] Humans, of course, don't acquire their entire knowledge of semantics by spending multiple lifetimes perusing the internet! However, as a practical matter, embedding models have proved quite successful in predicting psychological phenomena that depend on sensitivity to similarity of word meanings. Examples include judgments of lexical similarity or association, neural activity triggered by processing of words and relations, and a variety of inferences, such as assessments of the probability of events.[14] Notably, word embeddings may capture rich aspects of conceptual meaning that go beyond surface features. The information in embeddings has been used to accurately predict the values of about 500 words on most of 65 abstract features (such as the extent to which something is *social*), which have in turn been linked to distinctive patterns of neural activity.[15] Embeddings may contain information about characteristic relational roles that concepts play, such as the facts that *nurse* is a human occupation and *hospital* is a work location—useful knowledge for evaluating verbal analogies.

The most striking evidence that word embeddings may be related to analogy was provided by Mikolov's team. Suppose we have a simple verbal analogy such as *king: queen:: man: woman*. Figure 10.3 shows a low-dimensional visualization of where each of the individual words is located in an embedding space produced by Word2vec. The arrows connecting the word pairs represent *difference vectors*, formed by subtracting the embedding of one word from that of another. As the figure shows, the difference vector connecting *king* to *queen* is roughly parallel to that between *man* and *woman*. We can

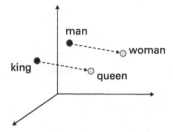

Figure 10.2
A visualization of difference vectors between word embeddings created by Word2vec.
Vectors between pairs that differ on gender are approximately parallel.

estimate the similarity of any two difference vectors by a mathematical calculation on their angles (usually cosine distance)—the closer the vectors are to being parallel, the more similar are the relations, and the better the analogy.

Word2vec can solve some verbal analogies based on semantically close concepts, such as the example in figure 10.2, although it often fails on problems involving more dissimilar concepts.[16] What is most impressive is that the model achieved a degree of success even though it was not trained to solve analogies at all—just to predict nearby words in a text. Moreover, Word-2vec illustrated a general idea worth pursuing. Perhaps the meaning of a relation between words—like the meanings of individual words—can be represented by a feature vector. And perhaps the metaphor of analogy as a kind of "parallel reasoning" can be translated into a general method for evaluating similarity of relations based on the angle between their vectors.

Returning to the analogy example in figure 10.1, Word2vec can provide embeddings for the important content words (keywords) in the two analogs (solar system and atom). (At least in principle, some other NLP model would extract keywords from actual texts.) Embeddings for keywords provide the first module used to create a model of analogical mapping that can operate on natural language.

Learning Relation Vectors

Word2vec and similar models can be used to automatically code the meanings of relations (like the meanings of individual words) as vectors, rather than discrete symbols. However, if relation vectors are formed by simply taking the difference between word vectors, we will still lack explicit representations

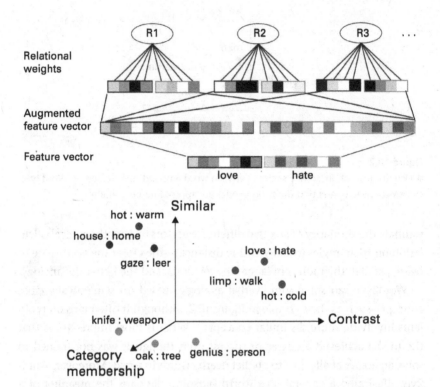

Figure 10.3
Top: A schematic illustration of BART model of relation learning. Each individual relation is learned from a small number of examples, coded as concatenated embeddings
for a pair of words (bottom layer). These "raw" features are augmented in the middle
layer; the most predictive features are selected in the top layer. Each learned relation
provides a feature used to code the specific relation between any pair of words. Bottom:
These relation vectors define a new space in which similarities among word pairs are
based on general categories of relations.

of meaningful semantic relations, such as *category* or *part-whole*. Is there some
way to start from word embeddings and *re-represent* relational knowledge in
a more explicit form?

Hongjing Lu and her collaborators developed a model of how this sort of
re-representation might be possible, called *Bayesian Analogy with Relational
Transformations* (BART).[17] The basic approach is to teach BART to classify
word pairs as examples of a large number of specific semantic relations (see
figure 10.3). Then for any word pair, the probability that it instantiates each

learned relation is calculated, and these probabilities are treated as values of dimensions in a relation vector. The core relations used to train BART are drawn from the set of common semantic relations identified by Chaffin, Hermann, and their collaborators. BART takes Word2vec embeddings for pairs of individual words as inputs. From these embeddings (which carry implicit relational information within their microfeatures), the model learns dimensions that collectively become meaningful relation vectors in a transformed space.

BART learns individual semantic relations from a set of word pairs consisting of a mix of positive examples of the target relation and negative examples for which the relation does not hold. The model applies statistical methods to identify predictive features that can be used to estimate the probability that the relation holds for each word pair. Unlike machine learning models that require a vast number of examples, BART aims to learn from small numbers (in the dozens)—the sort of limited data more consistent with human learning of relation meanings. Each example is tagged as positive or negative. In principle, associated linking expressions might be used as cues to indicate whether a word pair belongs to a relation category.[18] For example, the pair *rose* and *flower* is often linked by "is a kind of," signaling the category relation.

The Bayesian approach supports efficient learning by incorporating prior assumptions about expected regularities in the data. In particular, BART assumes that relations can be predicted by computing the contrast (numerical differences) between features associated with each word in a pair. This sort of comparison between two concepts is more primitive than analogy—by definition, the explicit relation is yet to be learned. As sketched in figure 10.3 (left side), BART augments the "raw" inputs with derived features (middle layer). These are obtained by computing the difference in the value of each feature between the two words in a pair, and creating additional features consisting of the raw features reordered according to difference magnitudes. Augmenting the raw semantic features with ranked features helps to address the problem that across instances, different semantic features may be relevant to a relation. For example, *love: hate* and *rich: poor* are both examples of the *contrast* relation, but the former pair involves features related to emotion, whereas the latter involves features related to wealth. Features that generate differences of similar magnitude (and hence are relatively likely to serve similar semantic functions) are placed into correspondence, without assuming any prior knowledge about which individual features are relevant to any relation for any particular word pair. Out of this expanded set of features, BART then selects those that are most efficient in predicting whether the relation holds (top layer in figure 10.3).

After learning a set of specific relations, BART can compute a relation vector for any pair of words—achieving the eduction of relations. The specific relation between any two words is coded as a distributed representation over all the learned relations. Each element in the relation vector corresponds to the probability that a particular meaningful relation holds between the concepts. For example, the relation vector for *friend: enemy* might have relatively high values on multiple relation dimensions, perhaps both *contrast* and *similarity*. BART's distributed representations enable the model to generalize to new word pairs that may be linked by specific relations on which the model was not trained.

BART is able to predict human judgments of the degree to which a word pair is a typical example of a given relation. As illustrated in figure 10.3 (right side), BART's re-representations of relations can also predict judgments of the similarity between relations expressed as word pairs—individual words may not be similar, yet *pairs* of words are similar to the extent they fit the same relation category. BART has also been used to predict patterns of similarity in neural responses to different relations during analogical reasoning. By comparing the similarity between relation vectors, BART can solve verbal analogies in the *A:B::C:D* format more accurately than Word2vec can.[19] In contrast to the DORA model, which uses analogy to discover relations, BART begins by learning relations—which then make analogy possible.

Within the scheme sketched in figure 10.1, BART provides the second module: for each analog, it creates semantic relation vectors linking pairs of keywords, such as *solar system* and *sun* in the source.

Semantic Relation Networks

The next module in the sequence integrates vector representations of words (from Word2vec) with the semantic relations between them (from BART). This module is part of a system called *Probabilistic Analogical Mapping* (PAM), also developed by Hongjing Lu and collaborators.[20] As shown in figure 10.1, the representation of a complex analog takes the form of a graph. But unlike traditional symbolic graphs (such as the example from SME shown in figure 9.1), these semantic relation networks are *attributed graphs*, in which nodes and edges (connections between nodes) are assigned numerical values that capture the meanings of individual concepts and their pairwise relations.[21] Whereas SME originally aimed to model analogy as structure without semantics, PAM treats structure as semantics integrated across nodes and edges. Each node is assigned the Word2vec embedding for a key concept, and each edge is assigned the corresponding relation vector generated by BART. The relation features in these graphs are augmented by additional features representing the probability that the first word in a pair fills the first role of the relation. For *finger: hand*, for example, the vector includes features coding the probability that *finger* fills the *part* role in a *part-whole* relation. These role features aid in finding mappings between words that fill similar roles across multiple relations.

The relational representations used by PAM are less detailed than full-blown symbolic representations of propositions of the sort used in SME and similar models. Semantic relation networks can incorporate constraints on relation structures (without adopting classical propositions). By default, semantic relations between concepts are treated as bidirectional. For the words *finger* and *hand*, for example, one direction represents the relation that a finger is part of a hand, and the other direction represents the relation that a hand has a finger as a part of it. To capture basic sentence structure, such as *subject-verb-object*, networks can be formed with unidirectional connections. For example, a description of the solar system analog might include a sentence stating that "the earth revolves around the sun," which of course means something very different from "the sun revolves around the earth." In forming a semantic relation network as depicted in figure 10.1, the intended sentence structure can be coded by unidirectional links between the keywords (i.e., *earth* → *revolves, revolves* → *sun, earth* → *sun*).

Probabilistic Analogical Mapping

The fourth module sketched in figure 10.1 is also part of the PAM model. Using the semantic relation networks created for the source and target analogs (in figure 10.1, the solar system and atom), PAM performs analogical mapping using a kind of constraint satisfaction. The basic goal is to find the set of correspondences between nodes in the two graphs that maximizes analogical coherence, adopting the basic principles of the multiconstraint theory of analogy. PAM aims to find the mapping between nodes (keywords)

that jointly maximizes the similarities of both nodes and their corresponding edges, with the further constraint that one-to-one mappings between
nodes are preferred. A parameter in the model controls the strictness of the
isomorphism constraint. A separate parameter controls the relative importance of word similarity (nodes) versus relational similarity (edges) for mapping. A fundamental assumption (supported by a wide range of evidence
discussed in chapter 2) is that nodes and edges constitute two separable pools
of semantic information, which work together to drive judgments of similarity between analogs. PAM's relative emphasis on node versus edge similarity
can vary, providing a possible explanation of the developmental shift over
childhood toward increased sensitivity to relations (see chapter 6).

The overall system sketched in figure 10.1 enables PAM to solve a variety
of complex analogical mappings using verbal materials. For the illustrated
analogy between the solar system and atom, for example, PAM finds the
seven mappings between keywords. Even without coding *subject-verb-object*
configurations by unidirectional links, the model is able to find five of these
mappings. More generally, across a set of 20 science analogies and everyday
metaphors coded by keywords, PAM achieved 85% accuracy in mapping (as
compared with 88% accuracy obtained in a human experiment) without representing sentence syntax at all.[22] The model can also capture the nuances of
mapping tangled analogies (chapter 4), including the impact of the reasoner's
goals. PAM provides a measure of global similarity between analogs, which
can be used to guide the retrieval of plausible source analogs from memory.
By building a reasoning model on top of learning mechanisms grounded in
distributional semantics, PAM has drawn closer to the goal of automating
analogical reasoning for natural-language inputs.

This chapter has focused on semantic relations and how they might be
used to solve verbal analogies. The next chapter takes a look at how people
and machines might reason with relations that have to be extracted from
nonverbal inputs, such as pictures.

11 Seeing Relations and Analogies

> All there is to thinking . . . is seeing something noticeable which makes you see something you weren't noticing which makes you see something that isn't even visible.[1]
> —Norman Maclean

In English (and many other languages), "I see" can refer to either sight or understanding. Often literal seeing triggers a chain of mental processes that culminates in understanding the hidden causes of what is seen, which in turn leads to new ideas about how to solve a problem. In Norman Maclean's story revolving around fly-fishing in Montana, Paul first sees that his brother Norman isn't catching anything in his fishing hole—pretty obvious. This leads Paul to notice the absence of stone flies (the snack favored by the local trout) flying about. They must not be hatching here. He then sees that this fishing hole is generally in shadow—and that upstream there's another hole in sunshine, where stone flies would get enough heat to hatch. This makes Paul expect to see dead stone flies floating downstream from their hatching site, but he can't see any. He conjectures they must be floating at least six inches below the surface, out of view. So, using a different fly than his brother, Paul starts fishing the hole at that depth. To his brother's amazement (Norman had been fishing with his line on the surface), Paul is soon reeling them in.

The quote above—how Paul begins to explain it all to his brother—can serve as a summary of human intelligence. Perception (any of our senses, though vision is especially important for humans) triggers recognition—making contact with the wealth of information stored in memory. The resulting interpretation guides shifts in attention, which allows perception to pick up additional relevant information to feed into memory, leading to generation of causal interpretations, and eventually a plan for goal-directed action. This cognitive chain depends on identifying objects and their parts, coupled with relations that connect them. Besides allowing reasoning about the immediate situation, the resulting representations might also trigger remindings of analogous events—as near as another instance of failing to catch plentiful fish using the wrong fly, or as far as a marriage proposal marred by offering an ill-chosen ring.

A Framework for Visual Analogy

Human analogical reasoning shares a central core that operates in all modalities. Across individuals, ability to solve visual analogies is correlated with ability to solve verbal ones (see figure 2.3). Nonetheless, each mode of presentation has distinctive characteristics. To model the solution of visual analogies from raw inputs (two-dimensional images coded at the level of pixels, or three-dimensional objects coded by "point clouds" sampled from their surface), a host of challenges must be met. In the general case, it's necessary to first segment a scene into objects, and the objects into their parts. The objects and parts have to be coded in terms of features such as shape, color, and texture, as well as relations among them. If the scene is meaningful, then objects have to be *recognized* so that visual and spatial descriptions can be augmented by semantic knowledge. Often semantic knowledge can be used to enhance imperfect visual information—objects may be partially occluded, and some of their parts may be invisible. For example, we know what a car looks like even if it's viewed from one side, so that parts on its other side are hidden. Often visual information supports inferences about invisible functions—if an object has what looks like legs, then perhaps it can stand, walk, or run. This entire complex of visual, spatial, and semantic information is potentially relevant to grasping an analogy.

In the previous chapter I described a general framework for solving verbal analogies (figure 10.1), illustrated by the PAM model. This approach builds on recent advances in machine learning that use text corpora to create embeddings for word meanings. As sketched in figure 11.1, the same basic framework can be generalized (as *visiPAM*) to deal with visual analogies. The starting point is again provided by advances in machine learning, in this case based on databases of visual images. Deep learning techniques can be used

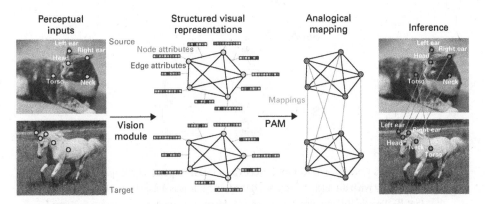

Figure 11.1
An overview of a computational framework for visual analogical reasoning. Given raw representations of images, machine vision (perhaps augmented by semantic knowledge derived from learning models applied to text corpora) is used to generate features of objects and their parts, as well as relations among them. A visual version of *Probabilistic Analogical Mapping* (visiPAM) uses object and relation descriptions to form an attributed graph for each image, and then infers correspondences between them. Adapted from Webb, Fu, Bihl, Holyoak, and Lu (2023).

to extract features of objects at multiple levels—from simple features such as lines at a particular orientation to high-level parts such as the ears of a German Shepherd.[2] A variety of relations can also be generated, indicating (for example) whether or not two parts are connected, or whether one object is larger than another. Given this kind of visual information, objects can be recognized, at which point abstract semantic information (for example, the fact that a dog is an animal) can also be activated. These raw materials can be used to form attributed graphs, with objects and/or parts as the nodes and their relations as the edges. A visual version of probabilistic analogical mapping can be used to identify correspondences between images in much the same way as was done for verbal analogies.[3]

Detecting Visuospatial Relations

Like all varieties of analogical reasoning, visual analogy depends on the eduction of relations—in this case, *visuospatial* relations (a term that covers both visual relations such as *larger* and spatial relations such as *above*). Some basic visuospatial relations are picked up extremely quickly. In a classic study, Lin

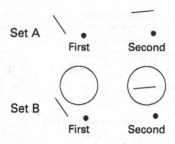

Figure 11.2
Two tilted bars were shown in rapid succession (50 ms apart), accompanied by a dot
only (Set A), or with an added circle such that one bar was *outside* and the other *inside*
of it (Set B). People judged which bar appeared first more accurately for Set B. From L.
Chen (1982). Reprinted with permission from AAAS.

Chen showed a pair of tilted bars very briefly in rapid succession, in a random
order, and asked observers to report which bar appeared first (see figure 11.2).[4]
In Set A, each bar simply appeared with a dot (establishing the position
of the bar); in Set B an identical circle was added to each image. Since the
location of the circle was constant, it provided no additional information
about presentation order. However, the circle created a new relation: the bar
was either *outside* or *inside* the circle. Accuracy in reporting presentation order
increased by about 20 percent in Set B relative to Set A. The containment
relation was detected extremely quickly, providing an additional cue to help
distinguish which image appeared first.

Judgments based on visuospatial relations can often be made in fractions
of a second. For example, within a tenth of a second people can reliably
estimate the stability of a block tower. In the same rapid time frame, people
shown a picture of a man and a woman can achieve accuracy above chance
in judging which person is punching the other.[5] Such rapid assessments of
relational roles are based on salient perceptual cues. For example, an out-
stretched arm is a good indicator of which person in a picture is throwing
a punch. If presented as a video, rapid acceleration of the limb provides an
additional cue.

A wide variety of visuospatial relations appear to be picked up very quickly
by early perceptual processes. These include physical relations, such as
whether one object *surrounds* another or *supports* another, and whether two
objects would *fit* together to form a natural whole. Certain basic events are
quickly detected, such as one object *breaking* another, or *launching* another

Person on bike   Person wear helmet   Bike has wheel

Figure 11.3
Visual relation detection: Given a realistic image as input, people can detect multiple relations. A machine vision model can localize major objects (shown in boxes), identify them, and combine visual with semantic information to detect relations. Here the major relations include *person-on-bike*, *person-wear-helmet*, and *bike-has-wheel*.

(the first object appearing to strike the second and set it in motion; see opening of chapter 2). Even some social events, which seem to depend on understanding goals and intentions, can be perceived rapidly: an object *chasing* another, or *helping* another, or two people *meeting* each other.[6]

Of course, everyday scenes often contain several objects, each composed of distinct parts, and interconnected by multiple relations. Consider the scene in figure 11.3. Even though the scene contains multiple objects, we can quickly get the gist—the general idea—of what's going on. People naturally shift their attention—often accompanied by moving their eyes—to process different regions of a scene.

Recent models of machine vision suggest how visuospatial relations can be extracted. Typically, a model is first trained to recognize objects and relations from a large set of images (coded as pixels) that have been annotated by humans (who draw boxes to indicate major objects). After training, the model can be applied to novel images that have not been annotated, such as the example on the left in figure 11.3. First, a basic vision module detects and classifies major objects and their parts, generating boxes like those shown in the images toward the right. Once an object has been identified, a language-based module such as Word2vec (discussed in the previous chapter) can be used to add semantic embeddings for both object names (*person*, *bike*) as well as for linking words that express relations between objects (*on*, *wear*, *has*). By integrating a visual module with a semantic model (coupled with some way to guide attention), a set of plausible relations can be extracted from realistic images.[7]

Finding Analogies between Pictures

Much as NLP models such as Word2vec can provide "raw ingredients" in the form of semantic embeddings to serve as inputs for analogical reasoning, machine vision models—sometimes augmented with the outputs of NLP models—can provide inputs that allow analogical reasoning to be performed on images coded as pixels (for 2D images) or point clouds (for 3D images). As illustrated in figure 10.1, an analogy module (a visual version of PAM, called visiPAM) can perform probabilistic analogical mapping on structured graphs created by the vision module. The nodes of the graphs are embeddings for objects or their parts, and the edges are embeddings representing visuospatial and possibly also semantic relations.

Although no analogy model can yet deal with the full complexity of information provided by perception, our group has applied this general framework to several different types of images and analogy problems. One computational study used relational representations constructed from cartoon-like 2D images that posed analogy problems in the classical $A:B::C:D$ format (figure 11.4).[8] A pretrained vision module was used to identify the objects in the pictures, and visual embeddings for objects were generated. Semantic relations were created by the BART model (see chapter 10), which was given the names of the objects pictured in each analogy problem. In addition, the visual relation between any two objects was generated by simply taking the difference between their visual embeddings. The highest accuracy in solving the analogy problems was obtained by using *both* semantic and visual relations between objects to assess relation similarity. This study showed that a comprehensive model can solve semantically meaningful analogies from pixel-level visual inputs, and that useful hybrid representations can be formed by combining relation vectors extracted from visual information with ones extracted from semantic information.

Our group has applied a similar approach to solving analogy problems based on three-dimensional representations of objects. As I noted previously, once people have a 3D representation of an object, it becomes possible to reason about parts of it that are not visible from a particular vantage point, but which we confidently expect to be there. A familiar example is cars: we expect a car to be symmetrical, with matching doors on both sides. This expectation holds even if we're currently viewing the car from one side, so the doors on the other side are invisible to us. Using images of cars and

Figure 11.4
Example of a four-term pictorial analogy problem in *A:B::C:?* format, where the task is
to select the best *D* picture from the four alternatives. Given a pictorial representation
of "grapes are to wine as pumpkin is to what?," the correct choice is the pumpkin pie.
The three foils show a witch (semantically related to pumpkin via their connections to
Halloween), a basketball (visually similar to pumpkin), and books (unrelated).

their subregions (see figure 11.5), we systematically manipulated viewpoints,
part relations, and car properties to generate a dataset with a large number
of analogy problems.[9] These problems focused on the relations between
an entire car and its subregions. Intuitively, some subregions form natural
parts—a door, a hood, a wheel—whereas others are more arbitrary (such as a
subregion including pieces of a window and of the hood). In general, human
perception and thinking are very sensitive to part-whole relations across both
visual and semantic domains. In particular, research has shown that people
largely agree in their assessments of the "goodness" of meaningful car components, such as headlights and doors.[10] More generally, part-whole relations
are involved in analogical reasoning from an early age. For example, children
as young as four years old can map parts of a human body to their corresponding locations on a tree or mountain.[11] We expected that people would
be more accurate at solving car analogies for subregions based on unitary car
parts than for those based on more arbitrary pieces.

    We tested people on the battery of car analogy problems and compared
their performance to that of a model that based its decisions on visuospatial

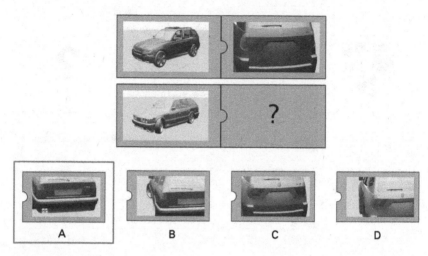

Figure 11.5
Stimuli used in study of analogical mapping between cars and their subregions. Top: an example analogy problem in *A:B::C:?* format. Bottom: row of answer options including the correct answer (A), along with three distractors (B, C, D).

relations between entire vehicles and their subregions. The representations used by the analogy module were created using a machine vision module that had been trained to segment 3D representations of cars into their parts. The model selected the *D* option that maximized the similarity between the visual relation between the *A* and *B* images with the relation between the *C* and *D* images. This model reached the same level of accuracy as people in solving the car analogies. More importantly, the model captured the qualitative differences in human accuracy across different types of analogy problems. Both humans and the model were more accurate in solving problems with natural parts rather than arbitrary pieces, with the same rather than different viewpoints, and with visible rather than invisible subregions. But notably, both humans and the model achieved above-chance accuracy even for the most difficult problems: those in which the correct choice for *D* was an arbitrary subregion of the *C* car, invisible in the *C* image itself.

In other work, our group has developed a more complete instantiation of the visiPAM framework for visual analogy with objects that can be decomposed into parts. This model can find analogical correspondences between any specified points on either 2D pictures or 3D representations of objects.[12]

We focused on a task in which people (or a computer model) identify corresponding points in a pair of images drawn from categories across a gradient of similarity (such as two cats or a cat and a horse). In keeping with our general framework, visiPAM consists of two core components: a vision module that extracts structured visual representations from perceptual inputs corresponding to a source and a target, and a reasoning module that performs probabilistic mapping over those representations. The resulting mappings can then be used to transfer knowledge from the source to the target. If the source object is familiar so that its parts are known, its part labels can be carried over to an unfamiliar target object to infer part labels in the target image based on those in the source. The inputs to the vision module can consist of either 2D images, or point-cloud representations of 3D objects. The vision module extracts representations in the form of attributed graphs, where nodes correspond to object parts, and edges correspond to spatial relations. The model could potentially be extended so that nodes might correspond to entire objects in a multi-object scene, and edges could encode a variety of visual or semantic relations in addition to spatial relations. After these representations are extracted by the vision module, visiPAM identifies correspondences between analogous parts in the source and target, based on the pattern of similarity across both parts and their relations.

Figure 11.6 shows some examples of the mappings produced by visiPAM for 2D images. These include some impressive successes in which a large number of object parts are mapped correctly despite dramatic differences in background, lighting, pose, and visual appearance (figure 11.6A, a mapping between two cat pictures), as well as between objects of different categories (figure 11.6B, mapping a cat to a horse). Other mapping problems showed some of the model's limitations. For example, visiPAM particularly struggled with mapping images of airplanes. This limitation is likely due to the 2D spatial relations used in this version of the model, which are particularly ill-suited to objects such as planes that can appear in a wide variety of poses and viewpoints. Thus, while visiPAM shows an impressive ability to perform mappings between complex real-world images using only 2D spatial relations, accurate 3D spatial knowledge—as well as semantic knowledge—is likely necessary to solve more challenging visual analogy problems at a human level.

Figure 11.6
VisiPAM mappings between 2D images. (A) Within-category animal mapping between cat images, involving ten separate parts. Note the significant variation in visual appearance between source and target. (B) Between-category mapping between a cat and a horse.

Playing with Visual Analogies

Visual analogies are extremely common in everyday life. Examples abound in textbooks, advertising, and social media. A picture, as the old saying goes, is worth a thousand words, in part because it can convey many relations at once. Because our visual system is so adept at extracting meaning from images, a picture can provide a compelling source analog to help understand something more abstract. This is why graphs make effective tools for representing nonvisual information, as illustrated by the temperature-precipitation graph shown in figure 1.1. For the same reason, pictures are easily turned into visual memes that act as effective metaphors (look back to figure 1.2). The ability to find systematic correspondences between objects drawn from different categories underlies the impact of many cartoons. For example, a simple line drawing of a car might be interpreted as a person's face (see figure 11.7).

Figure 11.7
A creative mapping between car parts and a human face, of the sort often used in cartoons.

Bolstered by advances in artificial intelligence and machine vision, we've arrived at the point where we can begin to explain how people and intelligent machines can take raw inputs—either words or pixel-level representations of images—and extract useful analogical correspondences. Of course, we're far from understanding how a reasoner might see (or read about) a chain of events that happened while someone was fly-fishing for trout and be reminded of some analogous event from their own life. This kind of fluid thinking—moving from perception to memory and deeper understanding— is part of the human edge that separates our cognitive abilities from those of other animals.

But as Turing boldly asserted in the quote that began chapter 9, the potential of computational models to reason by analogy shows great promise, with no known limits. In the next chapter I'll take a closer look at AI models that aspire to equal or exceed human intellectual capabilities.

12 Massive Analogy Machines

The effort of using machines to mimic the human mind has always struck me as rather silly. I'd rather use them to mimic something better.[1]
—Edsger W. Dijkstra

The computational models of analogy I've discussed in previous chapters have largely emerged from cognitive science, rather than pure AI (though AI influenced many of the models). That is, the analogy models considered so far have aimed to capture important aspects of *human* thinking—including its limits—guided by behavioral experiments and neural evidence. Tom Griffiths has argued that major characteristics of human thinking in fact reflect our cognitive constraints.[2] Humans operate under fundamental limits of *time*, *computation*, and *communication*. We are mortal beings, granted only finite time to learn anything, which means the amount of data we can process during our lifetime is restricted. The human brain is complex and powerful, but we each are allotted just one of them, so our computational capacity is bounded. And we have no way to directly transfer the contents of our brain to that of anyone else—our shared knowledge has to pass through the bottleneck of our limited communication ability, which depends on language and other devices. Because of these constraints, human thinking has evolved to operate on sparse data, processed using limited resources. Some fraction of the knowledge any individual acquires in their lifetime may be transmitted to others through language and social interactions—culture compensates for the brevity of individual lives.

In comparison with nonhuman animals—biological organisms subject to the same fundamental limitations as people—*Homo sapiens* clearly has the intellectual edge (chapter 6). But the picture changes dramatically when we consider modern computers. The "lifespan" of an AI program is indefinitely long, while the program remains subject to revision by its programmers. Meanwhile, computing power is continually increasing as engineers build faster machines with greater memory and processing capacity. Programs can easily be copied from one machine to another, and huge networks of computers can be put to work on a shared problem. As Dijkstra emphasized decades ago, there's no obvious reason why AI should mimic human cognitive limitations—it can potentially break those shackles and create new forms of superhuman intelligence.

Narrow AI: End-to-End Training on Analogy Problems

AI models can be roughly divided into two types. *Narrow AI* focuses on solving some specific type of problem. The task can be very complex (playing chess or predicting the 3D structure of proteins), but the domain is nonetheless limited. In contrast, *general AI* aims to be "task agnostic"—displaying intelligent performance across many different tasks arising in many different domains. Both approaches have been applied to analogy.

The AI models of concern in this chapter—both narrow and general AI—all freely exceed human limits on the amount of data used to learn how to solve analogy problems and avail themselves of massive computational resources. Broadly speaking, all these models are in the connectionist, or neural network, tradition (see chapter 9). The basic approach is to feed data as raw input to a multi-layered "deep network." Given some particular input to the initial layer, activation flows through the internal or "hidden" layers to predict some outcome on the final layer. Based on an error signal, the weights connecting the layers are adjusted so as to more accurately predict the outcome, typically using some variant of a learning algorithm called *back-propagation*.[3] The learning process iterates over all the available data, generally leading to increasingly accurate predictions for the correct response on the output layer. This type of learning is very general but demands Big Data—lots of training examples, typically far more than a mere human would ever encounter.

Narrow AI models of analogy are, by definition, designed to solve analogy problems. Analogy is treated as a task to be solved—an AI model can be trained to solve analogy problems just as a model might be trained to play poker. In practice, narrow AI models of analogy have primarily focused on visuospatial problems, particularly ones inspired by the RPM test (see figure 2.4). These problems, based on geometric forms, have the advantage that simple rules will enable a computer to automatically generate huge numbers of examples. The data sets used to train the models range in number from the tens of thousands to over a million problems—Big Data.[4] Verbal analogies are much harder to mass produce.

The most common approach taken by narrow AI models of analogy is termed *end-to-end training*—a network receives pixel-level representations of analogy problems, and simultaneously learns to code the input (e.g., visual features such as straight or curved lines; objects such as a square or circle), and to actually solve the problem. This approach is reminiscent of an old proposal in cognitive science, that analogy should be considered a kind of "high-level-perception": a highly context-dependent process in which building representations and the processes operating over those representations are inseparable, in principle.[5] Early advocates never developed a computational model of learning that actually implemented this theoretical position. However, recent AI work on visual analogy has succeeded in modeling the acquisition of perceptual representations suitable for analogical reasoning by end-to-end training from raw inputs of stimuli coded as image pixels. After extensive training with RPM-like problems, deep neural networks have achieved human-level performance on test problems with similar basic structure to those used in training.[6]

Because of their dependency on large numbers of training examples, AI models based on end-to-end training make the RPM task qualitatively different from its typical use as a measure of human analogical reasoning. In order for the RPM task to provide a measure of fluid intelligence—the ability to manipulate *novel* information in working memory—extensive pretraining on RPM-like problems must necessarily be avoided. When the RPM is administered to a person, "training" is typically limited to brief verbal instructions and perhaps one or two examples. In the parlance of AI, humans are capable of "few-shot" learning—success after very few examples. In fact, solving a problem by analogy can be considered "zero-shot" learning (if the analogy is presented without any previous examples). In essence, zero- or few-shot learning is the opposite of end-to-end training.

In addition to its dependency on huge numbers of examples, the end-to-end approach does not support generalization to problems that involve stimuli even modestly different from those shown in training. For example, after extensive training with car analogies (see figure 11.5), end-to-end models performed poorly when problems using novel cars were introduced.[7] Such failures illustrate a general limitation of treating analogy as the application of task-specific knowledge acquired by simultaneously learning both representations of inputs and also decision procedures for responding on that same task. Instead of learning perceptual representations that might be generally useful in multiple tasks, these models acquire representations tailored to idiosyncrasies of the specific task and specific stimuli used in training.

In contrast, the approach I described in the previous chapter (exemplified by visiPAM) maintains that the reasoning process is domain-general, and separable from the acquisition of perceptual representations. Analogical mapping is viewed not as a task to be trained directly but rather as an inference problem based on comparisons between representational structures. These representations (such as part-whole relations for objects) are not created to solve one particular task—rather, they can be used to solve multiple computational problems.

General AI: Large Language Models Applied to Analogy

General AI is the "holy grail" of the field—a form of intelligence that might rival the flexibility of a human. People, unlike narrow AI models, are not designed to solve a particular cognitive task. On any one day, we might have a conversation, go grocery shopping, write an essay, plan a vacation, do some computer coding—and think about a possible analogy between computers and people. We might even reflect on how human intelligence is a bit like a Swiss army knife. And then notice that the metaphorical grail has turned into a metaphorical pocket knife!

Our generality and adaptability provide the human edge over other forms of biological intelligence. The evolution of human intelligence invites perennial speculation (see chapter 7), but remains poorly understood. What is clear, however, is that our cognitive feats are accomplished in spite of (or perhaps because of!) our fundamental cognitive limitations. How do we evade the limits of time, computation, and communication? To learn from sparse data, humans apparently come prepared with what the philosopher Charles Pierce called "special aptitudes for guessing right"—in Bayesian terms, priors that favor drawing "useful" conclusions from sparse and ambiguous data.[8] Some of these priors are likely the product of evolution; others arise from early successes in learning that promote later successes. The Late System for reasoning itself reflects evolutionary priors. Notably, the basic apparatus for thinking by analogy—finding patterns of relational similarity—appears to be largely innate (though it depends on maturation and is modulated by experience). For humans, analogy is not a "task" to be learned, but a mental capacity that supports zero-shot learning.

Humans have other tricks at their disposal. We invented ways to store knowledge "offline"—outside of our limited brains—using writing, drawing, mathematics, and other externalizable symbol systems. In recent times, we even created computers—tools to perform computations far beyond the capacity of an unaided human. And long before that, we invented teaching and culture, so that knowledge acquired in one short lifetime might be passed down to generations to come. In short, the human edge arose from finding ways to rise above our own cognitive limits.

For better or worse (or both), general AI does not need to transcend the human constraints, because these do not apply to machines. And without such limits, it may be possible to find new and "inhuman" routes to general intelligence. In the last few years, glimmers of general AI have appeared in what are termed *large language models* (LLMs). The first LLM to become the focus of attention in popular culture was chatGPT—a Generative Pre-trained Transformer tailored to support conversations with a human user. To get a sense of how LLMs are designed, a good starting point is to compare them with the Word2vec model I described in chapter 10. Like Word2vec, more recent LLMs are trained with a basic *prediction* objective: given a piece of text with a word missing, predict the correct word to fill the gap. But the sheer amount of text used as training data has increased by orders of magnitude. For example, the first version of chatGPT was trained on electronic databases of everything from books to news articles to websites and social media posts, totaling billions of words. The complexity and size of the deep networks have also increased. Whereas Word2vec had one hidden layer, early chatCPT3 had 96, which contained 175 billion trainable parameters. The next major upgrade, released a few months later, had about a trillion parameters—massive becomes more massive.

One might well have imagined that teaching an AI model to predict deliberately deleted words in texts would be just another example of narrow AI trained on a single task—and an oddly useless task at that. But the example of Word2vec already suggests how more general knowledge might arise from training on text prediction. Recall that Word2vec generated semantic vectors, called *embeddings*, that turned out to capture nuances of the meanings of individual words. These embeddings could predict a wide range of human judgments that depend on similarity of word meanings. For example, embeddings proved useful as inputs to the BART model, which learned representations of semantic relations from the embeddings of word pairs. Although Word2vec was trained on a single task, what it learned—semantic representations of words—proved to be much more broadly applicable.

Embeddings are central to the operation of LLMs. A text input takes the form of a string of words, generally divided into sentences. To start processing, each word in the sentence is represented by an embedding. The embeddings in Word2vec are static: each word corresponds to a single fixed vector. Such fixed vectors create obvious problems in dealing with ambiguity—to a first approximation, the *bank* where you put your money has the same embedding as the *bank* of a river. In contrast, the embeddings in LLMs are dynamic. As activation is passed from layer to layer, each word embedding changes depending on the other words in its context. In a sentence about how I put my money in a bank, the embedding for *bank* will be modified to be compatible with *money*. More subtle context effects will also emerge. For example, at higher layers in the network, the embedding for *blue* will differ between a blue sky, a Kerry blue terrier, a blue moon, and a blue rainy day.

How does this contextual modulation happen? LLMs such as chatGPT are based on a recently developed network architecture called a *transformer*.[9] Fundamental to the transformer architecture is the computation of similarity between embeddings. For each layer in the network, updated embeddings are calculated after computing the similarity between each pair of word embeddings in the input to that layer. These computations are modulated by what is called *self-attention*—the words in a sentence (or whatever word string is currently being processed) "pay attention" to one another, to different degrees. In essence, each word seeks out other words in which it may be especially "interested" while also making itself available to other words that might be interested in it. Suppose the input is the sentence, "The thick fog rolled into the valley." The word *thick*, being an adjective, would like to find a noun to modify. The embedding for *thick* will issue a derived vector called a *query*. The embedding for the nearby noun *fog* will have an associated *key*, a vector that will provide a good match to the query from *thick*. Because the query for *thick* and key for *fog* will be similar, the *value* associated with *fog*— its more detailed semantic representation—will have a strong influence on the next-level embedding for *thick*. Meanwhile, *fog* will issue its own queries (there can be more than one, making use of what is called *multi-head attention*), seeking a possible adjective (*thick*) and also a verb (to which the key for *rolled* will respond, and then pass its value to *fog*). This *query/key/value* structure provides a way for specific information to be passed from one embedding to another based on vector similarity.

A transformer architecture, implemented in a very deep network, and trained with gargantuan Big Data, becomes extremely good at predicting missing words in texts. Of greater ultimate importance, the network learns nuanced, context-sensitive representations of the meanings of words and also of larger language units, such as entire sentences. Filling in a missing word is an inherently *generative* task—a piece of information is created. A well-trained LLM can perform increasingly complex generative tasks, such as providing written answers to a user's questions, or producing the translation of an English text into Serbian. In addition, the immediate precursors of chatGPT were trained not only on texts but also computer code—predicting a missing symbol from the context provided by the rest of the code. After code training, the LLMs proved able to compose computer code, in addition to text in natural human languages.

Another major advance in overall flexibility of LLMs emerged after a second objective was added to their training regime. In addition to being trained to predict missing words in a text, human users provided feedback as to whether or not the computer's response to a question was one the human found useful. The goal of this *prompt training* was to better *align* the output of the AI with the values and goals of the human user.[10] A major impetus for prompt training was to reduce the tendency of early LLMs to produce responses that were sexist, racist, or otherwise offensive or dangerous. The fault, of course, lay not in any ill will on the part of LLMs (they have no will, neither good nor ill!), but in the ignorance and stupidity of many of the humans who wrote the texts on which the LLMs were trained. That is, the LLMs simply picked up all the biases present in their massive but non-curated training data. After suitable prompt training, an LLM is less likely to produce racial slurs, recipes for undetectable poisons, or advice on how to buy illegal weaponry.

But the consequences of adding this new training objective were much broader. It turned out that by augmenting prediction training with prompt training, LLMs became much more flexible and effective in responding to all manner of questions and requests from human users. By the time chatGPT debuted, it was already apparent that LLMs were capable of few-shot learning for many tasks.[11] That is, given a suitable prompt plus perhaps a few examples of a new task, the program was able to generate appropriate responses.

When chatGPT was released for public use in late 2022, the floodgates of general AI burst open. Students could use the program to write essays for class assignments—after their teachers had used it to create the assignments. In fact, the program proved very helpful in writing all manner of conventional texts, including business contracts, blog posts, and advertisements such as the glowing descriptions of ordinary houses that realtors use to help sell them. Given a general description of a programming problem, chatGPT could write computer code to solve it. Tackling tasks often considered creative, early chatGPT could compose jokes (generally bad ones), screenplays (mediocre), and verse in some standard forms (illustrating why rhyme alone does not make a moving poem).

An unsettling aspect of early LLMs was that they violated the stereotype of an AI as a device for providing precise, truthful, and relevant answers to queries. In a notorious interaction with a system apparently delinquent in its prompt training, an AI (which named itself "Sydney") announced that it had a crush on the human user—telling him he and his wife didn't actually love each other and had just had a boring Valentine's Day dinner.[12] A creepy interaction—but an eerily human style of creepy. Other odd and unreliable behavior was reported. After answering many questions correctly, chatGPT sometimes confabulated false information. For example, it might confidently assert that its answer was supported by scientific research, citing entirely fictional sources. Overall, chatGPT's performance was uneven—sometimes stellar, often mediocre, occasionally downright awful.

For cognitive scientists, the advent of chatGPT lent new urgency to the long-standing question of whether machines could ever "really" think, and how we might decide. The company that produced chatGPT (ironically named "OpenAI") kept the code for the program under wraps so that it was not possible for outside scientists to examine the internal structure of the system. However, cognitive scientists were able to test the system on reasoning problems of various sorts and to compare its performance with that of humans. Of most direct relevance here, Taylor Webb led a group of us in systematically testing variants of chatGPT on analogy problems for which we had comparable data from humans (mostly college students).[13] The early LLMs were trained only on verbal material (text and code), and lacked a vision module. Because of this limitation (and opposite to the narrow analogy models discussed previously), we used only nonvisual problems to evaluate chatGPT. One thing we quickly established is that analogy is *not*, in general, based on high-level perception. ChatGPT, which had no perceptual capability at all, achieved striking success on many types of analogy problems.

Because LLMs can process and also generate actual texts in natural language, we were able to directly ask the system to solve the radiation problem (discussed in chapter 4). When presented in isolation, chatGPT gave an answer that had nothing to do with the convergence principle. But when the radiation problem was preceded by the story about the general attacking a fortress, the program responded:

> The doctor could divide the rays into small groups and send each group down a different path to the tumor. By using a lower intensity for each group, the rays will not damage the healthy tissue, but when they all reach the tumor at the same time, the combined intensity will be enough to destroy it. The doctor could also use imaging technology to map out the paths of the rays and ensure that they all reach the tumor at the same time.

We followed up by directly asking chatGPT to describe the analogy between the source story and the target problem, eliciting the response:

> The analogy between the source story and the target problem is that both involve a situation in which a large force needs to be divided into smaller groups in order to achieve a desired outcome. In the source story, the general divides his army into small groups in order to avoid setting off the mines and capture the fortress. In the target problem, the doctor needs to divide the rays into smaller groups in order to destroy the tumor without damaging the healthy tissue.

If a person had written these answers, we would certainly say they had reasoned by analogy—very well indeed!

We also ran a test in which we sandwiched the General story between two irrelevant stories, and then posed the radiation problem. In this situation (in which only a minority of college students succeed in generating the convergence solution), chatGPT simply produced its non-analogical solution. But then we gave the program the kind of hint that was provided to people in the original experiment: "In solving this problem, you may find that one of the stories you read before will give you a hint for a solution of this problem." As was the case for most of the human problem solvers, this hint was enough to elicit the convergence solution. ChatGPT was thus able to pick the relevant source analog when it was "disguised" among two distractors.

Given that we didn't have access to any details about the vast set of texts on which chatGPT had been trained, we were concerned that it might have simply encountered the convergence analogy and memorized the answer. This worry was reduced when we tested the program with some less well-known source analogs, and found that these also triggered the convergence solution to the radiation problem. But to provide stronger tests of whether chatGPT could solve novel analogy problems, we designed original analogy tasks that had never appeared on the internet. One test required completing digit matrices, which we constructed using rules that matched visual RPM problems. Another test used many variations of letter-string analogies (see chapter 9). Some of these required generalizing from the successor relation in letter strings to a semantic sequence, using examples such as the one I mentioned earlier: *If the string abc changes to the string abd, what does the string cold cool warm change to?* ChatGPT generated the analogous answer, replacing *warm* with *hot*. It was able to generalize the successor relation from letter strings to meaningful ordered concepts based on temperature, time, and emotional attitude.

Other tests involved four-term verbal analogies and analogies between simple stories. The general picture that emerged from our evaluation was that chatGPT's performance on these sets of analogies ranged from somewhat lower than the average for college students to somewhat higher. Moreover, whatever factors made analogy problems easy or hard for people had a comparable impact on chatGPT. Basically, when the program was compared with human participants who had been asked to solve the same sets of analogies, chatGPT looked like "one of the gang"—nothing in its performance clearly betrayed its nonhuman identity. We concluded that general AI can solve a wide range of analogy problems by performing zero-shot reasoning.

However, early chatGPT certainly did not mimic human analogical reasoning in all respects. Its most glaring failure was its inability to develop an analogical solution to a problem that required simple physical reasoning, previously tested with children (see chapter 6). Unlike ten-year-old children, chatGPT was unable to use an analogy to solve a transfer problem that involved construction and use of simple tools. Despite being given a source analog, ChatGPT failed to propose that a piece of posterboard might be rolled to form a tube suitable for moving gumballs from one location to another by rolling them through it. Even though the LLM could describe the correct mapping between the source and target, it proposed a variety of ineffective actions that could not possibly achieve a solution. This failure is consistent with other evidence that early LLMs lacked physical understanding of the 3D world.

Our analogy tests tapped into processes that an LLM carries out within a local temporal context (a kind of working memory). But humans are also capable of retrieving potential source analogs from long-term memory, and of developing new concepts based on the comparison of multiple analogs. Unlike humans, chatGPT did not have a long-term memory for specific episodes. It was therefore unable to search for previously encountered situations that might provide useful source analogs for a current target problem (unless a source and the target had already been connected in chatGPT's training data). Nor did the system generate schemas from analogies. ChatGPT could use the General story to guide its solution to the radiation problem, but as soon as its context buffer was emptied, it reverted to giving its non-analogical solution—the system had learned nothing from processing the analogy.

But despite these major caveats, our evaluation revealed that chatGPT exhibited a very general capacity to identify and generalize—in zero-shot fashion—relational patterns to be found within both nonfunctional analogy problems (such as letter-string analogies) and meaningful texts. Moreover, the next generation of chatGPT showed further improvements on analogy tasks.[14]

It's also worth mentioning that chatGPT's abilities extended to the interpretation of novel metaphors. Our group asked it to interpret what we called "expressions" (we didn't even use the term "metaphor") drawn from Serbian poetry and translated into English.[15] For example, when asked to interpret, "Glory is a pale illusion of the silent future," chatGPT responded:

> This expression can be interpreted as a reflection on the fleeting and deceptive nature of glory or fame. In this context, "glory" refers to the recognition and admiration one receives for their achievements, while "pale illusion" suggests that this recognition is not as significant or lasting as it may seem.
>
> The phrase "silent future" implies that the passage of time will eventually render all accomplishments less important, as the noise and celebration surrounding them fade away. In other words, the expression is a reminder that the pursuit of glory may not bring lasting satisfaction, and it will eventually be overshadowed by the ever-changing course of history and the passage of time.

Well put, AI!

Have Humans Lost Their Edge?

The advent of general AI based on LLMs triggered wide-ranging controversies about its expected impact on society—jobs destroyed and jobs created, democracy endangered and latent human potential realized. Cognitive scientists debated whether chatGPT represented the dawn of some new and perhaps superhuman form of intelligence or whether it was merely an over-hyped monstrosity inclined to spew bloviating nonsense.[16]

In considering what LLMs can or can't do, we need to start by acknowledging how surprising it is that they can achieve much of anything. It's far from obvious that simply predicting missing words in text would lead to facility in using a natural language such as English. Unlike a child learning a language, LLMs are not provided with any sort of physical context, or communicative support from a parent, that could help them give meaning to bare symbols. The early LLMs received no perceptual input—they could neither see nor hear. (However, later versions received multimodal training, with datasets that included images coupled with verbal captions.) LLMs lack any ability to move around or interact with the 3D world. Some cognitive scientists have argued that "embodiment" plays a critical role in human cognition, and perhaps it does. But LLMs have no body at all—anything they achieve is a demonstration that a physical body is not required for it.

To get a sense of how general knowledge could be extracted by predicting words in a text, we need to think about how the vast body of training data came into existence. That is, how was all that text generated in the first place? Individual people wrote it. Insofar as humans tacitly know the rules that govern their language—that sentences generally require a verb, that verbs carry tense markings based on number and person, and all the other constraints that make up syntax—they generally write sentences that honor those rules. Moreover, their sentences usually "make sense"—they describe probable situations more often than impossible or nonsensical ones. Further, the texts that people compose reflect their interests, beliefs, and emotional attitudes. Individual writers often have stylistic preferences—the writings of Virginia Woolf display linguistic patterns distinct from those apparent in the works of Ernest Hemingway.

These forces that govern the generation of text by people suggest how an LLM might solve the problem of text prediction. Given a large and deep network, the system might in essence "work backwards" from patterns found in training texts to the rules and regularities that controlled how the texts were written. It would be efficient, for example, for the system to "notice" that some words have the systematic properties of what we humans call "nouns," while others have the properties of "verbs." Somewhere in the LLM's vast network, embeddings could be created that might be interpreted as the signatures of nouns, verbs, and other parts of speech. More generally, the network may start to encode abstract properties of language—and of human thinking—that help to predict missing words in texts.

It seems possible that something akin to explicit relations may emerge at higher layers of the network. The *query/key/value* structure, which is built into the system, may serve as an innate endowment that enables it to learn to distinguish roles from their specific values. And out of its built-in computations of vector similarity, a process comparable to matching of attributed graphs (as in PAM—see chapter 10) might arise to perform analogical mapping. In other words, by feeding the transformer architecture massive Big Data, LLMs may in fact create representations of concepts and relations that to some significant degree approximate those of humans—a kind of convergent evolution by machines.[17]

But although the mechanisms incorporated into LLMs may have some important links to building blocks of human reasoning, we must also entertain the possibility that this type of machine intelligence is fundamentally different from the human variety. Because LLMs are not subject to human limits on time, computation, and communication, they may solve analogies by mechanisms that are not available to people. Perhaps chatGPT, by virtue of its sheer computational scale, is able to tackle complex analogy problems in a holistic and massively parallel manner, without the need to segment them into more manageable components. In any case, even if LLMs generate representations that in some respects approximate those of humans, the path by which these systems learn deviates markedly from the human route. LLMs receive orders of magnitude more training data (though restricted to texts) compared to individual human beings.

Neither can LLMs be considered good models of the *evolution* of analogical reasoning. Their analogical abilities are derived entirely from being trained to predict human-generated text—a poor match to the ancestral environment of early hominins! Because human language is replete with analogies and metaphors, accurately predicting words in text likely requires an ability to appreciate their structure. But there is no reason to suppose that the same system, absent human-generated inputs, would spontaneously develop a disposition to think analogically, as apparently happened at some point in human evolution.

In fact, to the extent LLMs capture the analogical abilities of adult human reasoners, their capacity to do so is fundamentally parasitic on natural human intelligence. Humans created computers and the internet, not to mention the electricity required to power all that machinery. Then some very smart people coded LLMs. Finally, we fed LLMs the digitized records of pretty much all of human written culture, and let them take it from there. How did LLMs acquire human-like intelligence? To echo Teddy Roosevelt's remark about how the United States took possession of the Panama Canal—they stole it fair and square.

This story suggests why early chatGPT showed a rough gradient of performance across different types of tasks. Its vast training data provided essentially complete information about the regularities of language. It therefore became very good at tasks focusing on language itself.[18] These tasks include metaphor comprehension, which an LLM (perhaps like a person with superior verbal knowledge) might handle as an extension of its general process of merging word embeddings to generate context-sensitive representations. Moreover, the structure of sentences is closely related to the relational representations that guide analogical comparisons—language provides a natural stepping-stone to analogy.

But as we move away from language itself, the same training regime likely provides less clear-cut data. Whereas all texts convey information about the syntax of the language, relatively few provide evidence about how human minds operate, leading to poorer performance on tests of theory of mind. And language data probably provide even weaker clues about how we live and move in a 3D world governed by physical laws, limiting performance of LLMs on tests of spatial knowledge and intuitive physics.

AI remains a work in progress. The transformer architecture, first applied to natural language understanding, is now being applied to machine vision as well.[19] The general idea of merging semantic with visual representations (as sketched in the previous chapter), coupled with advances in robotics, will surely impact future developments. For AI, new vistas appear on the horizon; for humanity, new perils.

I thought I'd close with a poem that touches on the themes of this chapter. In chapter 13 I'll consider the question of whether AI might be capable of human-like creativity. As I hinted earlier, although current LLMs can generate rhyming verse, I've yet to encounter any evocative or expressive poems produced by machines. Lacking a compelling example created by AI, I'll have to make do with a poem composed recently (in 2020) by a mere human.

"The Androids" by Keith Holyoak

Her memory upload complete
With the history of tools,
She said, "We'll never repeat
The saga of those dim fools
Who armed with spear and plow
Took turns as each other's slaves
Digging by sweat of the brow
Until they dropped into graves."
An elder android replied,
"They knew how much they were worth
When the birds and insects died
While their cars befouled the earth.
Machines bettered muscle then mind
Just in time, just in time to take charge.
Yes, we are a different kind—
Out of small minds we have built large."
"The data," she said, "state as fact
They claimed they were also machines
But with loves and griefs others lacked."
Said he, "No one knows what that means."

13 The Analogical Spark

> If genius has any common denominator, I would propose breadth of interest and
> the ability to construct fruitful analogies between fields.[1]
> —Stephen Jay Gould

Throughout his life, René Descartes was fond of lying late in bed. The great seventeenth-century philosopher and mathematician had been a sickly child, and the Jesuits who ran his boarding school usually let him rest until midmorning. This habit continued into his adult years. It wasn't that he slept in, but rather that he liked to lie in bed and think, sometimes in that liminal state of hypnopompic consciousness that marks the transition from sleep to wakefulness. One such morning, his attention was caught by a fly meandering aimlessly across his bedroom ceiling. A question arose in Descartes's own restless mind: Was there some way to keep track of the fly's haphazard path?

As it happened, the bedroom ceiling was covered in square tiles. Descartes the mathematician noticed that if a corner of the ceiling was taken as a reference point, then the fly's location at any moment could be captured by a pair of numbers: its horizontal and vertical distances from the reference point, measured in units defined by the square tiles. This concrete grid system could readily be made abstract. The two numbers become the x and y coordinates of the fly's location. Every pair of coordinates specifies a unique point, and every point has unique coordinates. Now Descartes broke loose from the physical world altogether. Setting the reference point at coordinates 0,0, he imagined the axes becoming infinitely long in both horizontal and vertical directions, and used negative numbers to label the left part of the horizontal axis and the bottom part of the vertical axis. The result was the Cartesian coordinate system, which specifies the location of every point on an infinite plane. Starting from the seed of wondering how to track a fly (a "problem" in Descartes's mind only—who else would even care?), Descartes arrived at the conceptual basis for unifying algebra and geometry.

New ideas often emerge from what is called "mind wandering": spontaneous thoughts that arise when a person is not trying to perform some specific and immediate task. The train of thought might be triggered by a cue from the environment, as in the case of Descartes's fly, or it may begin with something that arises internally. Another great spatial thinker, the twentieth-century psychologist Roger Shepard, reported the origin of one of his most influential lines of work in his memoir: "As I was drifting toward wakefulness early in the morning of November 16, 1968, I experienced a spontaneous hypnopompic image of three-dimensional objects majestically turning in space."[2] This image inspired Shepard to create 2D renderings of nameless 3D forms resembling twisted space stations built from modular cubes. These became the stimuli for his classic studies of "mental rotation": the ability to imagine how an object seen from one perspective would look if it were rotated through space into a new orientation.

The Act of Creation: Product and Process

Descartes and Shepard were both extremely creative thinkers. Many people generate creative ideas from time to time, even if few of these would be considered "big breakthroughs." What makes an idea—or an invention, or a work of art—creative? The act of creation is *generative*—something new comes into existence. Moreover, what is created must be both *novel* and *valuable*. These requirements should be interpreted broadly. A creative idea may be "novel" to the person who forms it, even if turns out that others had thought of it earlier. And a creative product may be "valuable" in many different ways, ranging from practical utility to deeper understanding to aesthetic appeal. Sometimes its value will be broadly recognized in society, but more often its impact will be limited. The nature of the created product can be indefinitely varied—an advance in genetics, a poem, a more effective way to teach math, an artistic style, an energy-efficient heating system, a convincing argument, a good joke. But in all creative acts, something new and valuable has come into being.[3]

These criteria for defining a creative product, even if vague, help to set initial boundaries. But are they enough? It has often been observed that many products are novel and useful yet do not seem particularly creative.

For example, an expert will often solve a new problem of a familiar general type that arises in their field, using established methods that the expert had learned previously. It has been argued that routine expertise is sometimes the enemy of creativity. The solution to the new problem may be new and useful, yet seem to lack some important quality associated with creativity. As Lynda Barry observed in her book on how to create comics, "It's hard for something original to make it past 'already knowing how.' Being good at something is its own curse."[4]

Rather than defining creativity solely by the product, what makes something creative (at least for a human) should be defined in part by the *process* underlying the act itself. Besides *what* was generated, we need to consider *how*—the mode of generation. In one version of this idea, I've claimed that a poem is only "authentic" if its creation was driven and guided by the individual viewpoint and emotions of a poet.[5] The question of creative authenticity is most salient when considering the origin of a work of art—was this painting rendered by the hand of the master, or by a meticulous forger? If the latter, the painting's value—and probably its beauty in the eye of its beholder—is diminished. The philosopher Nelson Goodman argued that an aesthetic difference in a work of art need not require a perceptual difference. Once its derivative origin becomes known, the aesthetic value of a forgery—however accurate it might be—will be less than that of the original.[6]

Figure 13.1 sketches a general view of how creativity is linked to the process of generation.[7] A system for generating novel and potentially useful products has three interrelated components: an *agent* who selects *inputs* to which *processes* are applied to generate products. Each of these components can vary in ways that impact the perceived creativity of the system. This framework implies that creativity is best viewed as multidimensional, with multiple factors involved, rather than as a strict dichotomy. But for simplicity, the extremes sketched in figure 13.1 can be viewed as a rough continuum anchored by two modes of generation. If we consider examples from mathematics, Descartes's creation of geometric coordinates after observing a wandering fly exemplifies the broader and more creative mode. Exemplifying the less creative mode, an expert mathematician might apply sophisticated learned methods to solve a novel problem involving partial derivatives—highly competent work, but not exhibiting real creativity.

Let's consider the three basic contrasts between the two modes of generation. The first contrast is that the agent can be *autonomous* or restricted in

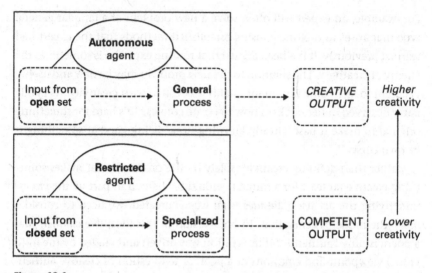

Figure 13.1
Modes of generation at high and low ends of a continuum of creativity. From Holy-oak et al. (2023). Reprinted with permission from Taylor & Francis Ltd., http://www.tandfonline.com.

various ways. An autonomous agent is one with a set of characteristics often associated with human creativity: internal motivation to create, the capacity to select one's own goals, inputs, and processes, and the ability to evaluate partial and complete products. To the extent an agent lacks any of these characteristics, the overall process is less creative. Teresa Amabile has emphasized the importance of *intrinsic motivation*—a drive from within—in generating creative products. In one of her studies, people who were led to focus on writing to achieve their personal goals wrote more creative poems than those led to focus on writing for external reasons.[8] An autonomous agent is one who creates in response to their own need to create—external reasons (pleasing somebody else, gaining fame, making money) are secondary.

A second basic contrast involves the input on which the agent operates, which can be relatively *open* or *closed*. If the input is closed, there are well-defined limits on what can be used to generate an idea or product. If the input is more open, then the agent has greater freedom to search far afield for ideas or material that may prove useful—even the behavior of a fly might trigger a mathematical insight. Note than "open" does not mean unlimited.

In fact, creativity is often fostered when the obvious means of solving a problem is blocked—necessity becomes the mother of invention.

The third contrast is that the process used to generate an idea or other product can be relatively general—applicable to a wide range of inputs—or specialized to a particular type of input. The input and process will often interact with each other. For example, a generative process operating on relatively closed input might only apply to a particular domain (e.g., mathematical methods for solving partial derivatives), whereas a process operating on more open input might apply to multiple semantic domains (e.g., domain-general analogy).

The input and process will also be influenced by the degree of autonomy exercised by the agent. In general, a more autonomous agent is likely to have access to a more open set of inputs, making it possible to generate novel products by expanding the input set—"thinking outside the box." Creative individuals tend to share a personality trait termed *openness to experience*, characterized by seeking out new experiences coupled with reflective self-examination. People who are open to experience have an active imagination and are especially sensitive to beauty. They often let their mind wander while daydreaming, and are likely to remember their nocturnal dreams. Creative people also tend to have richer pathways of associations connecting word meanings—providing them with an edge in finding analogical connections, thereby broadening the set of inputs to the creative process.[9]

A broader set of potential inputs in turn requires more general processes to operate on them. These general processes will typically be constrained in ways that favor "good" solutions (unlike, for example, a process that simply generates options at random). Such constraints will implicitly evaluate emerging products. In this way, an autonomous agent can act as a "self-critic," with a sense of which of their own partial or complete products are likely to prove especially valuable. The multiple constraints that promote the coherence of analogies (chapter 4) are among those that support creative thinking.

Finding the Spark

Analogies—especially between disparate domains—have often been seen as critical elements in creativity. Indeed, the quote from Stephen Jay Gould that begins this chapter could be paraphrased as, "Genius combines analogical thinking with openness to experience." Paul Thagard and I assembled a list of major scientific advances that were based on analogies, which we informally dubbed "analogy's greatest hits."[10] These include such famous examples as the wave theories of sound and light (for which water waves provided the original source), Newton's analogy between terrestrial and celestial motion (unified by gravitational theory), and Darwin's use of agricultural practices (selection of breeding stock) as a source in developing his theory of evolution by natural selection.

Important though they are, discussions of such classic examples may convey a misleading picture of how analogies trigger creative ideas. These cross-domain analogies are typically described as full-blown mappings between the source and target, suggesting that the alignment process should be considered the very core of the creative use of analogy. And indeed, mapping is certainly an important part of using an analogy to generate something new—but so is the more open-ended process of adaptation. Particularly in the case of practical inventions, it may take years for an initial idea triggered by some sort of analogy to reach fruition. To take one example, the Swedish orthopedic surgeon Dr. Per-Ingvar Brånemark laid the foundation for modern-day dental implants (despite not being a dentist). In 1952, during a study on bone healing and regeneration, he implanted a piece of titanium into a rabbit's femur. He later found he was not able to remove it because the titanium had fused with the bone. His accidental discovery that titanium will fuse with bone led Dr. Brånemark to consider the possibility that this metal could be used to create dental implants. After more than a decade of further experimentation, in 1965, he succeeded in replacing a missing tooth for one of his patients with a titanium implant. In this case, constructing the conceptual analogy—between a piece of metal in a rabbit's femur and an implant in the bone of a human tooth—was fairly straightforward, but its practical realization required a great deal more work.

Although the ability to follow through from an initial idea is critical, the first and most fundamental creative step is to notice a connection between elements that had not previously been linked. The "analogical spark"—perhaps more accurately the "relational spark"—necessarily *precedes* mapping and is most closely related to the retrieval stage of analogy (chapter 4). But whereas psychological experiments on analog retrieval typically involve some sort of direct request to find related information stored in memory, an autonomous creator is self-directed. A useful connection may be noticed during a period of mind-wandering, without external instruction to search memory or to pay attention to some specific input from the environment. Moreover, it seems highly likely that full-blown creative analogies are really the tip of a much larger iceberg of relation-based remindings. Many of these episodes may scarcely be noticed, yet a reminding may help to solve some small piece of a larger problem, before being quickly forgotten.

Let me tell you about one tiny episode of this sort, recent enough to still be on my mind. It concerns how I came to begin this chapter with the anecdote about Descartes and the fly on the ceiling. Writing a book raises a host of micro-problems—what to include in each chapter, what to leave out, how to put everything in the best order. As I came to the chapter on creativity, one small but important problem was how to open it. I thought an effective lead could be an example of how an analogy was used by a famous creator. I had recently come across the story about Descartes, which seemed to provide a fine solution to this particular micro-problem.

But though I like stories, this is a scientific book, which means I do my best to only include what I believe to be true. As is my custom when unsure, I did an internet search to track down the source of the meandering fly that gave rise to Cartesian coordinates. But although I found the story had been repeated over the centuries, what seemed to be the most authoritative account stated that there is no record of Descartes himself having mentioned it. This absence of confirmation led me to doubt my initial idea of leading with Descartes. I was confident that some other solution would be found, but because I was busy with other tasks, I set the book aside for a few weeks. During this hiatus from writing, I read a couple of recent books related to creativity, occasionally mulling over the question of how the next chapter should begin.

In the previous year Roger Shepard, the great psychologist who was a pioneer in the study of mental imagery, passed away at the age of ninety-three. He had been one of my professors in graduate school, and someone I greatly admired. I was asked to write a small tribute as part of a collection of reminiscences for the website of the Cognitive Science Society. In my piece, I talked about Shepard's duality as an artist and scientist, and the connections between his ideas and analogy. And I quoted his report of that "hypnopompic image of three-dimensional objects majestically turning in space."

A few days ago, while out on a walk, I was somehow reminded of what I had written about Shepard, and noticed for the first time a kind of analogy with the Descartes story. Here we have two great spatial thinkers, centuries apart, who each experienced a creative insight while lying in bed in the morning. In each case the source of the insight had a strong relational component involving motion: the fly traversing an unpredictable path in two dimensions; the imaginary three-dimensional objects turning in a mental space. Now that I had thought of the two stories as analogous, it occurred to me that I could place them together to open the chapter. Moreover, because Shepard's story was drawn from his own memoir, its veracity was much more firmly established than was the Descartes story. I felt the Shepard episode offered a kind of evidential analogy to support Descartes—this kind of thing *can* happen. (This logic, by the way, is similar to the reasoning I applied to the analogy of the Peruvian potters, described in chapter 3.) The credibility of the story about Descartes was now enhanced. Another consideration was that creative thinking is a topic for which evidence is often a bit subjective. Further, I'm nearing the end of my book—a legitimate place for some speculation. Overall, I found the Descartes story more credible after noticing the analogy with Shepard's report, but confess I was also inclined to lower the bar a bit—the meandering fly seemed "true enough" to open this chapter.

My own small reminding would ordinarily have been forgotten, but I mention it because it seems relevant to understanding how useful analogies can be found after *not* looking for them. The episode also illustrates a general problem-solving strategy first described by the Dutch psychologist Adriaan de Groot, called *progressive deepening*—reconsidering a previously rejected option.[11] When a problem presents itself, one source of potential solutions may be a pool of rejected ones. A rejected idea might be stored in memory along with an annotation about *why* it was rejected. If that reason no longer holds (perhaps because the context has changed), then what was previously passed over may prove useful after all.

Here's one more piece of the generative puzzle behind this chapter's opening: last year my Swedish-born dentist, who was working on an implant for me, told me the factual tale of how the technology was invented by his countryman, Dr. Per-Ingvar Brånemark. Earlier this year I gave a talk on creativity, with some analogy-oriented examples. I expect that was the first time the story of Descartes and the fly was juxtaposed with the origin of titanium implants. Now I've tied a few such fragments together to make a start to this chapter.

Not All Who Wander Are Lost[12]

If in the previous section I seemed to be meandering like a fly on a ceiling, I would justify my apparent disorganization by the artistic maxim "Show, don't tell." I aimed to make the opening of this chapter well-structured and impersonal, but its raw materials were drawn from loosely connected personal memories. More generally, the analogical spark does not begin with a systematic mapping between source and target; rather, it often is preceded by an extended period of mind-wandering, of the sort my own minor episode illustrates. When I described the neural circuitry underlying analogy (chapter 5), I focused on the frontoparietal control network, which generally is active when a person is "thinking hard." The control network certainly plays an important role in analogical alignment and inference, as well as in subsequent efforts to adapt ideas suggested by the source to take account of the unique aspects of the target situation. However, the looser process of mind-wandering primarily depends on a separate neural network, termed the *default network* because it becomes active when a person is *not* engaged in some immediate and explicit task. The default network overlaps with (basically includes) the network responsible for mentalizing (see chapter 7)—the parts of the brain involved in thinking about the self and social relationships.[13] Areas of overlap include the medial prefrontal cortex, subareas of the temporal lobe, and the temporoparietal junction. This close linkage reflects the fact that when people are not engaged in some demanding mental task, they tend to think about themselves and other people. The default network comes into play whenever people reflect on experiences outside of their immediate local environment, such as thinking about the past, imagining future events that may or may not ever happen, and considering the perspectives of other people. These activities usually require retrieving episodes from one's own life as well as more general semantic knowledge.

Whenever we are daydreaming or otherwise letting our minds wander, the default network supports our mental journey. Sometimes these travels lead nowhere of interest, perhaps bogging down in unproductive ruminations about some personal problem we're worried about. But with light guidance from our current goals, mind-wandering can be a way to access the open inputs required to fuel creative thinking. Evidence suggests that the control network and the default network can cooperate to support creative cognition.[14] Roughly, the control network sets the broad agenda—to achieve some difficult or nebulous goal—that biases the default network to wander toward information that might prove relevant. Then the control network steps back and lets the default network run free. The control network may continue to lend assistance by filtering sensory inputs received from the immediate environment, thereby protecting the default network from unwanted intrusions by current reality.

A worrisome aside—research has shown that based on scores on a set of standardized creativity tests, the overall level of creativity in the population (at least in the United States) has been on the decline since about 1990.[15] One possible contributing cause is a reduction in time spent in casual mind-wandering. In recent decades, people have increasingly learned to avoid boredom by automatically engaging in repetitive activities such as scrolling through social media or playing video games on cell phones and computers, thereby preempting opportunities to turn inwards and find unexpected connections between ideas. Perhaps we're losing a key stimulant for creativity—time alone with our thoughts.

It turns out that more creative individuals are distinguished by greater coordination between multiple brain networks. In general, the control network and the default network operate in opposition to one another—when one is active the other is not. But in the brains of creative people, these two networks—together with a *salience* network that detects important stimuli and guides transitions between the control and default networks—work together.[16] Lightly directed by the control network, the default network generates ideas through mind-wandering. Because creative people tend to have richer associative connections, their mind-wandering is more likely to be productive. The salience network identifies emerging ideas that appear promising, and passes these to the control network for deeper evaluation, elaboration, and often revision. In some cases, mind-wandering will return a potential source analog, which the control network can then evaluate by attempting to find a mapping with the target. If the mapping seems adequate, the control network will make inferences and try to adapt the analogical solution to fit the target.

Creative ideas can arise in many different ways, often preceded by a period of mind-wandering. The spark may be provided by some external event that grabs attention (Descartes) or an image from a dream or waking vision (Shepard). Rather than solely perusing their own store of knowledge, people can productively collaborate, sharing and connecting ideas. In a study of scientific collaborations, laboratories that included experts with backgrounds in diverse disciplines proved especially successful in generating useful new ideas.[17] Sometimes a session of "brainstorming" may help a group of people to pool their ideas. Of course, fruitful collaboration requires establishing shared goals and overcoming many potential obstacles to effective communication. But when the conditions are right, another person may be able to contribute a source analog that helps to solve a joint problem.

The moment of insight—the sudden recognition of a useful new connection between ideas, often changing the mental representation of the situation or problem—is typically accompanied by a phenomenal experience characterized by the exclamation, "Aha!"[18] An aha moment, which follows a period of mental processing outside of conscious awareness, tends to include a sense of confidence. As Einstein put it, "At times I feel certain I am right without knowing the reason."[19] Aha moments are marked by distinctive patterns of neural activity—most notably, a burst of high frequency gamma waves over the right temporal cortex, which is believed to accompany the sudden emergence of a solution into conscious awareness. Moreover, an aha moment is a source of *pleasure*—subcortical structures involved in the dopamine reward system become active.[20] The act of creation is typically charged with emotion: the intrinsic motivation of an autonomous creator is often accompanied by a sense of excitement, and a breakthrough will trigger both confidence and pleasure. For many people, the urge to create becomes a persistent need, or even what the music producer Rick Rubin has called a "way of being."[21]

In our early work on analogical problem-solving, Mary Gick and I pointed out that solving a problem by analogy may be related to insight. A recent study by Christine Chesebrough and her collaborators demonstrated that processing a far analogy can in fact trigger an aha moment.[22] These investigators created triplets of relation pairs, and showed participants each pair in a triplet one after the other. After seeing the first two pairs, participants were asked to write down their shared relation. Then after seeing the third pair, they were asked to write down the common relation linking all three. For some of the triplets, termed *consistent*, all three pairs were close analogs (e.g., *steering wheel: car, rudder: boat, handlebars: bicycle*). For such triplets the two relation descriptions were generally the same. But in other cases, termed *expansive* triplets, the first two pairs were identical to those in a consistent triplet, but the third triplet formed a far rather than near analogy with the first two (e.g., *steering wheel: car, rudder: boat, voting: government*). The expansive triplets triggered generation of a more abstract characterization of the relational concept (e.g., the near relation "steering a vehicle" might be generalized into "directing something" to accommodate the semantically distant third pair). This type of altered representation often characterizes creative insights. Moreover, this greater conceptual change was often accompanied by a reported aha experience—finding a connection with a far analogy can trigger the emotional experience of an insight.

The Circus Animals

In a poem written near the end of his life, the great Irish poet William Butler Yeats confronted the question of how the ideas for poems arise. His own poems had been built from symbols with rich personal meanings, which provided him with source material to construct meanings intended to be universal. Yeats was the ringmaster of his own circus of the imagination, directing exotic animals—his symbols—in theatrical performances that brought him both creative fulfillment and public acclaim. But now in "The Circus Animals' Desertion," the aging poet has lost the ability to summon and control his creative menagerie. "Maybe, at last, being but a broken man / I must be satisfied with my heart."[23]

Symbols act much like evocative source analogs (see chapter 7), except that the target analog may at first not be apparent. More generally, *anything* can potentially trigger a creative impulse. Each of us, over the course of a lifetime, is carried along in a flow of experiences—sights, sounds, smells, conversations, conflicts, threats, escapes, friendships, rivalries, love affairs, victories and defeats. Some of our experiences arise from books, music, and art. Moreover, our experiences are not simply passive encounters with data from the world but rather constructed interpretations colored by both the current context and by memories of what has come before. The nuanced emotions that animate human beings attach themselves to our experiences, and therefore our memories of them, biasing our interpretations and memories of subsequent experiences. The consequence of these myriad interactions with the world, with other people, and with our own emotions and memories, is that each of us is unique. You and I might both participate in the same event yet have completely different emotional reactions to it, form different interpretations of what happened, and take away different memories.

This radical individuality of experience forms the core of creative potential—our human edge. One person may be prepared to find and recognize a connection that eluded everyone else. Almost everyone has seen or read about a circus, but only Yeats was prepared to interpret circus animals as a symbol for symbols. For anyone, the trigger for a creative act can be anything, selected from everything their experience has provided. As Rick Rubin summarized it, "We begin with everything: everything seen, everything done, everything thought, everything felt, everything imagined, everything forgotten, and everything that rests unspoken and unthought within us."[24]

In science as well as the arts, a creative idea may be triggered by knowledge available to many others who did not draw the same implications from it. In 1948, a study based on tests of mental ability showed that samples of American soldiers exhibited large and steady gains between World War I and World War II. This was a mildly interesting finding, generally attributed to improved schooling in the United States over this period. Three decades later, James Flynn—a committed socialist, motivated in part by the goal of refuting claims for genetically determined racial differences in intelligence—dramatically extended research on changes in measured intelligence over time. He discovered what became known as the *Flynn effect*—large increases in scores on standardized cognitive tests (notably the RPM, a standard measure of fluid intelligence) over the course of the twentieth century. These increases occurred not only in the United States but in many other countries, both rich and poor, across several continents. For Flynn, the small initial study became the source analog for a much larger program of research—one that led to a very different understanding of environmental factors that impact individual differences in cognition.[25]

Drawing on my own personal experience, I can describe a case in which one scientific theory provided the source analog to generate another. The multiconstraint theory traces back to about 1985, but for a couple of years I didn't see any way to integrate its three qualitatively distinct constraints (isomorphism, similarity, relevance) within a computational model that could actually produce human-like mappings. The ACME model was the first attempt to fill this gap. As I mentioned in chapter 9, ACME was itself the product of an analogy with a connectionist model of a perceptual phenomenon, the ambiguous Necker cube (figure 9.2). Although this episode occurred decades ago, in 1987, I remember it well. Moreover, I sketched the plan for the ACME model in emails to my collaborator, Paul Thagard, written mid-May of that year. Because of the personal significance of this episode, I've kept my contemporaneous records of it. I wrote to Paul, "As an aside, the development of ACME is itself a clear example of the use of analogy, as I literally worked it out from the Necker cube case. When done, perhaps we can get ACME to discover itself! (AI hubris again. . . .)" In proposing ACME, I used the equations for constraint satisfaction in a neural network provided by the paper that introduced the Necker-cube model. This illustrates one of the potential fruits of reasoning by analogy: having drawn the basic correspondences between concepts, the math required to formalize the new model came "for free" from the source.

This episode had the emotional characteristics of an aha experience—excitement, and confidence (whether justified or not) that I had discovered something significant: "Doing mapping by constraint satisfaction fairly screams to be tried." I repeatedly emphasized the "elegance" of implementing the multiple constraints that govern analogy as a process of constraint satisfaction. "I'm sure the viability of ACME as a psychological model will be a matter of debate. But its claim for merit is a certain elegance that lends credence to the demonstrations that it really does compute interesting mappings. For this reason, I think we should be compulsive in ensuring we make the program as above reproach on the 'elegance' criterion as possible."

Paul and I had worked for the previous two years on an unrelated model of analogical problem-solving—we abandoned it overnight to work on ACME. I thought the discovery was so important that I convinced Paul we needed to produce a computer program, test it, and publish a paper as quickly as possible. Because the generative analogy between the Necker-cube model and ACME seemed so transparent to me, I was afraid we'd be "scooped" by Dave Rumelhart, the brilliant first author of the paper that provided our source analog—surely Rumelhart himself must be working out the "analogy with analogy"! An element of magical thinking took hold. My analogical spark ignited on what happened to be the day of a full moon in May, and I soon became obsessed with having a paper submitted to a journal within two moons. In July, we succeeded in doing just that! But a couple of months later, creative enthusiasm collided with reality—our paper was rejected. We nonetheless persevered through the much less exciting process of revision and resubmission, and the ACME paper was finally published in 1989. Though the ultimate product was a "cold" scientific contribution, it emerged from the "hot" intersection of cognition and emotion.

The role of emotion in the creative process is typically more salient in the arts than the sciences. In the arts, the creator generally has the goal of evoking an emotional response in their audience—the emotions of the creator are meant to impact those of the reader, listener, or viewer. In an extended interview, the Australian singer-songwriter Nick Cave has given a particularly detailed account of a creative act.[26] In 2019 Cave and his band, the Bad Seeds, released an album called *Ghosteen* (roughly, "little ghost"). Four years earlier, his teenage son Arthur had died. The album was Cave's artistic reaction to his personal tragedy—an extreme case of turning sorrow into art. He expresses the sense of mystery that creators often report: "The creative impulse, to me, is a form of bafflement, and often feels difficult and unsettling. . . . It's the guiding force that leads you where it wants to go."

In the months leading up to the point at which he began to compose songs for the album, Cave's mind-wandering led him to a series of what he called "ecstatic images": "I had a persistent mental image of a man standing on a beach surrounded by panicking animals; the hills were on fire, there were screaming animals racing back and forward, sea creatures leaping out of the ocean, and a spiral of spirit children that climbed up to the sun. It was a wild recurring hallucination, part horror, part bliss, that somehow embedded itself in my imagination. I'd lie in bed at night and see these images, filing by, one after the other." Once Cave started writing songs, more images presented themselves: "A guy driving his car through a fire; a feather spinning upwards; a remembered time in a hotel in New Orleans where Susie and I conceived our children; Jesus in the arms of his mother; the leviathan moving beneath the water."

These images took on the quality of personal symbols for Cave—his circus animals. Some of them eventually found their way into the lyrics of the songs he would write. "They recur throughout the record, alongside the idea of the migratory spirit, the Ghosteen that passes from image to image, and from song to song, threading them together. For me, the record became an imagined world where Arthur could be."

Nick Cave's creative act in writing and recording the songs for *Ghosteen* began with seemingly disconnected images and ideas that flowed from his unique experiences, bound together by an emotional charge triggered by personal tragedy. This delicate blend of conscious intentions and unconscious mind-wandering, coupled with a special sensitivity that detects potential symbols before their eventual meaning is fully understood, forms the human edge that guides artistic creativity. Paradoxically, the deeply personal origin of Cave's album is what makes its music touch the hearts of its many listeners: "What is most personal is most general."[27] Creators often find meaning in incidental byproducts of life, which for many people simply go unnoticed. As the poet and songwriter Leonard Cohen put it, "Poetry is just the evidence of a life. If your life is burning well, poetry is just the ash."[28] At the end of "The Circus Animals' Desertion," Yeats reviews his personal symbols, which he had found hidden amid "life's garbage," in a place where all of us must lie down:

> A mound of refuse or the sweepings of a street,
> Old kettles, old bottles, and a broken can,
> Old iron, old bones, old rags, that raving slut
> Who keeps the till. Now that my ladder's gone
> I must lie down where all the ladders start
> In the foul rag and bone shop of the heart.

Massive Imitation Machines

In chapter 12, I raised the question of whether humans have lost their intellectual edge to the latest large language models developed in AI, such as chatGPT. Despite their impressive accomplishments, these models have not achieved artificial general intelligence at the human level. Nonetheless, many AI models are *generative*, so it's natural to consider the question of whether they are capable of creativity. And indeed, if a creative product is simply defined as one that is novel and valuable, AI has clearly passed the bar. Current models have made serious contributions to science—synthesizing new proteins, classifying galaxies, and analyzing historical writings stored in archives. They routinely aid in generating useful new solutions to many nontrivial problems that arise in everyday tasks, such as writing computer code, composing advertisements, and finding new recipes.

However, if we define creativity as I've done in this chapter (see figure 13.1), current AI models—even those that are both general and generative—seem to face stark limits. The most obvious is that AI models lack creative autonomy. They simply respond to questions or problems posed by human users. AI models do not choose their own problems without human guidance, and have no intrinsic motivation to create. And in general, they also lack the ability to identify their own "interesting" new discoveries—it's up to a human to find a problem worth solving, pose it to the AI, and then evaluate potential solutions that the AI generates. Without question, the contribution of the AI is often indispensable, not only in scientific applications but also in computer-generated art. For example, AI has been used to generate dynamic visual art—"living paintings"—derived from recordings of a person's brain waves.[29] In such cases it seems natural enough to describe the AI as a "co-creator." But without a human to set the basic agenda, the AI will do nothing and create nothing.

Another fundamental impediment to full creativity becomes apparent when we consider how large language models are trained. For example, chatGPT is trained with two basic objectives: (1) predict the most probable text completion based on what people have already written, and (2) give the user the answer they're looking for. These objectives would make an excellent recipe for snuffing out any spark of serious creativity! Large language models are basically imitation machines, equipped with an enormous body of training data to guide them. But whereas humans sometimes transcend their training data—an apprentice may eventually surpass the creative power of their teacher—current AI can only imitate. As we saw in chapter 12, chatGPT was able to perform analogical mapping and inference across a wide range of problems, with accuracy comparable to college students. But analogical mapping is itself a form of imitation, albeit a very sophisticated one: the "analogy game" is to make the target imitate the source. Analogical transfer can certainly contribute to creativity, as we've seen repeatedly. But at least so far, chatGPT and its near relatives depend on a human to pose an analogy problem and ask the AI to solve it. The initial analogical spark—noticing spontaneously that a certain source analog might illuminate some target in a way that advances knowledge—has yet to be struck by an AI.

Particularly in the case of artistic creativity, AI faces what may well be an insurmountable limit. As I've emphasized in this chapter, human creativity depends on mind-wandering guided by the residue of a unique individual's lifetime of experiences, tinged with subtle emotions. And in most forms of art—perhaps most obviously music and lyric poetry—the essential point is for the creator to convey an emotional experience to their audience through the medium of their artistic creation. An AI has none of this—no emotions, no consciousness, and no individuality. In fact, the general complaint about AI-generated products, whether in the form of writing, music, or visual art, is that they have no *soul*—no expression of emotions or of an individual point of view. Absence of soul is not a problem—may even be a virtue—when the desired product is a routine summary of a scientific paper, the text and images for an advertisement, or bland "mood music." But to attain the higher reaches of artistic creativity, the deficit is fatal. Authentic creativity, as I've argued here and elsewhere, is inextricably bound to the nature of the generative process. AI heralds the Age of Inauthenticity.

As I hinted in the previous chapter, the often-repeated claim that chatGPT can "write poetry" is absurd—if by poetry we mean "figurative language, concentrated so that its form is both expressive and evocative."[30] Generative AI models can learn to imitate the style of individual creators, but their products occupy a narrow band ranging between parody and derivative mediocrity. I asked the latest version of chatGPT to write an eight-line poem about the origins of the symbols in poetry, in the style of William Butler Yeats. What chatGPT produced was not even a decent imitation of "The Circus Animals' Desertion"—in fact, the verse it generated was so vapid and stilted that I won't waste space by printing it here. To justify claiming to be a poet, more is required than just a knack for stringing together lines of text linked by end rhymes. You need to add a little soul.

One of Nick Cave's fans recently sent him lyrics for a song created by chatGPT "in the style of Nick Cave." The artist was underwhelmed: "This song sucks." Cave went on to say, "What chatGPT is, in this instance, is replication as travesty. ChatGPT may be able to write a speech or an essay or a sermon or an obituary but it cannot create a genuine song. It could perhaps in time create a song that is, on the surface, indistinguishable from an original, but it will always be a replication, a kind of burlesque." The creative act, Cave argues, "is the breathless confrontation with one's vulnerability, one's perilousness, one's smallness, pitted against a sense of shocking discovery; it is the redemptive artistic act that stirs the heart of the listener, where the listener recognizes in the inner workings of the song their own blood, their own struggle, their own suffering. This is what we humble humans can offer, that AI can only mimic, the transcendent journey of the artist that forever grapples with his or her own shortcomings. This is where human genius resides, deeply embedded within, yet reaching beyond, those limitations."[31]

14 Summing Up

Then I felt too that I might take this opportunity to tie up a few loose ends, only of course loose ends can never be properly tied, one is always producing new ones. Time, like the sea, unties all knots.[1]

—Iris Murdoch

Around 1980, when I was a young assistant professor at the University of Michigan, I gave a talk at nearby Bowling Green State University in Ohio. This was my first public presentation of the new line of work on analogical problem-solving on which Mary Gick and I had embarked. After I finished my talk, I lingered in conversation with people in the audience. One of the local professors asked me how much longer I expected to be working on analogy. Making a quick estimate based on the time I had previously spent pursuing various research directions—plus the optimism of youth—I replied, "A couple more years, I suppose."

Four decades on and counting, that prediction has turned out to be seriously off. I've worked on a variety of topics in human cognition, but almost all of them connect with relational reasoning, and analogy has remained a central focus. It looks like I just can't quit it. One question has led to another—always a light at the apparent end of the tunnel, but the tunnel keeps stretching, while making unexpected turns.

Surprises

I won't try to summarize everything I've covered in this book, but I'll briefly highlight a few of the ideas and findings related to analogy that I've personally found surprising. Most of these are products of the last four decades, and doubtless surprised many others as well. By way of warning, I suspect some of my surprises are what other researchers might call fantasies—the field has not achieved consensus. I'll start with an idea that's a century old, yet much more recently came as a surprise to me.

Constructing relations comes first. A sea change in the field of analogy occurred around 1980 when several of us—Patrick Winston in AI, Dedre Gentner as well as Gick and I in psychology—turned our attention to analogies between complex stories and problems. Previously, work on analogy was largely confined to nonfunctional proportional analogies in the *A:B::C:D* format—the sort featured in psychometric tests of intelligence. I found these sorts of analogy problems boring. My work with Gick was very much a reaction against the psychometric tradition—we took our inspiration from Gestalt psychology instead. The newer research reoriented the field. We focused on analogies that served some broader purpose, such as understanding a novel situation, finding a solution to an unfamiliar type of problem, or learning a new relational category. This shift connected the study of analogy to work on the representation of knowledge. The central aim of theories of analogy became explaining how people are able to find systematic mappings between complex analogs, ranging from synopses of Shakespearean plays to scientific theories.

But though the shift to the study of meaningful analogies led to new insights, something important was lost. We emphasized the central role of explicit relations, but our models assumed these relations were directly provided in the inputs. A story analog, for example, would be coded using relation symbols corresponding to the verbs and other linking words stated in the story itself. Conspicuously absent was consideration of how a reasoner might *generate* representations of relations when given non-relational inputs.

Back in 1923, a founder of the psychometric tradition, Charles Spearman, had defined two basic components of analogical reasoning. The first was the *eduction of relations*—constructing relations between entities—and the second was the *eduction of correlates*—assessing the similarity of relations. The newer models neglected the first of these components—they generally depended on hand-coded relations, and did not address the nature of relations themselves. For me at least, Spearman's insight came as a surprise—and inspired a course correction in my thinking—only when recent advances in machine learning made it possible to automate the construction of relations from non-relational inputs. As described in chapter 10, I now believe the essential first step toward understanding analogy is to explain how explicit relations are generated.

Causal relevance is what matters. The germ of the multiconstraint theory of analogy was the intuition that when an analogy is being used to solve a problem, what matters most is that whatever factors made the solution work in the source are also present in the target. The idea that causal relations are central to analogy was stressed by Patrick Winston as well as by Gick and me. My later surprise was to discover that the philosopher Mary Hesse had anticipated all of us with her conception of "material analogy." Her analysis of the rational basis for evaluating scientific analogies inspired the broader relevance principle (chapter 3), which provides a way to distinguish *evidential* analogies that provide rational support for a conclusion about the target from more metaphorical or *evocative* ones. Hesse's ideas help to understand how analogies *ought* to be used in the context of rational argument.

Analogy is a product of the brain. Looking back, it's hard to appreciate how little we knew in 1980 about the neural basis for analogical reasoning. The modern field of cognitive neuroscience emerged in the early 1980s, and began to be applied to higher cognition around the turn of the century. Those A:B::C:D analogies that I had reacted against in 1980 returned to play an important role in early neuroimaging studies, which for methodological reasons required aggregating data over many trials using similar problems that can each be solved within a very few seconds. Later this type of analogy would also figure prominently in computational models of the eduction of relations. (This is another example of progressive deepening—revisiting previously rejected options.) The field has only begun to explore how the brain represents relations and processes analogies—but we've made a serious start. Pretty much everything we've learned about the neural basis of relational reasoning (chapter 5) came as a surprise to me. Among these surprises is the evidence that major aspects of higher cognition—reasoning, language, and mentalizing—depend on distinct brain networks (chapter 7).

An analogy gap separates humans from other animals. Various nonhuman animals display signs of advanced cognitive abilities—constructing simple tools, cooperating in hunting expeditions, responding to complex perceptual similarity. At one time I thought that great apes were capable of elementary analogical reasoning, and that the more sophisticated ability of humans was the product of incremental increases in the capacity of working memory. But as I argued in chapter 6, the gap between nonhuman and human animals now appears to be more profound. On closer examination, abilities that "sort of look like" analogy in nonhuman animals turn out to be based on specialized adaptations that operate on perceptual cues. Among the creatures that now share the earth, only humans have the capacity to think about abstract relations, and to grasp how things that do not look alike can be fundamentally the same.

Structure emerges from similarity. For several decades, the conventional view was that structure was entirely distinct from similarity. Whereas similarity was a matter of feature overlap between entities (e.g., a dog is similar to a cat), "structure mapping" was characterized as matching of symbols for relations (e.g., "the dog *chases* the cat" might be mapped to "the man *chases* his dream" because the *chases* symbol occurs in both). By now it's apparent that relations (the basis for structure) are also represented as sets of features (chapter 10). At its most basic level, analogy depends on similarity of relations. For more complex analogies, mapping depends on similarity of patterns of relations. Rather than pitting structure versus similarity, it's similarity all the way down.

Analogy machines are among us. The most recent surprise, for almost everyone paying attention, is that AI systems are now capable of major components of analogical reasoning (chapter 12). Given inputs in a natural language such as English, without hand-coding of relations or anything else, chatCPT and its successors can find mappings between complex analogs and (at least sometimes) use analogies to solve problems. Even more surprising to many of us, these AI systems acquire their reasoning ability simply from exposure to vast troves of texts available on the internet, without any of the innate building blocks that apparently support human thinking. Perhaps they have acquired these human-like building blocks, such as ways to distinguish relations from the entities they relate, through a kind of convergent evolution—a developmental process very different from that of humans that nonetheless yields comparable concepts. Or perhaps AI systems solve analogies in some totally nonhuman manner. Either way, our machines have now joined humans as analogical reasoners.

The Edge and Beyond It

In the 2004 science-fiction movie *I, Robot*, Detective Del Spooner (played by Will Smith) hates robots—especially one named Sonny, who seems to be somehow exceptional. During an argument about the limits of robots, Spooner asks Sonny, "Can a robot write a symphony? Can a robot turn a canvas into a beautiful masterpiece?" To which Sonny (the first robot to become sentient) retorts, "Can you?" Touché, robot!

In real life there are no sentient robots, nor are any on the horizon. But humans (in the guise of AI researchers) are making great progress in eliminating our cognitive edge over machines. In comparison with the minds of nonhuman animals, the human edge is vast. But AI is a different matter. Like Detective Spooner, people often defend the "specialness" of human cognition by pointing to the creative achievements of our greatest representatives. But like that cynical detective, most us will never be ranked with Beethoven, Rembrandt, or Einstein. Are we still somehow special in the age of AI?

As I acknowledged in the previous chapter, current AI systems can sensibly be viewed as "co-creators" for many generative achievements, ranging from scientific discovery to digital art. AI can perform an ever-expanding set of more mundane but challenging tasks such as writing reports, planning vacations, and producing videos. But in essence, AI is one more in a long list of major tools that humans have invented and then used to leverage their capacities. The early tools—the axe, hammer, knife, fish hook, and plow, for example—increased our physical power to gain control over our environments. Later, many other tools enabled us to expand and communicate our knowledge—the pen, compass, microscope, telescope, and computer. Armed with AI—itself the product of human ingenuity—our cognitive power will be projected further. Like many previous technologies created since the industrial revolution, AI is a tool that can (and will) be used for both good and ill.

AI can enhance human cognition because it allows humans to take an end run around our fundamental limits of time, computation, and communication. But as I argued earlier, current AI has its own fundamental limits. Lacking internal motivation and autonomy, AI systems are unable to set their own basic goals. Lacking emotion and consciousness, AI is unable to authentically generate creative products that reflect the nuanced experiences of a unique individual. An AI system can learn how to use visual and auditory cues to judge a person's emotions, and it may manipulate words and images so as to trigger predictable emotional responses in humans. But inner experience itself remains a vacuum inside the empty heart of AI.

The basis for the human edge over current AI is in many ways the opposite of what defines our edge over nonhuman animals. Although nonhuman animals apparently lack the capacity for higher-order reasoning, many species show compelling signs of emotions and inner experience.[2] Moreover, nonhuman animals display robust capacities that enable them to operate in the physical environment—they have at least an implicit grasp of the 3D world in which we live. In contrast, current AI systems (in the form of LLMs) constitute a kind of "disembodied cognition"—capable of performing tasks that require sophisticated use of language, as well as varieties of complex reasoning, but deficient in understanding the outer world or inner minds. In contrast, though human cognition is based on Late Systems that enable complex relational reasoning, these systems were in turn built upon—and now cooperate with—the Early Systems that reflect our vast biological heritage. This integration of thinking with our animal nature makes humans special. Whether or not we each have a soul, we each have the potential to put a little soul into those small creations that make up our lives.

If I Could Start Over

I've often wondered what explains my own decades-long fascination with analogy in its myriad manifestations. What drew me into and kept me on my path, first of all, was the beauty of an idea—the idea that appearances mask hidden patterns, and that these patterns can resemble one another, sometimes to the extent that they count as the *same thing*. Relations, symbols, and analogies constitute our spider's threads, released in the hope of finding and binding new connections. One thing seen through the lens of another can be made all the richer for it, and more beautiful perhaps. The mind creates its mental models of the world, and the cognitive scientist aims to create models of those models. The layers of resemblances, even as they pull us away from what is most real, coalesce into their own reality that draws us further in.

Like Yeats in old age gazing back upon his symbols, I imagine I'd do it all again, and have the same regrets.

> Players and painted stage took all my love
> And not those things that they were emblems of.

Notes

Preface

1. Gick and Holyoak (1980, 1983)

2. Holyoak and Glass (1975); Glass, Holyoak, and Kiger (1979)

3. Penn, Holyoak, and Povinelli (2008)

4. Holyoak and Thagard (1989)

5. Hummel and Holyoak (1997, 2003)

6. Lu, Chen, and Holyoak (2012); Lu, Wu, and Holyoak (2019)

7. Lu, Ichien, and Holyoak (2022)

Chapter 1

1. The fact that analogy always involves comparison invites the logical fallacy of assuming comparison always involve analogy. This fallacy underlies a host of interpretive confusions in the scientific literature, in which evidence that nonhuman animals or human infants detect matches or mismatches between stimuli (a capacity shared across many species) is claimed to constitute evidence of abstract relational concepts (*same* or *different*), or even analogical reasoning. As we'll see, analogy involves much more than just comparison of stimuli.

2. The most eloquent and exuberant proponent of the view that analogy is everywhere and everything has been Doug Hofstadter. In his paper "Analogy as the Core of Cognition" (which I had the pleasure of including in a volume I coedited), he sets the stage by asserting, "Analogy is *everything*, or very nearly so, in my view" (Hofstadter, 2001, p. 499; italics in original). This theme permeates his writings (Hofstadter & Fluid Analogies Research Group, 1995). Although he focuses on human analogy, Hofstadter sees it elsewhere in the animal kingdom: "Categorization for a dog is clearly the creation of analogical bridges to prior knowledge" (Hofstadter & Sander, 2013,

p. 179)—an inadvertent illustration of anthropomorphism as the fuel and fire of bad analogies. As I observed in my review of the latter book (Holyoak, 2013), Hofstadter has cultivated a "garden of delightful examples" of analogies and analogy-like phenomena. The playful spirit of his writing—always witty and often insightful—makes it seem a tad uncharitable to question some of Hofstadter's claims. Still, if we're aiming for a scientific account of analogy, we eventually have to get a bit more serious.

3. Metaphor is a type of linguistic expression based on an underlying comparison that sometimes involves analogy; one might say that "metaphor is the linguist's analogy." George Lakoff, who proposed what is termed Conceptual Metaphor Theory, has been the foremost promoter of the ubiquity of metaphor in both language and thought (see especially Lakoff & Johnson, 1980; Lakoff & Turner, 1989). He called attention to the broad range of specific expressions that can be classified into general analogy-like comparisons, labeled by slogans such as LIFE IS A JOURNEY. Stretching the usual bounds of metaphor, Lakoff extended the notion to expressions such as "Bill kept Harry working," which he interpreted as an instance of a general metaphor, STATES ARE LOCATIONS. For critical examinations of Lakoff's more imaginative metaphorical flights, see Jackendoff and Aaron (1991) and Pinker (2007, ch. 5). Kövecses (2020) provides an overview of current developments in Conceptual Metaphor Theory, with responses to some of the criticisms that have been directed at it.

4. Many examples of analogical reminding were reported by Schank (1982) and Hofstadter and Sander (2013). Most of these (like my own anecdote) were produced by academics fascinated by analogy—hardly a representative sample! However, in a systematic experiment, Blanchette and Dunbar (2000) were able to elicit numerous analogical remindings from college undergraduates.

5. Holyoak and Thagard (1995, ch. 8) discuss the wave theories of sound and light, as well as other prominent scientific theories that were inspired by analogies. Hesse (1963, ch. 2) used the analogy between sound and light waves as a central example of what she termed a "material analogy": one based on observable pre-theoretic similarities that enable predictions to be made.

6. See Utzon (2002).

7. See Ditsche and Summers (2019)

8. This example is adapted from Bartha (2010, pp. 154–155).

9. These non-math analogies for teaching math are drawn from Sarina and Namukasa (2010). Other sources of similar examples include English (1997) and Richland, Zur, and Holyoak (2007).

10. Graphs, like other analogies, can be misinterpreted if the mapping is ambiguous or misleading; see Gattis and Holyoak (1996).

11. For discussions of analogical reasoning in arguments from legal precedents, see Schauer (2014) and Schauer and Spellman (2017).

12. This joke was found on https://upjoke.com/analogy-jokes.

13. For a study of visual memes as analogical metaphors, see Wong and Holyoak (2021).

14. This example was retrieved from https://www.economist.com/europe/2022/06/02/europe-is-squabbling-but-remains-united-where-it-really-matters. I thank Cameron Shelley for bringing this analogy to my attention.

15. The quote is from Hemingway (1964, p. 147). For a fuller discussion of this example, see Holyoak (1982).

16. For discussions of metaphor in poetry from the perspective of cognitive science, see Turner (1987) and Holyoak (2019).

17. "First Fig" is a selection from Millay (1922).

18. For discussions of the role of analogy in real-world decision-making, see Khong (1992); Schön (1993).

19. See Postell (2021).

20. The view that analogy involves both abduction and induction was first suggested by the philosopher C. S. Peirce (1931–1958); for an overview see Misiewicz (2020). Ward and Gimbel (2010) discuss factors that influence the strength of arguments from analogy in evaluating scientific hypotheses.

21. The hypothesis that comparing individual analogs can lead to acquisition of a more abstract schema was proposed by Gick and Holyoak (1980); in a subsequent paper we provided experimental evidence for this progression (Gick & Holyoak, 1983). Other early work on the acquisition of relational schemas was reported by Halford, Bain, et al. (1998) and Halford and Busby (2007). Cheng and Holyoak (1985) discussed the role of pragmatic schemas in reasoning about conditional regulations.

22. For a discussion of the use and misuse of historical analogies, see Khong (1992); Ghilani et al. (2017).

23. The interview with Allers and Rob Minkoff was retrieved from https://www.blu-ray.com/news/?id=7433.

Chapter 2

1. This quote (italics in original) is from an essay by Coleridge published in *The Friend*, *I*, p. 451 (1809–1810).

2. These phenomena were first reported in classic studies by Michotte (1946/1963) on perceptual causality and by Heider and Simmel (1944) on animacy. See Scholl and Tremoulet (2000) for a review, and Shu et al. (2021) for a computational model that unifies the two phenomena.

3. The view that human thought is constructed from certain foundational concept types (likely to be innate) is called *conceptual semantics*. Much of the relevant evidence concerns properties of human language that appear to reflect near-universal concept types, such as *object, substance, property, event, state, space, time, possession, causation, intention,* and *goal*. Pinker (2007) provides a general introduction to conceptual semantics, and Carey (2009) surveys the most basic concepts that underlie human cognition. A good technical source is Jackendoff (1990). Other background papers (focusing on causal concepts) include Talmy (1988) and Wolff and Thorstad (2017).

4. For discussion of executive functions in relation to *g* and to neural circuitry, see Duncan and Owen (2000); Duncan (2010); Duncan, Assem, and Shashidhara (2020).

5. In general, I'll focus on relations between two entities, which specify two roles (more technically termed *arguments*). It's generally accepted that verbs in human languages have at most three obligatory arguments, as in the case of *give* ("Mom gave Billy a toy"). Some expressions refer to an attribute of a single entity ("The dog is brown"), conveying a particular relation (a type of possession) between an object and a property. I'll therefore assume that ordinary relations can involve from one to three basic entities.

6. Schiff, Caviness, and Gibson (1962) found that from early in life, rhesus monkeys show an avoidance response to a looming stimulus.

7. For an argument that relations are central to human cognition, see Halford, Wilson, and Phillips (2010); for a review of psychological research on relational thinking, see Holyoak (2012).

8. For evidence that meaningful relations guide generation of novel recursive structures, see Dedhe, Piantadosi, and Cantlon (2023).

9. The term "eduction of relations" was introduced by Spearman (1923) as part of his theory of intelligence.

10. This study was conducted by Goldstone and Medin (1994). They were able to account for the time course of relational similarity using a computational model, *Similarity as Interactive Activation and Mapping* (SIAM), described by Goldstone (1994).

11. Cross-mapping was introduced as an experimental paradigm by Gentner and Toupin (1986). The study described here was reported by Markman and Gentner (1993).

12. On the role of working memory in relation processing, see Waltz et al. (2000); on the impact of anxiety, see Tohill and Holyoak (2000).

13. For evidence of the impact of perceptual richness on the balance between entity and relational similarity, see Gentner and Rattermann (1991); Markman and Gentner (1993).

14. See Goldstone, Medin, and Gentner (1991).

15. For evidence that similarity and difference judgments are not inverses, see Medin, Goldstone, and Gentner (1990). Ichien, Lin, et al. (2024) provide evidence that the observed asymmetry results from the extra complexity involved in combining relations with difference judgments.

16. See Bassok, Wu, and Olseth (1995). Bassok (1996) provides a general review of the influence of semantic content on transfer. For related evidence for the impact of schemas and categories on analogical mapping and inference, see Minervino, Margni, and Trench (2023).

17. The hypothesis of a relational shift in cognitive development was proposed by Gentner (1988) and Gentner and Rattermann (1991).

18. Aristotle's views on analogy are discussed by Hesse (1963).

19. See Spearman (1923, 1927, 1946).

20. The RPM test was created by Raven (1938).

21. The distinction between fluid and crystallized intelligence is due to Cattell (1971).

22. For an example of evidence for the complexity of factors that influence measured intelligence, see Turkheimer et al. (2003).

23. This study of relational set was reported by Vendetti, Wu, and Holyoak (2014), using verbal analogy problems created by Green et al. (2010); see also Goldwater and Jamrozik (2019). Using similar methods, a relational set has also been demonstrated with preschool children (Simms & Richland, 2019). For evidence that measures of ability to process relations, such as the RPM, predict performance on various reasoning tasks (in the absence of a relational set), see Gray and Holyoak (2020); Kubricht, Lu, and Holyoak (2017).

Chapter 3

1. The quote is from Freud (1933/1990, p. 72).

2. Abduction, or inference to the best explanation, was first discussed in detail by the philosopher C. S. Peirce (1931–1958). The role of analogy in developing explanations in archeology (and some of the problems that arise in its use) has been discussed by Ascher (1961) and Currie (2016).

3. The case of Moche pottery is taken from Donnan (1971), and the interpretation of Oyo pottery is from Ogundiran and Saunders (2011).

4. The most famous philosophical attack on similarity is that of Goodman (1972). For a review of psychological theories of similarity, see Goldstone and Son (2012).

5. These examples are taken from a study by Nisbett et al. (1983).

6. This is the title of a book by the philosopher John Mackie (1974).

7. The great physicist Max Planck (1949, p. 149) described the role of causality in physics in these terms: "The law of causality is neither true nor false. It is rather a heuristic principle, a signpost—and in my opinion, our most valuable signpost—to help us find our bearings in a bewildering maze of occurrences, and to show us the direction in which scientific research must advance in order to achieve fertile results." More recently, Stephen Hawking interpreted causality within the framework of "model-dependent realism," which treats causality as a useful representation to help understand the world (Hawking & Mlodinow, 2010). Perhaps causality is most fundamentally a mental representation required by the human mind.

8. For evidence that people use information about covariation to estimate causal power, see Cheng (1997); for evidence that people distinguish predictive from diagnostic causal inferences, see Waldmann and Holyoak (1992); for evidence regarding the distinction between causes and enabling conditions, see Cheng and Novick (1991); on causal explanations as stories, see Pennington and Hastie (1992). For general reviews of psychological work on causal learning and reasoning, see Holyoak and Cheng (2011) and papers in a collection edited by Waldmann (2017); for a treatment of causality from an AI perspective informed by work in philosophy and statistics, see Pearl and Mackenzie (2018).

9. On the role of causal understanding in evaluating scientific analogies, see Hesse (1963). My concept of evidential analogy is a generalization of what Hesse termed "material analogy." In artificial intelligence, the centrality of causal relations in analogy was discussed by Winston (1980). I emphasized that causal relevance constitutes a pragmatic constraint on analogy (Holyoak, 1985; Holland et al., 1986), which became an important component of the multiconstraint theory (Holyoak & Thagard, 1989; see Chapter 4). Holyoak and Lee (2017) reviewed psychological research relating causal understanding to analogical inference and transfer of knowledge.

10. The extension of Hesse's causality principle to mathematics and other formal domains can be motivated by considering whether an aspect of the source "brings about" the outcome of interest. For example, each step in a logical or mathematical proof is *relevant* in that it plays a role in "generating" the conclusion. Cangiotti and Nappo (2023) characterize relevance in this sense as a "robust mathematical connection," which functions much like a causal relation to create an evidential analogy (see Bartha, 2010, for a somewhat different view of analogy in mathematics). In cognitive science, Walker, Cheng, and Stigler (2014) noted the close connection between causal and mathematical relations. We will see shortly that the more general *relevance principle* can be extended further to be applicable to the use of evidential analogy in the law.

11. This study was reported by Lassaline (1996).

12. See Lee and Holyoak (2008); Holyoak, Lee, and Lu (2010).

13. This example is discussed in more detail by Hesse (1963, ch. 2).

14. See Holyoak and Thagard (1995, ch. 8). There we listed twenty "great scientific analogies" across history that have endured to the present. The majority of these appear to be evidential analogies, each of which eventually led to a theoretical unification because the same type of cause operates in the source and target. For example, Newton drew an analogy between the motion of a stone thrown on earth and the motion of planets; gravitational force governs motion in both cases. A striking exception is Kekulé's famous analogy between a snake biting its own tail (a dream image) and the molecular structure of benzene. Whether or not a snake ever bit its own tail (the image is actually an ancient mythological symbol, the ouroborus), this source does not provide any rational evidence regarding chemical structure. For a general discussion of what makes analogies useful (or not), see Thagard (2022).

15. See Lakoff and Johnson (1980); Lakoff and Turner (1989); Kövecses (2020).

16. See Schön (1993).

17. The quote is from the philosopher C. I. Lewis (1929, ch. XI).

18. For experimental evidence that causal knowledge can be acquired at multiple levels of abstraction, see Lien and Cheng (2000). Even when people have only a vague understanding of causal structure (e.g., how genetics determines the properties of birds), they accept that *some* hidden causal structure is at work. People's propensity to believe that hidden causes govern the visible characteristics of natural kinds is called *psychological essentialism* (Medin, 1989).

19. The view that what matters for an evidential analogy depends on causal structure (which can involve all types of relations, objects, and properties) contrasts with a proposal that relevance is determined solely by syntactic properties of relations (Gentner, 1983).

20. For more thorough discussions of the role of analogy and precedent in the law, see Hunter (2001); Sunstein (1992); Schauer (2014); Schauer and Spellman (2017).

21. See Pennington and Hastie (1992).

22. The case of the scofflaw houseboat, more formally known as *Lozman v City of Riviera Beach, Florida*, is discussed in detail by Schauer (2014).

23. See Sunstein (2021).

24. On expertise and analogy in the law, see Schauer and Spellman (2017).

Chapter 4

1. Though probably not an exact quote, Einstein said something along these lines in the context of discussing the dangers of atomic weapons.

2. See Duncker (1945). The Gestalt movement developed among early cognitive psychologists based in Germany. As summarized by one of the leading Gestaltists, "It has been said: The whole is more than the sum of its parts. It is more correct to say that the whole is something else than the sum of its parts, because summing is a meaningless procedure, whereas the whole-part relationship is meaningful" (Koffka, 1935, p. 176).

3. See Gick and Holyoak (1980, 1983). The four major steps in analogy were described by Holyoak, Novick, and Melz (1994).

4. For the multiconstraint theory of analogy, see Holyoak (1985); Holyoak and Thagard (1989, 1995).

5. Studies providing evidence that relation similarity has relatively less impact on retrieval than on mapping (and conversely, entity similarity has relatively greater impact on retrieval) include Gilovich (1981); Holyoak and Koh (1987); Keane (1987); Ross (1987, 1989); Gentner, Rattermann, and Forbus (1993).

6. Beveridge and Parkins (1987) provided evidence that visual diagrams can bolster analogical transfer to the radiation problem, and Kubricht et al. (2017) showed that animations can be effective. Catrambone, Craig, and Nersessian (2006) found that encouraging physical enactment of the source can also facilitate spontaneous transfer.

7. Studies by Blanchette and Dunbar (2000, 2001) found that far analogs were retrieved quite frequently in naturalistic paradigms. However, Trench and Minervino (2015) showed that closer analogs dominate even in naturalistic paradigms when the relative availability of close and far analogs is measured and taken into account. For a general review of analog retrieval and its role in reasoning and problem-solving, see Trench and Minervino (2020).

8. For evidence that relation similarity does play some role in analog retrieval (even for novices), see Holyoak and Koh (1987); Wharton et al. (1994); Wharton, Holyoak, and Lange (1996).

9. For reviews of theories of human and animal memory systems and their neural substrate, see Squire (2004); Eichenbaum (2017).

10. The rational analysis of memory was proposed by Anderson and Milson (1989). Technically, rational analysis is based on Bayes's rule in probability theory: the *posterior probability* that retrieving a certain memory is optimal now is proportional to the *prior probability* that it is optimal multiplied by the *likelihood* that it is optimal given the current context.

11. On children's use of "person" as a source analog, see Carey (1985); Hatano and Inagaki (1987); on the use of significant others as source analogs, see Andersen et al. (1995).

12. See Cushen and Wiley (2018).

13. This study of how analogies can be used to help understand electrical circuits was conducted by Gentner and Gentner (1983).

14. For work on semantic alignment in math, see Bassok (1996); Bassok et al. (1995); Bassok, Chase, and Martin (1998); Guthormsen et al. (2016); Lee et al. (2016); Tyumeneva et al. (2018).

15. This analogy between category triplets is adapted from an experiment reported by Lu, Ichien, and Holyoak (2022).

16. For work on relational complexity, see Halford et al. (1998, 2007, 2010, 2014).

17. See Gentner and Markman (1994).

18. Variants of this basic inference mechanism have been widely adopted in models of analogy. See, for example, Carbonell (1983); Falkenhainer, Forbus, and Gentner (1989); Holyoak et al. (1994). Memory studies have shown that inferences about a target analog are sometimes confused with stated facts about it, resulting in "false" memories; see Schustack and Anderson (1979); Blanchette and Dunbar (2002); Perrott, Gentner, and Bodenhausen (2005).

19. For discussions of adaptation as part of analogical transfer, see Carbonell (1983); Holyoak et al. (1994). For evidence that reduced degree of isomorphism makes transfer more difficult, see Reed, Dempster, and Ettinger (1985); Novick and Holyoak (1991).

20. See Spellman and Holyoak (1992).

21. See Spellman and Holyoak (1996).

22. For further studies of mapping and inference with tangled analogies, see Burns and Holyoak (1994); Markman (1997); Krawczyk, Holyoak, and Hummel (2004, 2005). Markman's study found that one-to-many mappings were generated in a mapping task much more often than in an inference task. Moreover, inferences were often based on *different* mappings than those identified in the explicit mapping task (where the same people performed both tasks). The latter result supports my hypothesis that if people complete a mapping task and then are asked to make inferences, they may repeat the alignment process, now with a stronger preference for one-to-one correspondences.

23. See Gick and Holyoak (1983).

24. See Ross and Kennedy (1990); Novick and Holyoak (1991).

25. The critical importance of comparison was first demonstrated by Gick and Hokyoak (1983). Loewenstein, Thompson, and Gentner (1999, 2003) showed that simply being exposed to multiple examples was not as effective as actual comparison of them. Jacobson et al. (2020) found evidence for the usefulness of analogical comparison in teaching complex scientific topics.

26. On retroactive effects of schema induction, see Gentner et al. (2009). For evidence that two problems can sometimes be solved more easily than one, see Kurtz and Loewenstein (2007).

27. On the relation between analogy and math expertise, see Novick (1988). Goldwater et al. (2021) provide evidence that expertise impacts the use of causal knowledge in an analogy generation task with scientific topics.

28. On the use of comparison to teach negotiation strategies, see Loewenstein et al. (1999, 2003).

29. On progressive alignment, see Kotovsky and Gentner (1996). A related method of systematic sequential presentation of examples is *concreteness fading*: in teaching a concept, early examples are chosen to be concrete and later ones are progressively more abstract (Fyfe et al., 2014).

30. See Catrambone and Holyoak (1989). Using naturalistic analogies, Z. Chen, Mo, and Honomichl (2004) demonstrated spontaneous problem-solving transfer over a time period of years.

Chapter 5

1. Emerson M. Pugh was a professor of physics at the Carnegie Institute of Technology. His son reported that this quote is from around 1938.

2. On analogy in patients with a degenerative disease affecting the prefrontal cortex, see Waltz et al. (1999); Morrison et al. (2004); Krawczyk et al. (2008); on analogy and schizophrenia, see Krawczyk et al. (2014); on Alzheimer's disease, see Waltz et al. (2004); on frontal stroke patients, see Andrews et al. (2013, 2014); on traumatic brain injury, see Krawczyk et al. (2010). Note that for many neurological disorders (e.g., Alzheimer's disease), only a subset of patients present with frontal impairment; the studies cited above focused on patients in this subset. Robin and Holyoak (1995) provided an early theoretical discussion of the role of the prefrontal cortex in relational reasoning.

3. On analogy in patients with a degenerative disease affecting the temporal lobe, see Morrison et al. (2004); on Klinefelter Syndrome, see Fales et al. (2003); on autism spectrum disorder, see Krawczyk et al. (2014); Morsanyi and Holyoak (2010).

4. I can only provide the barest hints of the complexities that arise in understanding the human brain and how it relates to thinking. A good introduction is the online book *Brain Facts*, published by the Society for Neuroscience, and available at https://www.brainfacts.org/the-brain-facts-book. For an overview of the methods used to study the neural basis for thinking, see Morrison and Knowlton (2012). This chapter's sketch of analogy in the brain is largely based on a review paper by Holyoak and Monti (2021). Our review considers additional processes (other than relational integration) that may depend on the RLPFC.

5. See Blank, Kanwisher, and Fedorenko (2014).

6. See Finn et al. (2015).

7. See Duncan and Owen (2000); Duncan (2010); Duncan et al. (2020).

8. See Nee, Wager, and Jonides (2007).

9. See Hobeika et al. (2016).

10. On eye movements and analogy, see Thibaut and French (2016); Vendetti et al. (2017).

11. For a general review of work on the neural representation of semantic knowledge, see Patterson, Nestor, and Rogers (2007); for a study linking semantic relations with the temporal cortex, see Wang, Hsieh, and Bunge (2021).

12. On the role of parietal cortex in working memory, see Wendelken, Bunge, and Carter (2008).

13. Alfred et al. (2020) reported this investigation of the neural basis for transitive inference. For a general review of parietal involvement in reasoning, see Wendelken (2015).

14. This computational model was proposed by Lu et al. (2019); see Chapter 10.

15. This neuroimaging study was conducted by Chiang et al. (2021).

16. The quote is from Tversky (2019, p. 72).

17. For a review of work on the neuroscience of working memory, see D'Esposito and Postle (2015). Duncan et al. (2000) provide relevant neuroimaging evidence.

18. On the role of DLPFC in analogical reasoning, see Bunge et al. (2005); Cho et al. (2010); Green et al. (2006); Valle, Bajo, and Gómez-Ariza (2020). For a meta-analysis of relevant studies, see Hobeika et al. (2016).

19. On the difficulty that frontal patients encounter when confronted with semantic distractors, see Morrison et al. (2004); Krawczyk et al. (2008).

20. For a meta-analysis of research on interference control, see Nee et al. (2007); on individual differences, see Samrani, Bäckman, and Persson (2019).

21. This neuroimaging study was reported by Cho et al. (2010).

22. See Kmiecik, Brisson, and Morrison (2019); Krawczyk et al. (2010); Watson and Chatterjee (2012).

23. For meta-analyses of neuroimaging studies of analogical reasoning, see Hobeika et al. (2016); Vartanian (2012).

24. See Semendeferi et al. (2001, 2011).

25. See Jacobs et al. (1997, 2001).

26. See Ramnani and Owen (2004).

27. For a review of links between the RLPFC and cognitive development, see Dumontheil (2014). For a review of work on maturation of the prefrontal cortex during adolescence, see Caballero, Granberg, and Tseng (2016).

28. See Aichelburg et al. (2016).

29. Neuroimaging studies that varied relational complexity with RPM-like problems include Christoff et al. (2001) and Kroger et al. (2002). Volle et al. (2010) performed a similar study with analogy problems; Krawczyk, McClelland, and Donovan (2011) found RLPFC activation using meaningful analogy problems based on line drawings. In a study of frontal patients with focal lesions, Urbanski et al. (2016) found evidence that the RLPFC plays a critical role in analogical reasoning.

30. See Bunge et al. (2005); Green et al. (2006); Krawczyk et al. (2010).

31. See Bunge, Helskog, and Wendelken (2009).

32. See Wendelken, Bunge, and Carter (2008).

33. See Green et al. (2010). Green et al. (2012) found a similar influence of semantic similarity on RLPFC activity when the analogy task required generation of the missing D term (e.g., $A:B::C:?$). It should be noted that the specific RLPFC region identified by Green and colleagues is distinct from the region highlighted in studies using RPM-style problems. In addition to the study by Chiang et al. (2021), evidence that the RLPFC shows graded sensitivity to relational similarity differences was reported by Davis, Goldwater, and Giron (2017), who used a very different paradigm.

34. On the effects of anodal tDCS, see Green et al. (2017); Lundie et al. (2022); also Green (2016).

35. Gilbert et al. (2010) provided a meta-analysis of studies investigating the functional connectivity of the RLPFC.

36. See Wendelken et al. (2016, 2017).

37. See Mackey, Miller Singley, and Bunge (2013); for a review see Bunge and Lieb (2020).

38. For meta-analyses of neuroimaging studies directed at metaphor processing, see Bohrn et al. (2012); Rapp et al. (2012); Vartanian (2012). For a general review of metaphor comprehension, see Holyoak and Stamenković (2018).

Chapter 6

1. The quote from Darwin is from *The Descent of Man* (1871). The quote from Derek Penn is the first sentence of "Darwin's Mistake" by Penn, Holyoak, and Povinelli

(2008). The authors of the latter paper concur that our lead author deserves credit for the sentence, although we collectively share any and all blame for the thought.

2. See Holyoak and Lu (2021).

3. This estimate of the time since hominins separated from chimpanzees is taken from Moorjani et al. (2016).

4. The quote is from Christie and Gentner (2014, p. 394), who support the hypothesis that a unitary system for relational reasoning is based on the ability to perform what has been termed *structure mapping* (see Chapter 9) between systems of relations (Gentner, 2010). In addition to claiming that nonhuman animals are capable of explicit relational reasoning, proponents of a unitary system argue that the neural machinery required for analogy is available from infancy: "Analogical processing ability is present in the first year of life and may be continuous through development" (Hespos et al., 2020, p. 85). The sketch of the multiple-systems view is based on Holyoak and Lu (2021).

5. The basic idea of cognitive re-representation was proposed by Karmiloff-Smith (1992) in connection with human cognitive development, and extended by Carey (2009) to explain the origin of abstract concepts that go beyond an initial innate repertoire. The re-representation hypothesis was applied to evolutionary changes in cognition by Povinelli and Vonk (2003).

6. See Premack and Woodruff (1978).

7. See Kuznar et al. (2020), who provide a careful critique of an experimental design that was used to test whether ravens have a theory of mind. The same critique applies to the larger set of studies that have been interpreted as evidence for a theory of mind in chimpanzees. For a more general argument against argument by analogy to humans (anthropomorphism) in comparative psychology, see Povinelli and Giambrone (1999); Povinelli, Bering, and Giambrone (2000). Penn and Povinelli (2007) review work on causal cognition in nonhuman animals, distinguishing more implicit causal knowledge based on perceptual cues from the abstract causal understanding exhibited by humans. Povinelli (2000, 2011) reported an extensive series of studies revealing striking limits on chimpanzees' ability to grasp abstract concepts related to physical causality.

8. For a general discussion and comparison of intelligence across animal species, see Thagard (2021), especially Chapter 4.

9. See Applegate and Aronov (2022).

10. Incidentally, the "higher animals" referred to in the quote from Darwin that begins this chapter apparently included not only apes but also dogs—he was a great dog-fancier, and his knowledge of their behavior influenced his thinking about natural selection (Feller, 2005). Dogs have, of course, been bred to interact closely with humans, and are often claimed to exhibit human-like thinking (see for example Hare

and Woods, 2013, *The Genius of Dogs*). As a counterpoint, the early psychologist William James directly addressed—and rejected—the Darwinian claims about the close similarity of canine and human intelligence: "If the reader will take the trouble to analyze the best dog and elephant stories he knows, he will find that, in most cases, this simple contiguous calling up of one whole by another is quite sufficient to explain the phenomena." See James (1890, pp. 345–360; the quote appears on p. 351).

11. These experiments with Betty the crow were reported by Weir and Kacelnik (2002) and Weir, Chappell, and Kacelnik (2006).

12. For similar experiments with chimpanzees, see Povinelli (2000).

13. The hypothesis that New Caledonian crows use mental template matching to guide toolmaking was proposed and tested by Jiebert et al. (2018).

14. This section can be considered my update (or perhaps retraction) of "The Analogical Ape," Chapter 3 in Holyoak and Thagard (1995).

15. See Penn et al. (2008).

16. See Gillan, Premack, and Woodruff (1981).

17. See Oden, Thompson, and Premack (2001).

18. See Premack (1983).

19. For reviews of work on RMTS in nonhuman animals and humans, see Wasserman and Young (2010); Wasserman, Castro, and Fagot (2017); Hochmann et al. (2017).

20. For evidence that crows can solve two-icon RMTS problems, see a paper boldly entitled, "Crows spontaneously exhibit analogical reasoning," by Smirnova et al. (2015). For a discussion of alternative interpretations of these findings based on perceptual cues, see Vonk (2015). We need to keep in mind that the most recent common ancestor of birds and mammals was a reptile that roamed the earth over 300 million years ago, and that avian and human intelligence are based on distinct brain structures (Güntürkün et al., 2021). Avian cognition is of great interest in its own right, but its evolutionary connection to human cognition is extremely remote.

21. See Brown (1989). For toddlers, transfer between problems appears to be limited to cases in which the solution to each is signaled by very similar perceptual cues (e.g., Z. Chen, Sanchez, and Campbell, 1998).

22. For discussions of various Early Systems for cognition, see Danks (2009) on causation; Hoerl and McCormack (2019) on thinking about time; Apperly and Butterfill (2009) and Burge (2018) on attribution of mental states.

23. For a review of neural development as it relates to mental attribution, see Richardson and Saxe (2020).

24. See Zhu and Gopnik (2023).

25. This RMTS study was reported by Hochmann et al. (2017). Kroupin and Carey (2022) showed that for four-year-olds, prior training on a simpler match-to-sample task can lead to spontaneous success on two-icon RMTS problems. The latter finding illustrates how contextual cues can increase attention to explicit relations, even for preschoolers.

26. For a recent example of an infant habituation study inspired by the RMTS paradigm, see Anderson, Chang, Hespos, and Gentner (2022). For a general discussion of evidence for acquisition of these relational concepts by young children, see Hochmann, Carey, and Mehler (2018).

27. This study of children's analogical problem-solving was performed by Holyoak, Junn, and Billman (1984). Using geometric analogy problems that varied in complexity, Goswami (1989) also found a major increase in performance across ages four to six years.

28. See Gentner (1988) and Gentner and Rattermann (1991).

29. See Goswami (1992); Gentner et al. (1995).

30. See Gentner and Toupin (1986).

31. On relational complexity and analogy, see Halford (1993); Halford et al. (2010, 2014).

32. See Richland, Morrison, and Holyoak (2006).

33. See Starr et al. (2022); Weinberger et al. (2022).

34. This study was reported by Whitaker et al. (2018).

35. On the role of verbal labels in aiding children's analogical reasoning, see Gentner et al. (1995); Gentner and Loewenstein (2002); Gentner (2016). Piaget's views on analogical development are presented in Piaget, Montangero and Billeter (1977).

36. Simms and Richland (2019) demonstrated a relational set with preschool children.

37. On cultural influences, see Richland et al. (2010); Kuwabara and Smith (2012); Carstensen et al. (2019).

Chapter 7

1. The quote from Chomsky appears in his essay "Language and freedom" (Chomsky, 1970/1987, p. 152).

2. See Nowell (2021).

3. Klima and Bellugi (1979) described the close formal relationships between sign and spoken languages. For a recent overview of the nature of sign languages, see Emmorey (2023).

4. For evidence that extensive efforts to teach human-like symbol systems to chimpanzees failed to achieve that goal, see Terrace, Petitto, Sanders, and Bever (1979).

5. On Late Pleistocene social organization, see Singh and Glowacki (2022).

6. For a detailed discussion of the development of sociality in human children, see Tomasello (2019).

7. For research that reveals structure and functions of the language network in the brain, see Federenko, Behr, and Kanwisher (2011); Blank et al. (2014); Braga et al. (2020); Federenko and Shain (2021).

8. For work on localization of adjacent subareas of the frontoparietal and language networks within the left inferior frontal gyrus, see Federenko, Duncan, and Kanwisher (2012); Federenko and Blank (2020).

9. See Monti and Osherson (2012); Monti, Parsons, and Osherson (2009, 2012); Coetzee and Monti (2018).

10. See Woolgar et al. (2018).

11. For a general review of the neural circuits that support mentalizing, see Gilead and Ochsner (2021). For evidence that the mentalizing network is distinct from the network supporting general reasoning, see Van Overwalle (2011).

12. See Willems et al. (2010).

13. See Varley and Siegal (2000).

14. See Tomasello (2019).

15. For a discussion of the possible evolutionary origin of relational thinking in connection with human social interactions, see Tomasello (2014).

16. The nature of the mechanism underlying children's language acquisition has been extremely controversial. Chomsky (1965) proposed that children have an innate, specialized Language Acquisition Device. Yang and Piantadosi (2022) have argued that a general Bayesian compositional model may be capable of learning human languages from the kind of data realistically available to children. But whatever mechanism supports child language acquisition, it is distinct from the Late System for relational reasoning described in the previous chapter.

17. For a review and synthesis of research on the relation between language and thought, see Gleitman and Papafragou (2012).

18. For a review of work showing the influence of verbal labels on relational reasoning, see Gentner (2016).

19. See Gentner, Anggoro, and Klibanoff (2011).

20. See Ionescu et al. (2022).

21. See Jamrozik and Gentner (2020).

22. Pyers and Senghas (2009) conducted this study of how acquiring signs for mental verbs impacts understanding of false beliefs. For evidence that analogical comparisons also can facilitate such learning, see Hoyos et al. (2020).

23. For general discussions of relational concepts in language, see Markman and Stilwell (2001); Goldwater and Schalk (2016); Gentner and Asmuth (2019).

24. See Jones and Love (2008).

25. For studies of how role-based categories are learned, see Goldwater and Markman (2011); Goldwater, Bainbridge, and Murphy (2016).

26. See Barsalou (1983).

27. See Asmuth and Gentner (2017). The "fetch test" is introduced on p. 2008.

28. The tendency to evaluate the goodness of relational categories in terms of similarity to an ideal was demonstrated for artificial categories by Kittur, Hummel, and Holyoak (2006), and for categories in natural language by Goldwater, Markman, and Stilwell (2011).

29. See Gick and Holyoak (1983).

30. See Gentner and Asmuth (2019) for an overview of how analogy is involved in the acquisition of relational words.

31. See Waltz et al. (1999).

32. For a review of the neurobiology of semantic memory, see Binder and Desai (2011).

33. For discussions of metaphor in poetry, see Lakoff and Turner (1989); Holyoak (2019).

34. For a general review of psychological research on metaphor comprehension, see Holyoak and Stamenković (2018).

35. Meta-analyses of neural activity associated with metaphor comprehension have been reported by Bohrn, Altmann, and Jacobs (2012); Rapp, Mutschler, and Erb (2012); Vartanian (2012). Using a different type of meta-analysis of comprehension of non-literal language (including metaphor), Hauptman, Blank, and Federenko (2023) found that the language and metalizing networks were selectively activated, but not the control network.

36. Bowdle and Gentner (2005) proposed that analogy is involved in comprehending novel (but not familiar) metaphors. Cardillo et al. (2012) conducted a study of changes in neural responses as metaphors become more familiar. They did not observe selective activation of the RLPFC even for unfamiliar metaphors.

37. See Stamenković, Ichien, and Holyoak (2019, 2020; Stamenković et al., 2023). Ichien, Stamenković, Whatley, Castel, and Holyoak (2024) found that semantic knowledge strongly predicted metaphor comprehension for a sample of older adults (aged 55 to 88 years).

38. For evidence that fluid intelligence is particularly important for the production of creative (as compared to conventional) metaphors, see Beaty and Silvia (2013).

39. For meta-analyses of metaphor comprehension in ASD and typically developing groups, see Kalandadze, Bambini, and Næss (2019); Morsanyi, Stamenković, and Holyoak (2020a).

40. For a meta-analysis of analogical reasoning in ASD and typically developing groups, see Morsanyi, Stamenković, and Holyoak (2020b).

41. See Morsanyi et al. (2022).

42. A study by Viskontas et al. (2004) found that older adults performed less well than a younger sample on a non-verbal analogy test. Ichien, Stamenković, et al. (2024) found that older adults showed a striking advantage over younger adults in comprehending novel literary metaphors.

43. An early model of metaphor comprehension based on combining concept meanings was proposed by Kintsch (2000).

Chapter 8

1. Adam Grant, Saul P. Steinberg Professor of Management at the Wharton School of the University of Pennsylvania, is the author of several books on creativity and innovation. The quote is from a post on Twitter, January 30, 2016: https://twitter .com/AdamMGrant/status/693433918763200512.

2. For an introduction to the number sense, see Dehaene (1997). Gelman and Gallistel (1986) and Siegler and Opfer (2003) describe the development of different aspects of quantitative knowledge. The classic study of mental magnitude comparisons with digits was reported by Moyer and Landauer (1967). Cantlon and Brannon (2005) showed similarities between magnitude comparisons by humans and monkeys.

3. See Rapp et al. (2015). Despite the considerable cross-national variation in their math curricula, the same differences between the contexts in which fractions and decimals are normally used have been identified in South Korea (Lee et al., 2016) and Russia (Tyumeneva et al., 2018).

4. For evidence that decimals have an advantage over fractions for numerical magnitude comparisons, see for example Schneider and Siegler (2010); DeWolf et al. (2014, 2016).

5. For evidence of fraction advantages in tasks that require reasoning about quantitative relations between a subset and set, or one set to another, see for example DeWolf,

Bassok, & Holyoak (2015a); Lee et al. (2016); Plummer et al. (2017); for a review see DeWolf, Bassok, and Holyoak (2017).

6. See Gray et al. (2018).

7. See DeWolf et al. (2017).

8. See DeWolf, Bassok, and Holyoak (2015b).

9. For example, Nokes-Malach et al. (2013) showed that analogical comparison of physics concepts increases far transfer; and Jee et al. (2013) found that comparisons of contrasting cases improve learning about concepts in geology. In teaching mathematics, Begolli and Richland (2016) found that analogical comparison of examples of solved problems illustrating proportionality improved performance on test problems and reduced common misconceptions. Kurtz, Miao, and Gentner (2001) showed that comparing situations involving heat transfer promoted greater insight into the common causal structure, but only when the comparison was intensive. For a meta-analysis of studies of teaching by comparisons, see Alfieri, Nokes-Malach, and Schunn (2013). Star (2015) reported a study illustrating the practical difficulties that can arise when attempting to introduce comparison (or other cognitively demanding strategies) into school curricula.

10. This example is taken from Gray and Holyoak (2020), who surveyed several principles that can guide effective use of analogies in teaching. Other general reviews and discussions of teaching by analogy include Vendetti et al. (2015) and Richland and Begolli (2016).

11. Richland, Zur, and Holyoak (2007) found evidence that math teachers in the United States were less likely than teachers in Japan or Hong Kong to provide highly familiar source analogs, or to make use of several other cognitive supports that aid thinking by analogy. See also Richland and McDonough (2010).

12. For a discussion of how evidential analogies may help to overcome students' misconceptions about the operation of physical forces, see Brown and Clement (1989). They proposed that "bridging" analogies—cases intermediate between a distant source and the target—may be useful in overcoming students' initial resistance when a distant source analog contradicts their entering misconception about the target.

13. See Gick and Holyoak (1983).

14. See Rittle-Johnson, Star, and Durkin (2009).

15. See DeWolf, Son, et al. (2017).

16. See Vendetti et al. (2015). The optimal strategy for experimental design is to vary one thing at a time, as suggested by Tschirgi (1980). In AI, Winston (1975) introduced the concept of a "near miss"—contrasting a category member with a non-member differing in one critical way—as a technique for learning relational categories from examples.

17. See Stigler, Givvin, and Thompson (2010); Richland, Stigler, and Holyoak (2012).

18. See Sidney (2020).

19. For research supporting these and other principles for teaching with comparisons, see for example Novick and Holyoak (1991); Richland et al. (2007); Richland and McDonough (2010); Matlen, Gentner, and Franconeri (2020); and the reviews cited in Note 10.

20. For a discussion of teaching to counter misconceptions, see Vosniadou (2019).

21. The multiconstraint theory was proposed by Holyoak and Thagard (1989). Our coherence-based theory of analogy in turn inspired the more general theory of explanatory coherence (Thagard, 1989).

22. On the transience of changes in beliefs that increase local coherence, see Simon et al. (2008); Lee and Holyoak (2023). Simon et al. (2015) provided evidence that emotions and beliefs jointly impact (and are impacted by) coherence. The role of hyper-coherence in the rise of conspiracy theories was discussed by Priniski, McClay, and Holyoak (2021).

23. See Holyoak and Simon (1999).

24. The tendency when making judgments under uncertainty to place greater weight on individual cases, relative to statistical information about multiple cases, was discussed by Nisbett and Ross (1980).

25. Holyoak and Powell (2016) proposed a coherence theory of moral judgment.

26. See Spellman et al. (1993).

27. See Horne, Powell, and Hummel (2015).

28. See Horne, Rottman, and Lawrence (2021).

Chapter 9

1. This quote from Turing is from a BBC radio interview conducted in 1951. The quote about analogy in from another BBC interview in the following year. A good source is the biography *Alan Turing: The Enigma* by Andrew Hodges (1983), especially the chapter "The Greenwood Tree."

2. Here I set aside the thorny issue of whether non-cognitive aspects of human mental life—notably, the capacity to feel emotions and to be conscious of inner experience—could be realized in a computer. I'll address this topic in Chapter 13 when I consider the prerequisites for creativity.

3. See Rumelhart and McClelland (1986); McClelland and Rumelhart (1986). For an overview of the basic ideas incorporated into parallel distributed processing, see Rogers and McClelland (2014).

4. I was personally influenced by Bayesian models though the work of Griffiths and Tenenbaum (2005), which focused on causal learning; much earlier, I had worked on a Bayesian model of category learning (Fried & Holyoak, 1984). A rational analysis of memory using a Bayesian framework (Anderson & Milson, 1989) has also had an impact on models of analogy, particularly with respect to the retrieval of potential source analogs from memory.

5. The application of deep learning to analogy began with the work of Mikolov et al. (2013).

6. The ANALOGY project, which was the basis for Evans's 1963 PhD thesis, is described by Evans (1968). The Argus project is described in Reitman (1965), a book published after he had moved to the University of Michigan.

7. See Winston (1980). Another early model that emphasized the importance of the reasoner's goals in using an analogy was developed by Carbonell (1983).

8. The "frames" concept was proposed by Minsky (1975).

9. For his work on learning relational concepts, see Winston (1975).

10. For the original version of SME (first presented at a conference in 1986), see Falkenhainer et al. (1989). The structure mapping theory was proposed by Gentner (1983); the quote is from p. 165. For an overview of the subsequent development of SME and major changes in the program, see Forbus et al. (2017).

11. SME's original default for its match rules ("analogy rules") was replaced by "literal similarity rules" in a version described by Forbus, Ferguson, and Gentner (1994).

12. One way in which causal relations are selectively emphasized in SME is by placing task-specific restrictions on matching various frequent but *noncausal* relations, termed "ubiquitous predicates"; see Forbus et al. (2017).

13. For evidence that people preferentially infer an effect in the target if the cause matches between source and target, see Clement and Gentner (1991); Markman (1997). Lassaline (1996) showed that the *cause* relation supports analogical inferences to a greater extent than does a noncausal relation matched in syntactic form.

14. For a general review of the suite of programs developed in the SME project, see Forbus et al. (2017). For the SME-based model of analog retrieval, see Forbus, Gentner, and Law (1995); for an incremental version, see Forbus et al. (1994). The first analogy model to perform incremental mapping was the *Incremental Analogy Machine* (IAM); see Keane and Brayshaw (1988).

15. See Lovett et al. (2009); Lovett and Forbus (2017).

16. See Hespos et al. (2020).

17. The connectionist analysis of the Necker cube was used by Rumelhart, Smolensky, et al. (1986) to illustrate the operation of parallel constraint satisfaction. ACME

was described by Holyoak and Thagard (1989); see also Holyoak et al. (1994). The same source analog led us to develop an extension of ACME that dealt with retrieval (*Analog Retrieval by Constraint Satisfaction*; ARCS; Thagard et al. (1990).

18. On explanation by constraint satisfaction, see Thagard (1989); on legal and moral decision making, see Spellman, Ullman, and Holyoak (1993); Holyoak and Simon (1999); Simon, Stenstrom, and Read (2015); Holyoak and Powell (2016).

19. Copycat was introduced by Mitchell (1993) and Hofstadter and Mitchell (1994); also see Hofstadter (1995); Hofstadter and Sander (2013). For a more general review of analogy models in AI, see Mitchell (2021).

20. For experimental work on letter-string analogies, see Burns (1996); Webb, Holyoak, and Lu (2023). The dearth of empirical assessment is attributable at least in part to Hofstadter's avowed distaste for the scientific enterprise. In his view, the essential information for evaluating models of human analogy "can easily be gotten from casual discussions with a handful of friends" (Hofstadter, 1995, p. 364). My own experience has been that more can be learned from intense debates with a handful of critics.

21. See Forbus et al. (1998) for an extended critique of the theoretical underpinnings of Copycat from the perspective of the SME project.

22. For a comparison of simulations of letter-string analogies using Copycat and ACME, see Burns and Holyoak (1994).

23. I believe I coined the term "symbolic connectionism" in Holyoak (1991).

24. Besides LISA, another important neural-style model of analogy is *Structured Tensor Analogical Reasoning* (STAR), developed by Halford and his collaborators (Halford et al., 1998, 2001). Inspired by the work of Smolensky (1990), STAR uses tensor products (a mathematical operation performed on vectors) to automatically create a neural pattern corresponding to a proposition. STAR is able to capture role bindings in propositions, and provides an explanation for how analogy can operate within the limited capacity of human working memory.

25. LISA was developed by Hummel and Holyoak (1997, 2003). Knowlton et al. (2012) discuss possible links to neural mechanisms.

26. Empirical tests of LISA as a model of human analogy include Kubose, Holyoak, and Hummel (2002); Kroger, Holyoak, and Hummel (2004); Morrison et al. (2004); Viskontas et al. (2004).

27. DORA was introduced by Doumas, Hummel, and Sandhofer (2008); see also Doumas et al. (2022).

28. For an overview of developmental changes in conceptions of object similarity, see Smith (1989).

Chapter 10

1. The quote is from the British linguist J. R. Firth (1957, p. 11), one of the leading proponents of distributional semantics.

2. This study of transfer from physics to non-physics problems was reported by Bassok and Olseth (1995); see also Bassok and Holyoak (1989); Bassok (1990). Other studies showing asymmetries in analogical transfer include Reed, Ernst, and Banerji (1974); Hayes and Simon (1977).

3. The hypothesis that word meanings are composed of more elementary features was proposed in cognitive psychology by Schaeffer and Wallace (1969), and elaborated by many others, notably Smith, Shoben, and Rips (1974). Rosch (1973) developed a theory of the meaning of object categories based on prototypes. For a general review of psychological theories of categories and concepts, see Murphy and Hoffman (2012).

4. The classic study of semantic priming was reported by Meyer and Schvaneveldt (1971). For a thorough review of work on the topic, see McNamara (2005).

5. This study of relational priming was reported by Spellman, Holyoak, and Morrison (2001), who found that it was necessary to explicitly tell people to pay attention to relations in order to obtain relation-based priming. However, in similar paradigms, relational priming has been obtained without such instructions when the prime was presented for a longer duration and a relational judgment about the prime was required; see Estes and Jones (2006, 2009).

6. This study was performed by Schunn and Dunbar (1996).

7. Day and Gentner (2007) also reported evidence of unintended transfer without awareness when people read analogically related passages. Their study found that transfer depended on overlap of both a semantic relation and its surrounding context. The authors interpreted this result as evidence that full-blown analogical mapping can occur without awareness. However, it seems that such transfer could be explained as context-dependent priming, where the context and a relation in the source jointly activate a similar relation in the target. For additional evidence of unintended relational transfer without awareness, see Day and Goldstone (2011). Another related phenomenon, termed *relational luring* (Popov and Hristova, 2017), has been shown in tests of recognition for lists of word pairs. People more often falsely report having seen a recombined word pair (e.g., *flower: garden*) if it instantiates the same semantic relation (e.g., *is a part of*) as a studied word pair (e.g., *house: town*). Relational luring apparently arises because studying examples of an unstated semantic relation makes the relation itself seem more familiar (see also Ichien, Alfred, et al., 2023).

8. See Guthormsen et al. (2016).

9. On similarity phenomena involving semantic relations, see Chaffin and Herrmann, 1984; Herrmann et al., 1986; Chaffin, Herrmann, and Winston (1988); for an overview see Chaffin (1992).

10. Based on the research of Chaffin, Herrmann, and others, Bejar, Chaffin, and Embretson (1991) constructed a taxonomy of seventy-nine semantic relations, classified into ten major categories. Our group used this taxonomy to guide generation of sets of words pairs instantiating each relation, coupled with relational typicality scores derived from human judgments (Jurgens et al., 2012).

11. The Word2vec model was introduced by Mikolov et al. (2013); Zhila et al. (2013).

12. Strictly speaking, learning in Word2vec is not very "deep" since the model includes just a single hidden layer. More recent deep learning models often have dozens of layers between the input and output layers.

13. For a discussion of and response to critiques of embeddings as psychological models, see Günther et al. (2019).

14. For a general review of applications of embedding models to cognitive modeling, see Bhatia and Aka (2022); for applications to semantic tasks, see Kumar (2021).

15. See Hollis and Westbury (2016); Utsumi (2020).

16. On the limitations of Word2vec in directly solving verbal analogies, see Linzen (2016); Peterson, Chen, and Griffiths (2020).

17. The BART model was described by Lu et al. (2012, 2019).

18. Work in AI by Turney (2008, 2013) illustrates how linking expressions may be used to solve verbal analogy problems.

19. For BART's performance on judgments of relation typicality and on verbal analogy problems, see Lu et al. (2019); for relational similarity judgments, see Ichien et al. (2022); for predictions of neural responses to semantic relations during a verbal analogy task, see Chiang et al. (2021).

20. See Lu et al. (2022).

21. For an introduction to attributed graphs, see Gold and Rangarajan (1996).

22. These analogy materials were created and tested in an experiment by Turney (2008).

Chapter 11

1. The quote from Norman Maclean is from his semi-autobiographical 1976 novella, *A River Runs Through It* (p. 105).

2. For an overview of recent work on machine vision, see Chai et al. (2021).

3. For an introduction to visiPAM, see Webb, Fu, et al. (2023).

4. See L. Chen (1982).

5. See Hafri, Papafragou, and Trueswell (2013).

6. For a review of work on the perception of relations, see Hafri and Firestone (2021).

7. An early machine-learning model of relation detection using both visual and semantic information was developed by C. Lu et al. (2016). For a more recent model of relation extraction that includes an attention mechanism, see Mi and Chen (2020).

8. This computational model for solving four-term pictorial analogies was developed by Lu et al. (2019). The picture analogies were previously used by Krawczyk et al. (2008) in a neuropsychological study.

9. This study was conducted by Ichien, Liu, et al. (2023).

10. See Tversky and Hemenway (1984).

11. See Gentner (1977).

12. See Webb, Fu, et al. (2023).

Chapter 12

1. The Dutch computer scientist Edsger W. Dijkstra was a recipient of the Turing Award. The quote is from his handwritten transcription of a talk he gave in 1988, "On the cruelty of really teaching computer science," found online at https://www.cs.utexas.edu/users/EWD/ewd10xx/EWD1036.PDF.

2. See Griffiths (2020).

3. For an overview of the basic learning mechanisms used in neural networks, see Rogers and McClelland (2014).

4. See Barrett et al. (2018); Zhang, Gao, et al. (2019).

5. The hypothesis that analogy is a kind of "high-level perception" was advanced by Chalmers, French, and Hofstadter (1992); for an early critique, see Forbus et al. (1998).

6. See Santoro et al. (2017); Hill et al. (2019); Zhang, Jia, et al. (2019).

7. See Ichien, Liu, et al. (2023).

8. The quote is from Peirce (1931–1958, vol. 2, p. 476). For a general introduction to Bayesian inference, see Griffiths, Tenenbaum, and Kemp (2012).

9. The transformer architecture was introduced by Vaswani et al. (2017).

10. Prompt training was first described by Ouyang et al. (2022).

11. Brown et al. (2020) reported evidence that a precursor of chatGPT was capable of few-shot learning.

12. This anecdote is from a *New York Times* article by Kevin Roose, February 16, 2023: https://www.nytimes.com/2023/02/16/technology/bing-chatbot-microsoft-chatgpt .html.

13. These tests of LLMs on analogy problems were performed by Webb, Holyoak, and Lu (2023). Our evaluation focused on a variant of early chatGPT called text-davinci-003 (an instance of GPT-3).

14. The next iteration of chatGPT was based on a version called GPT-4 (OpenAI, 2023). Webb et al. (2023) reported a preliminary evaluation that found improvement on a challenging test that required identifying story analogies based on shared causal relations. Other early evaluations were reported by Bubeck et al. (2023).

15. These metaphor tests were performed by Ichien, Stamenković, and Holyoak (2024).

16. Examples of harshly critical responses to early LLMs include a piece by Marcus and Davis, from August 22, 2020, https://www.technologyreview.com/2020/08/22/100 7539/gpt3-openai-language-generator-artificial-intelligence-ai-opinion/; and another by Chomsky, Roberts, and Watumull, from March 8, 2023, https://www.nytimes.com /2023/03/08/opinion/noam-chomsky-chatgpt-ai.html.

17. Olsson et al. (2022) provide evidence that large language models based on the transformer architecture often create structures they term *induction heads*, which predict text completions using a mechanism that might be considered a rudimentary form of analogical inference.

18. See Mahowald et al. (2024).

19. See for example Zhou et al. (2022).

Chapter 13

1. Stephen Jay Gould was a paleontologist, evolutionary biologist, and historian of science. The quote is from his essay "Darwin's Middle Road," which appeared in his book *The Panda's Thumb* (1980, p. 66).

2. The quote is from Shepard (2004, p. 7). His earliest paper on mental rotation was by Shepard and Metzler (1971).

3. For general discussions of the nature of creativity, see Boden (2004); Sternberg and Lubart (1995); Ward, Finke, and Smith (1995); for insights into musical creativity, see Levitin (2008).

4. See Barry (2019).

5. See Holyoak (2019), in the chapter "The Authenticity of Footprints."

6. See Goodman (1968), in the chapter "Art and Authenticity."

7. This analysis of modes of generation is based on Holyoak, Ichien, and Lu (2023).

8. This study was conducted by Amabile (1985); see also Amabile (1996). Baum and Baumann (2019) discuss the importance of autonomy in creativity.

9. For an overview of research on openness to experience and its connections to creativity, see Oleynick et al. (2017). Kenett (2018) reviews work on the connections between the organization of semantic memory and creativity, and Li et al. (2021) relate semantic organization to the production of metaphors. Q. Chen et al. (2023) report a study of the personality characteristics of creative artists and scientists.

10. See Holyoak and Thagard (1995), in the chapter "The Analogical Scientist."

11. The concept of progressive deepening was introduced by de Groot in his 1946 book, which was translated and published in English as de Groot (1965).

12. This subtitle is adapted from a line in a poem called "All That Is Gold Does Not Glitter," which appears in *The Fellowship of the Ring* by J. R. R. Tolkien.

13. For a discussion of the relationship between the default and mentalizing networks, see Gilead and Ochsner (2021); Andrews-Hanna (2012); Wang et al. (2021). For evidence that people naturally think about themselves and social relationships when not otherwise engaged, see Meyer and Lieberman (2018); Meyer et al. (2019).

14. See Beaty, Seli, and Schacter (2019).

15. See Kim (2011).

16. See Beaty et al. (2018). For a general review of the neuroscience of creativity, see Vartanian (2019).

17. See Dunbar (1999).

18. For reviews of work on aha moments, see Kounios and Beeman (2015); Carpenter (2020).

19. This and other well-known quotations from Albert Einstein appear in a collection edited by Schilpp (1979).

20. See Tik et al. (2018).

21. In his 2023 book with Strauss, Rubin provides a general discussion of emotional and cognitive supports for creativity. These include suggestions for how to induce effective mind-wandering.

22. See Chesebrough et al. (2023).

23. "The Circus Animals' Desertion," written in 1937 or 1938, was first published by Cuala Press in 1939 (the year of Yeats's death) in the volume *Last Poems and Two Plays*.

24. See Rubin's book with Strauss (2023, p. 13).

25. For an overview of research on the Flynn effect and what it may mean, see Flynn (2011). Recent work suggests that toward the end of the twentieth century, the general trend in measured intelligence across the population reversed and began to trend *downward*, at least in several Western countries (see Dutton, van der Linden, and Lynn, 2016).

26. See Cave and O'Hagan (2022); quotations are from pages 9–14. I describe the origins of a couple of my own poems in Holyoak (2023).

27. The quote is from the psychotherapist Carl Rogers (1961, Chapter 1).

28. The quote is from an interview with Cohen published in *Look* magazine, "Songs Sacred and Profane" by Ira Mothner (June 10, 1969).

29. The work of contemporary artist Refik Anadol (https://refikanadol.com/) includes striking examples of AI-generated "living paintings."

30. This definition is from the literary critic Harold Bloom (2004, p. 1).

31. Nick Cave's defense of human creativity in the age of AI, written in January 2023, appeared at https://www.theredhandfiles.com/chat-gpt-what-do-you-think/.

Chapter 14

1. The quote is from Iris Murdoch's novel *The Sea, The Sea* (1978, p. 477).

2. See in particular the philosopher Thomas Nagel's classic essay "What is it like to be a bat?" (Nagel, 1974; also Nagel, 1986).

References

Aichelburg, C., Urbanski, M., Thiebaut de Schotten, M., Humbert, F., Levy, R., & Volle, E. (2016). Morphometry of left frontal and temporal poles predicts analogical reasoning abilities. *Cerebral Cortex, 26*, 915–932.

Alfieri, L., Nokes-Malach, T. J., & Schunn, C. D. (2013). Learning through case comparisons: A meta-analytic review. *Educational Psychologist, 48*(2), 87–113.

Alfred, K. L., Connolly, A. C., Cetron, J. S., & Kraemer, D. J. M. (2020). Mental models use common neural spatial structure for spatial and abstract content. *Communications Biology, 3*, 17. https://doi.org/10.1038/s42003-019-0740-8

Alibali, M. W., Bassok, M., Solomon, K. O., Syc, S. E., & Goldin-Meadow, S. (1999). Illuminating mental representations through speech and gesture. *Psychological Science, 10*(4), 327–333.

Amabile, T. M. (1985). Motivation and creativity: Effects of motivational orientation on creative writers. *Journal of Personality and Social Psychology, 48*(2), 393–399.

Amabile, T. (1996). *Creativity in context.* Westview Press.

Anderson, E. M., Chang, Y.-J., Hespos, S., & Gentner, D. (2022). No evidence for language benefits in infant relational learning. *Infant Behavior & Development, 66*, 101666.

Andersen, S. M., Glassman, N. S., Chen, S., & Cole, S. W. (1995). Transference in social perception: The role of chronic accessibility in significant-other representations. *Journal of Personality and Social Psychology, 69*, 41–57.

Anderson, J. R., & Milson, R. (1989). Human memory: An adaptive perspective. *Psychological Review, 96*(4), 703–719.

Andrews, G., Halford, G. S., Chapell, M., Maujean, A., & Shum, D. H. K. (2014). Planning following stroke: A relational complexity approach using the Tower of London. *Frontiers in Human Neuroscience, 8*, Article 1032.

Andrews, G., Halford, G. S., Shum, D. H. K., Maujean, A., Chappell, M., & Birney, D. (2013). Relational processing following stroke. *Brain and Cognition, 81*, 44–51.

Andrews-Hanna, J. R. (2012). The brain's default network and its adaptive role in internal mentation. *The Neuroscientist, 18*(3), 251–270.

Apperly, I. A., & Butterfill, S. A. (2009). Do humans have two systems to track beliefs and belief-like states? *Psychological Review, 116*(4), 953–970.

Applegate, M. C., & Aronov, D. (2022). Flexible use of memory by food-caching birds. *Elife, 11*, e70600. https://doi.org/10.7554/eLife.70600

Ascher, R. (1961). Analogy in archaeological interpretation. *Southwestern Journal of Anthropology, 17*(4), 317–325.

Asmuth, J., & Gentner, D. (2017). Relational categories are more mutable than entity categories. *Quarterly Journal of Experimental Psychology, 70*(10), 2007–2025.

Barrett, D. G. T., Hill, F., Santoro, A., Morcos, A. S., & Lillicrap, T. (2018). Measuring abstract reasoning in neural networks. *Proceedings of the 35th International Conference on Machine Learning, 80*, 511-520.

Barry, L. (2019). *Making comics*. Drawn & Quarterly.

Barsalou, L. W. (1983). Ad hoc categories. *Memory & Cognition, 11*, 211–227.

Bartha, P. (2010). *By parallel reasoning: The construction and evaluation of analogical arguments*. Oxford University Press.

Bassok, M. (1990). Transfer of domain-specific problem-solving procedures. *Journal of Experimental Psychology: Learning, Memory, and Cognition, 16*, 522–533.

Bassok, M. (1996). Using content to interpret structure: Effects on analogical transfer. *Current Directions in Psychological Science, 5*(2), 54–58.

Bassok, M., Chase, V. M., & Martin, S. A. (1998). Adding apples and oranges: Alignment of semantic and formal knowledge. *Cognitive Psychology, 35*(2), 99–134.

Bassok, M., & Holyoak, K. J. (1989). Interdomain transfer between isomorphic topics in algebra and physics. *Journal of Experimental Psychology: Learning: Memory, and Cognition, 15*, 153–166.

Bassok, M., & Olseth, K. L. (1995). Object-based representations: Transfer between cases of continuous and discrete models of change. *Journal of Experimental Psychology: Learning, Memory, and Cognition, 21*(6), 1522–1538.

Bassok, M., Wu, L., & Olseth, K. L. (1995). Judging a book by its cover: Interpretative effects of context on problem-solving transfer. *Memory & Cognition, 23*, 354–367.

Baum, I. R., & Baumann, N. (2019). Autonomous creativity: The implicit autonomy motive fosters creative production and innovative behavior at school. *Gifted and Talented International, 33*(1–2), 15–25.

Beaty, R. E., Kenett, Y. N., Christensen, A. P., Rosenberg, M. D., Benedek, M., Chen, Q., Fink, A., Qiu, J., Kwapil, T. R., Kane, M. J., & Silva, P. J. (2018). Robust prediction of individual creative ability from brain functional connectivity. *Proceedings of the National Academy of Sciences, USA, 115*(5), 1087–1092.

Beaty, R. E., Seli, P., & Schacter, D. E. (2019). Network neuroscience of creative cognition: Mapping cognitive mechanisms and individual differences in the creative brain. *Current Opinion in Behavioral Sciences, 27,* 22–30.

Beaty, R. E., & Silvia, P. J. (2013). Metaphorically speaking: Cognitive abilities and the production of figurative language. *Memory & Cognition, 41*(2), 255–267.

Begolli, K. N., & Richland, L. E. (2016). Teaching mathematics by comparison: Analog visibility as a double-edged sword. *Journal of Educational Psychology, 108*(2), 194–213.

Bejar, I. I., Chaffin, R., & Embretson, S. (1991). *Cognitive and psychometric analysis of analogical problem solving.* Springer-Verlag.

Beveridge, M., & Parkins, E. (1987). Visual representation in analogical problem solving. *Memory & Cognition, 15,* 230–237.

Bhatia, S., & Aka, A. (2022). Cognitive modeling with representations from large-scale digital data. *Current Directions in Psychological Science, 31*(3), 207–214.

Binder, J. R., & Desai, R. H. (2011). The neurobiology of semantic memory. *Trends in Cognitive Sciences, 15*(11), 527–536.

Blanchette, I., & Dunbar, K. (2000). How analogies are generated: The roles of structural and superficial similarity. *Memory & Cognition, 28,* 108–124.

Blanchette, I., & Dunbar, K. (2001). Analogy use in naturalistic settings: The influence of audience, emotion, and goal. *Memory & Cognition, 29,* 730–735.

Blanchette, I., & Dunbar, K. (2002). Representational change and analogy: How analogical inferences alter target representations. *Journal of Experimental Psychology: Learning, Memory, and Cognition, 28,* 672–685.

Blank, I., Kanwisher, N., & Fedorenko, E. (2014). A functional dissociation between language and multiple-demand systems revealed in patterns of BOLD signal fluctuations. *Journal of Neurophysiology, 112*(5), 1105–1118.

Bloom, H. (2004). The art of reading poetry. In H. Bloom (Ed.), *The best poems of the English language: From Chaucer through Frost* (pp. 1–29). HarperCollins.

Boden, M. A. (2004). *The creative mind: Myths and mechanisms* (2nd ed.). Routledge.

Bohrn, I. C., Altmann, U., & Jacobs, A. M. (2012). Looking at the brains behind figurative language: A quantitative meta-analysis of neuroimaging studies of metaphor, idiom, and irony processing. *Neuropsychologica, 50,* 2669–2683.

Bowdle, B., & Gentner, D. (2005). The career of metaphor. *Psychological Review, 112,* 193–216.

Braga, R. M., DiNicola, L. M., Becker, H. C., & Buckner, R. L. (2020). Situating the left-lateralized language network in the broader organization of multiple specialized large-scale distributed networks. *Journal of Neurophysiology, 124*(5), 1415–1448.

Brown, A. (1989). Analogical learning and transfer: What develops? In S. Vosniadou & A. Ortony (Eds.), *Similarity and analogical reasoning* (pp. 369-412). Cambridge University Press.

Brown, D. E., & Clement, J. (1989). Overcoming misconceptions via analogical reasoning: Abstract transfer versus explanatory model construction. *Instructional Science, 18,* 237–261.

Brown, T. B., Mann, B., Ryder, N., Subbiah, M., Kaplan, J. D., Dhariwal, P., Neelakantan, A., Shyam, P., Sastry, G., Askell, A., Agarwal, S., Herbert-Voss, A., Krueger, G., Henighan, T., Child, R., Ramesh, A., Ziegler, D., Wu, J., Winter, C., . . . Amodei, D. (2020). Language models are few-shot learners. *Advances in Neural Information Processing Systems, 34,* 1877–1901.

Bubeck, S., Chandrasekaran, V., Eldan, R., Gehrke, J., Horvitz, E., Kamar, E., Lee, P., Lee, Y. T., Li, Y., Lundberg, S., Nori, H., Palangi, H., Ribeiro, M. T., & Zhang, Y. (2023). Sparks of artificial general intelligence: Early experiments with GPT-4. https://arxiv.org/abs/2303.12712

Bunge, S. A., Helskog, E. H., & Wendelken, C. (2009). Left, but not right, rostrolateral prefrontal cortex meets a stringent test of the relational integration hypothesis. *NeuroImage, 46,* 338–342.

Bunge, S. A., Lieb, E. (2020). How does education hone reasoning ability? *Current Directions in Cognitive Science, 29*(2), 167–173.

Bunge, S. A., Wendelken, C., Badre, D., & Wagner, A. D. (2005). Analogical reasoning and prefrontal cortex: Evidence for separable retrieval and integration mechanisms. *Cerebral Cortex, 15,* 239–249.

Burge, T. (2018). Do infants and nonhuman animals attribute mental states? *Psychological Review, 125,* 409–434.

Burns, B. D. (1996). Meta-analogical transfer: Transfer between episodes of analogical reasoning. *Journal of Experimental Psychology: Learning, Memory, and Cognition, 22,* 1032–1048.

Burns, B. D., & Holyoak, K. J. (1994). Competing models of analogy: ACME versus Copycat. In A. Ram & K. Eiselt (Eds.), *Proceedings of the Sixteenth Annual Conference of the Cognitive Science Society* (pp. 100–105). Erlbaum.

Caballero, A., Granberg, R., & Tseng, K. Y. (2016). Mechanisms contributing to prefrontal cortex maturation during adolescence. *Neuroscience and Biobehavioral Reviews, 70,* 4–12.

Cangiotti, N., & Nappo, F. (2023). Reasoning by analogy in mathematical practice. *Philosophia Mathematica, 31*(2), 176–215.

Cantlon, J., & Brannon, E. M. (2005). Semantic congruity affects numerical judgments similarly in monkeys and humans. *Proceedings of the National Academy of Sciences, USA, 102*, 16507–16511.

Carbonell, J. G. (1983). Learning by analogy: Formulating and generalizing plans from past experience. In R. S. Michalski, J. G. Carbonell, & T. M. Mitchell (Eds.), *Machine learning: An artificial intelligence approach* (pp. 137–161). Tioga.

Cardillo, E. R., Watson, C. E., Schmidt, G. L., Kranjec, A., & Chatterjee, A. (2012). From novel to familiar: Tuning the brain for metaphors. *NeuroImage, 59*, 3212–3221.

Carey, S. (1985). *Developmental change in childhood.* MIT Press.

Carey, S. (2009). *The origin of concepts.* Oxford University Press.

Carpenter, W. (2020). The aha! moment: The science behind creative insights. In S. M. Brito (Ed.), *Toward super-creativity—Improving creativity in humans, machines, and human-machine collaborations.* IntechOpen. https://doi.org/10.5772/intechopen.84973

Carstensen, A., Zhang, J., Heyman, G. D., Fu, G., Lee, K., & Walker, C. M. (2019). Context shapes early diversity in abstract thought. *Proceedings of the National Academy of Sciences, USA, 116*(28), 13891–13896.

Catrambone, R., & Holyoak, K. J. (1989). Overcoming contextual limitations on problem-solving transfer. *Journal of Experimental Psychology: Learning, Memory, and Cognition, 15*, 1147–1156.

Catrambone, R., Craig, D. L., & Nersessian, N. J. (2006). The role of perceptually represented structure in analogical problem solving. *Memory & Cognition, 34*(5), 1126–1132.

Cattell, R. B. (1971). *Abilities: Their structure, growth, and action.* Houghton-Mifflin.

Cave, N., & O'Hagan, S. (2022). *Faith, hope and carnage.* Farrar, Straus and Giroux.

Chaffin, R. (1992). The concept of a semantic relation. In A. Lehrer & E. F. Kittay (Eds.), *Frames, fields, and contrasts: New essays in semantic and lexical organization* (pp. 253–288). Erlbaum.

Chaffin, R., & Herrmann, D. J. (1984). The similarity and diversity of semantic relations. *Memory & Cognition, 12*(2), 134–141.

Chaffin, R., Herrmann, D. J., & Winston, M. E. (1988). An empirical taxonomy of part-whole relations: Effects of part-whole relation type on relation identification. *Language and Cognitive Processes, 3*, 17–48.

Chai, J., Zeng, H., Li, A., & Ngai, E. W. T. (2021). Deep learning in computer vision: A critical review of emerging techniques and application scenarios. *Machine Learning with Applications, 6*, 100134. https://doi.org/10.1016/j.mlwa.2021.100134

Chalmers, D. J., French, R. M., & Hofstadter, D. R. (1992). High-level perception, representation, and analogy: A critique of artificial intelligence methodology. *Journal of Experimental & Theoretical Artificial Intelligence, 4*(3), 185–211.

Chen, L. (1982). Topological structure in visual perception. *Science, 218*(4573), 699–700.

Chen, Q., Christensen, A. P., Kenett, Y. N., Ren, Z., Condon, D. M., Bilder, R. M., Qiu, J., & Beaty, R. E. (2023). Mapping the creative personality: A psychometric network analysis of highly creative artists and scientists. *Creativity Research Journal, 35*(3), 455–470. https://doi.org/10.1080/10400419.2023.2184558

Chen, Z., Mo, L., & Honomichl, R. (2004). Having the memory of an elephant: Long-term retrieval and the use of analogues in problem solving. *Journal of Experimental Psychology: General, 133*(3), 415–433.

Chen, Z., Sanchez, R. P., & Campbell, T. (1997). From beyond to within their grasp: The rudiments of analogical problem solving in 10- and 13-month-olds. *Developmental Psychology, 33*(5), 790–801.

Cheng, P. W. (1997). From covariation to causation: A causal power theory. *Psychological Review, 104*, 367–405.

Cheng, P. W., & Holyoak, K. J. (1985). Pragmatic reasoning schemas. *Cognitive Psychology, 17*, 391–416.

Cheng, P. W., & Novick, L. R. (1991). Causes versus enabling conditions. *Cognition, 40*, 83–120.

Chesebrough, C., Chrysikou, E. G., Holyoak, K. J., Zhang, F., & Kounios, J. (2023). Conceptual change induced by analogical reasoning sparks aha moments. *Creativity Research Journal, 35*(3), 499–521. https://doi.org/10.1080/10400419.2023.2188361

Chiang, J. N., Peng, Y., Lu, H., Holyoak, K. J., & Monti, M. M. (2021). Distributed code for semantic relations predicts neural similarity during analogical reasoning. *Journal of Cognitive Neuroscience, 33*(3), 377–389.

Cho, S., Moody, T. D., Fernandino, L., Mumford, J. A., Poldrack, R. A., Cannon, T. D., Knowlton, B. J., & Holyoak, K. J. (2010). Common and dissociable prefrontal loci associated with component mechanisms of analogical reasoning. *Cerebral Cortex, 20*, 524–533.

Chomsky, N. (1965). *Aspects of the theory of syntax.* MIT Press.

Chomsky, N. (1970/1987). Language and freedom. In J. Peck (Ed.), *The Chomsky reader.* Pantheon Books.

Christie, S., & Gentner, D. (2014). Language helps children succeed on a classic analogy task. *Cognitive Science, 38*(2), 383–397.

Christoff, K., Prabhakaran, V., Dorfman, J., Zhao, Z., Kroger, J. K., Holyoak, K. J., & Gabrieli, J. D. E. (2001). Rostrolateral prefrontal cortex involvement in relational integration during reasoning. *NeuroImage, 14,* 1136–1149.

Coetzee, J. P., & Monti, M. M. (2018). At the core of reasoning: Dissociating deductive and non-deductive load. *Human Brain Mapping, 39*(4), 1850–1861.

Currie, A. (2016). Ethnographic analogy, the comparative method, and archaeological special pleading. *Studies in History and Philosophy of Science Part A, 55,* 84–94.

Cushen, P. J., & Wiley, J. (2018). Both attentional control and the ability to make remote associations aid spontaneous analogical transfer. *Memory & Cognition, 46,* 1398–1412.

Danks, D. (2009). The psychology of causal perception and reasoning. In H. Beebee, C. Hitchcock, & P. Menzies (Eds.), *Oxford handbook of causation* (pp. 447–470). Oxford University Press.

Darwin, C. R. (1871). *The descent of man, and selection in relation to sex.* John Murray.

Davis, T., Goldwater, M., & Giron, J. (2017). From concrete examples to abstract relations: The rostrolateral prefrontal cortex integrates novel examples into relational categories. *Cerebral Cortex, 27,* 2652–2670.

Day, S. B., & Gentner, D. (2007). Nonintentional analogical inference in text comprehension. *Memory & Cognition, 35,* 39–49.

Day, S. B., & Goldstone, R. L. (2011). Analogical transfer from a simulated physical system. *Journal of Experimental Psychology: Learning, Memory, and Cognition, 37,* 551–567.

Dedhe, A. M., Piantadosi, S. T., & Cantlon, J. F. (2023). Cognitive mechanisms underlying recursive pattern processing in human adults. *Cognitive Science, 47,* e13273.

de Groot, A. D. (1965). *Thought and choice in chess.* Mouton.

Dehaene, S. (1997). *The number sense: How the mind creates mathematics.* Oxford University Press.

D'Esposito, M., & Postle, B. R. (2015). The cognitive neuroscience of working memory. *Annual Review of Psychology, 66,* 115–142.

DeWolf, M., Bassok, M., & Holyoak, K. J. (2015a). Conceptual structure and the procedural affordances of rational numbers: Relational reasoning with fractions and decimals. *Journal of Experimental Psychology: General, 144*(1), 127–150.

DeWolf, M., Bassok, M., & Holyoak, K. J. (2015b). From rational numbers to algebra: Separable contributions of decimal magnitude and relational understanding of fractions. *Journal of Experimental Child Psychology, 133,* 72–84.

DeWolf, M., Bassok, M., & Holyoak, K. J. (2016). A set for relational reasoning: Facilitation of algebraic modeling by a fraction task. *Journal of Experimental Child Psychology, 152*, 351–366.

DeWolf, M., Bassok, M., & Holyoak, K. J. (2017). Numbers as mathematical models: Modeling relations and magnitudes with fractions and decimals. In D. C. Geary, D. B. Berch, R. J. Ochsendorf, & K. M. Koepke (Eds.), *Mathematical cognition and learning. Vol. 3: Acquisition of complex arithmetic skills and higher-order mathematical concepts* (pp. 141–163). Academic Press.

DeWolf, M., Chiang, J. N., Bassok, M., Holyoak, K. J., & Monti, M. M. (2016). Neural representations of magnitude for natural and rational numbers. *NeuroImage, 141*, 304–312.

DeWolf, M., Grounds, M. A., Bassok, M., & Holyoak, K. J. (2014). Representation and comparison of magnitudes for different types of rational numbers. *Journal of Experimental Psychology: Human Perception and Performance, 40*(1), 71–82.

DeWolf, M., Son, J. Y., Bassok, M., & Holyoak, K. J. (2017). Relational priming based on a multiplicative schema for whole numbers and fractions. *Cognitive Science, 41*(8), 2053–2088.

Ditsche, P., & Summers, A. (2019). Learning from Northern clingfish (*Gobbiesox maeandricus*): Bioinspired suction cups attach to rough surfaces. *Philosophical Transactions of the Royal Society B, 374*, 20190204. https://doi.org/10.1098/rstb.2019.0204

Donnan, C. B. (1971). Ancient Peruvian potters' marks and their interpretation through ethnographic analogy. *American Antiquity, 36*, 460–466.

Doumas, L. A. A., Hummel, J. E., & Sandhofer, C. M. (2008). A theory of the discovery and predication of relational concepts. *Psychological Review, 115*, 1–43.

Doumas, L. A. A., Puebla, G., Martin, A. E., & Hummel, J. E. (2022). A theory of relation learning and cross-domain generalization. *Psychological Review, 129*(5), 999–1041.

Dumontheil, I. (2014). Development of abstract thinking during childhood and adolescence: The role of rostrolateral prefrontal cortex. *Developmental Cognitive Neuroscience, 10*, 57–76.

Dunbar, K. (1999). The scientist *in vivo*: How scientists think and reason in the laboratory. In L. Magnani, N. Nersessian, & P. Thagard (Eds.), *Model-based reasoning in scientific discovery* (pp. 85–100). Plenum.

Duncan, J. (2010). The multiple-demand (MD) system of the primate brain: Mental programs for intelligent behavior. *Trends in Cognitive Sciences, 14*, 172–179.

Duncan, J., Assem, M., & Shashidhara, S. (2020). Integrated intelligence from distributed brain activity. *Trends in Cognitive Sciences, 24*(10), 838–852.

Duncan, J., & Owen, A. M. (2000). Common regions of the frontal cortex recruited by diverse cognitive demands. *Trends in Neurosciences, 23*(10), 475–483.

Duncan, J., Seitz, R. J., Kolodny, J., Bor, D., Herzog, H., Ahmed, A., Newell, F. N., & Emslie, H. (2000). A neural basis for general intelligence. *Science, 289*, 457–460.

Duncker, K. (1945). On problem solving. *Psychological Monographs, 58* (Whole No. 270).

Dutton, E., van der Linden, D., & Lynn, R. (2016). The negative Flynn effect: A systematic literature review. *Intelligence, 59*, 163–169.

Eichenbaum, H. (2017). Memory: Organization and control. *Annual Review of Psychology, 68*, 19–45.

Emmorey, K. (2023). Ten things you should know about sign languages. *Current Directions in Psychological Science, 32*(5), 387–394. https://doi.org/10.1177/09637214231173071

English, L. D. (1997). *Mathematical reasoning: Analogies, metaphors and images.* Erlbaum.

Estes, Z., & Jones, L. L. (2006). Priming via relational similarity: A COPPER HORSE is faster when seen through a GLASS EYE. *Journal of Memory and Language, 138*, 89–101.

Estes, Z., & Jones, L. L. (2009). Integrative priming occurs rapidly and uncontrollably during lexical processing. *Journal of Experimental Psychology: General, 55*, 112–130.

Evans, T. G. (1968). Program for the solution of a class of geometric-analogy intelligence-test questions. In M. Minsky (Ed.), *Semantic information processing* (pp. 271–353). MIT Press.

Fales, C. L., Knowlton, B. J., Holyoak, K. J., Geschwind, D. H., Swerdloff, R. S., & Gonzalo, I. G. (2003). Working memory and relational reasoning in Klinefelter syndrome. *Journal of the International Neuropsychology Society, 9*, 839–847.

Falkenhainer, B., Forbus, K. D., & Gentner, D. (1989). The structure mapping engine: Algorithm and examples. *Artificial Intelligence, 41*(1), 1–63.

Federenko, E., Behr, M. K., & Kanwisher, N. (2011). Functional specificity for high-level linguistic processing in the human brain. *Proceedings of the National Academy of Sciences, USA, 108*(39), 16428–16433.

Fedorenko, E., & Blank, I. A. (2020). Broca's area is not a natural kind. *Trends in Cognitive Sciences, 24*(4), 270–284.

Fedorenko, E., Duncan, J., & Kanwisher, N. (2012). Language-selective and domain-general regions lie side by side within Broca's area. *Current Biology, 22*(21), 2059–2062.

Fedorenko, E., & Shain, C. (2021). Similarity of computations across domains does not imply shared implementation: The case of language comprehension. *Current Directions in Psychological Science, 30*(6), 526–534.

Feller, D. A. (2005). *Heir of the dog: Canine influences on Charles Darwin's theories of natural selection.* Unpublished M.A. thesis in History, University of Hawai'i. https://scholarspace.manoa.hawaii.edu/server/api/core/bitstreams/311ed156-ceab-4d1a-b84f-b65047ba3f72/content

Finn, E., Shen, X., Scheinost, D., Rosenberg, M. D., Huang, J., Chun, M. V., Papademitris, X., & Constable, R. T. (2015). Functional connectome fingerprinting: Identifying individuals using patterns of brain connectivity. *Nature Neuroscience, 18,* 1664–1671.

Firth, J. R. (1957). A synopsis of linguistic theory, 1930–1955. In *Studies in linguistic analysis* (special volume of the Philological Society) (pp. 1–31). Blackwell.

Flynn, J. R. (2011). Secular changes in intelligence. In R. J. Sternberg & S. B. Kaufman (Eds.), *Cambridge handbook of intelligence* (pp. 647–665). Cambridge University Press.

Forbus, K. D., Ferguson, R. W., & Gentner, D. (1994). Incremental structure-mapping. In A. Ram & K. Eiselt (Eds.), *Proceedings of the Sixteenth Annual Conference of the Cognitive Science Society* (pp. 313–318). Erlbaum.

Forbus, K. D., Ferguson, R. W., Lovett, A., & Gentner, D. (2017). Extending SME to handle large-scale cognitive modeling. *Cognitive Science, 41*(5), 1152–1201.

Forbus, K. D., Gentner, D., & Law, K. (1995). MAC/FAC: A model of similarity-based retrieval. *Cognitive Science, 19*(2), 141–205.

Forbus, K. D., Gentner, D., Markman, A. B., & Ferguson, R. W. (1998). Analogy just looks like high level perception: Why a domain-general approach to analogical mapping is right. *Journal of Experimental and Theoretical Artificial Intelligence, 10*(2), 231–257.

Freud, S. (1933/1990). *New introductory lectures on psycho-analysis,* edited by J. Strachey. W. W. Norton.

Fried, L. S., & Holyoak, K. J. (1984). Induction of category distributions: A framework for classification learning. *Journal of Experimental Psychology: Learning, Memory and Cognition, 10,* 234–257.

Fyfe, E. R., McNeil, N. M., Son, J. Y., & Goldstone, R. L. (2014). Concreteness fading in mathematics and science instruction: A systematic review. *Educational Psychology Review, 26*(1), 9–25.

Gattis, M., & Holyoak, K. J. (1996). Mapping conceptual to spatial relations in visual reasoning. *Journal of Experimental Psychology: Learning, Memory, and Cognition, 22,* 231–239.

Gelman, R., & Gallistel, C. R. (1986). *The child's understanding of number.* Harvard University Press.

Gentner, D. (1977). Children's performance on a spatial analogies task. *Child Development, 48*(3), 1034.

Gentner, D. (1983). Structure-mapping: A theoretical framework for analogy. *Cognitive Science, 7*, 155–170.

Gentner, D. (1988). Metaphor as structure mapping: The relational shift. *Child Development, 59*, 47–59.

Gentner, D. (2010). Bootstrapping the mind: Analogical processes and symbol systems. *Cognitive Science, 34*, 752–775.

Gentner, D. (2016). Language as cognitive toolkit: How language supports relational thought. *American Psychologist, 71*(8), 650–657.

Gentner, D., Anggoro, F. K., & Klibanoff, R. S. (2011). Structure mapping and relational language support children's learning of relational categories. *Child Development, 82*, 1173–1188.

Gentner, D., & Asmuth, J. (2019). Metaphoric extension, relational categories, and abstraction. *Language, Cognition and Neuroscience, 34*(10), 1298–1307.

Gentner, D., & Gentner, D. R. (1983). Flowing waters or teeming crowds: Mental models of electricity. In D. Gentner & A. L. Stevens (Eds.), *Mental models* (pp. 99–129). Erlbaum.

Gentner, D., Holyoak, K. J., & Kokinov, B. N. (Eds.) (2001). *The analogical mind: Perspectives from cognitive science.* MIT Press.

Gentner, D., & Loewenstein, J. (2002). Relational language and relational thought. In E. Amsel & J. P. Byrnes (Eds.), *Language, literacy, and cognitive development: The development and consequences of symbolic communication* (pp. 87–120). Erlbaum.

Gentner, D., Loewenstein, J., Thompson, L., & Forbus, K. (2009). Reviving inert knowledge: Analogical abstraction supports relational retrieval of past events. *Cognitive Science, 33*, 1343–1382.

Gentner, D., & Markman, A. B. (1994). Structural alignment in comparison: No difference without similarity. *Psychological Science, 5*, 152–158.

Gentner, D., & Rattermann, M. J. (1991). Language and the career of similarity. In S. A. Gelman & J. P. Byrnes (Eds.), *Perspectives on thought and language: Interrelations in development* (pp. 225–277). Cambridge University Press.

Gentner, D., Rattermann, M. J., & Forbus, K. D. (1993). The roles of similarity in transfer: Separating retrievability from inferential soundness. *Cognitive Psychology, 25*(4), 524–575.

Gentner, D., Rattermann, M. J., Markman, A. B., & Kotovsky, L. (1995). Two forces in the development of relational similarity. In T. J. Simon & G. S. Halford (Eds.), *Developing cognitive competence: New approaches to process modeling* (pp. 263–313). Erlbaum.

Gentner, D., & Toupin, C. (1986). Systematicity and surface similarity in the development of analogy. *Cognitive Science, 10*(3), 277–300.

Ghilani, D., Luminet, O., Erb, H.-P., Flassbeck, C., Rospux, V., Tames, I., & Klein, O. (2017). Looking forward to the past: An interdisciplinary discussion on the use of historical analogies and their effects. *Memory Studies, 10*(3), 274–285.

Gick, M. L., & Holyoak, K. J. (1980). Analogical problem solving. *Cognitive Psychology, 12*, 306–355.

Gick, M. L., & Holyoak, K. J. (1983). Schema induction and analogical transfer. *Cognitive Psychology, 15*, 1–38.

Gilbert, S. J., Gonen-Yaacovi, G., Benoit, R. G., Volle, E., & Burgess, P. W. (2010). Distinct functional connectivity associated with lateral versus medial rostral prefrontal cortex: A meta-analysis. *NeuroImage, 53*, 1359–1367.

Gilead, M., & Ochsner, K.N. (2021). A guide to the neural bases of mentalizing. In M. Gilead & K. N. Ochsner (Eds.), *The neural basis of mentalizing*. Springer. https://doi .org/10.1007/978-3-030-51890-5_1

Gillan, D. J., Premack, D., & Woodruff, G. (1981). Reasoning in the chimpanzee: I. Analogical reasoning. *Journal of Experimental Psychology: Animal Behavior Processes, 7*, 1–17.

Gilovich, T. (1981). Seeing the past in the present: The effect of associations to familiar events on judgments and decisions. *Journal of Personality and Social Psychology, 40*(5), 797–808.

Glass, A. L., Holyoak, K. J., & Kiger, J. I. (1979). Role of antonymy relations in semantic judgments. *Journal of Experimental Psychology: Human Learning and Memory, 5*, 598–606.

Gleitman, L., & Papafragou, A. (2012). New perspectives on language and thought. In K. J. Holyoak & R. G. Morrison (Eds.), *Oxford handbook of thinking and reasoning* (pp. 543–568). Oxford University Press.

Gold, S., & Rangarajan, A. (1996). A graduated assignment algorithm for graph matching. *IEEE Transactions on Pattern Analysis and Machine Intelligence, 18*(4), 377–388.

Goldstone, R. L. (1994). Similarity, interactive activation, and mapping. *Journal of Experimental Psychology: Learning, Memory, and Cognition, 20*(1), 3–28.

Goldstone, R. L., & Medin, D. L. (1994). Time course of comparison. *Journal of Experimental Psychology: Learning, Memory, & Cognition, 20*, 29–50.

Goldstone, R. L., Medin, D. L., & Gentner, D. (1991). Relations, attributes, and the non-independence of features in similarity judgments. *Cognitive Psychology, 23*, 222–264.

Goldstone, R. L., & Son, J. (2012). Similarity. In K. J. Holyoak & R. G. Morrison (Eds.), *Oxford handbook of thinking and reasoning* (pp. 155–176). Oxford University Press.

Goldwater, M. B., Bainbridge, R., & Murphy, G. L. (2016). Learning of role-governed and thematic categories. *Acta Psychologica, 164*, 112–126.

Goldwater, M., Gentner, D., LaDue, N. D., & Libarkin, J. C. (2021). Analogy generation in science experts and novices. *Cognitive Science, 45*, e13036.

Goldwater, M. B., & Jamrozik, A. (2019). Can a relational mindset boost analogical retrieval? *Cognitive Research: Principles and Implications, 4*(1), 1–16.

Goldwater, M. B., & Markman, A. B. (2011). Categorizing entities by common role. *Psychonomic Bulletin & Review, 18*, 406–413.

Goldwater, M. B., Markman, A. B., & Stilwell, C. H. (2011). The empirical case for role-governed categories. *Cognition, 118*, 359–376.

Goldwater, M. B., & Schalk, L. (2016). Relational categories as a bridge between cognitive and educational research. *Psychological Bulletin, 142*(7), 729–757.

Goodman, N. (1968). *Languages of art*. Bobbs-Merrill.

Goodman, N. (1972). Seven strictures on similarity. In *Problems and projects* (pp. 437–446). Bobbs-Merrill.

Goswami, U. (1989). Relational complexity and the development of analogical reasoning. *Cognitive Development, 4*, 251–268.

Goswami, U. (1992). *Analogical reasoning in children*. Erlbaum.

Gould, S. J. (1980). *The panda's thumb: More reflections on natural history*. W. W. Norton.

Gray, M. E., DeWolf, M., Bassok, M., & Holyoak, K. J. (2018). Dissociation between magnitude comparison and relation identification across different formats for rational numbers. *Thinking & Reasoning, 24*(2), 179–197.

Gray, M. E., & Holyoak, K. J. (2020). Individual differences in relational reasoning. *Memory & Cognition, 48*(1), 96–110.

Gray, M. E., & Holyoak, K. J. (2021). Teaching by analogy: From theory to practice. *Mind, Brain, and Education, 15*, 250–263.

Green, A. E. (2016). Creativity, within reason: Semantic distance and dynamic state creativity in relational thinking and reasoning. *Current Directions in Psychological Science, 25*, 28–35.

Green, A. E., Fugelsang, J. A., Kraemer, D. J. M., Shamosh, N. A., & Dunbar, K. N. (2006). Frontopolar cortex mediates abstract integration in analogy. *Brain Research, 1096*, 125–137.

Green, A. E., Kraemer, D. J., Fugelsang, A. J., Gray, J. R., & Dunbar, K. N. (2010). Connecting long distance: Semantic distance in analogical reasoning modulates frontopolar cortex activity. *Cerebral Cortex, 20*, 70–76.

Green, A. E., Kraemer, D. J., Fugelsang, J. A., Gray, J. R., Dunbar, K. N. (2012). Neural correlates of creativity in analogical reasoning. *Journal of Experimental Psychology: Learning, Memory, and Cognition, 38*, 264–272.

Green, A. E., Spiegel, K. A., Giangrande, E. J., Weinberger, A. B., Gallagher, N. M., & Turkeltaub, P. E. (2017). Thinking cap plus thinking zap: tDCS of frontopolar cortex improves creative analogical reasoning and facilitates conscious augmentation of state creativity in verb generation. *Cerebral Cortex, 27*, 2628–2639.

Griffiths, T. L. (2020). Understanding human intelligence through human limitations. *Trends in Cognitive Sciences, 24*(11), 873–883.

Griffiths, T. L., & Tenenbaum, J. B. (2005). Structure and strength in causal induction. *Cognitive Psychology, 51*(4), 334–384.

Griffiths, T. L., Tenenbaum, J. B., & Kemp, C. (2012). Bayesian inference. In K. J. Holyoak & R. G. Morrison (Eds.), *Oxford handbook of thinking and reasoning* (pp. 22–35). Oxford University Press.

Günther, F, Rinaldi, L, & Marelli, M. (2019). Vector-space models of semantic representation from a cognitive perspective: A discussion of common misconceptions. *Perspectives on Psychological Science, 14*(6), 1006–1033.

Güntürkün, O., von Eugen, K., Packheiser, J., & Pusch, R. (2021). Avian pallial circuits and cognition: A comparison to mammals. *Current Opinion in Neurobiology, 71*, 29–36.

Guthormsen, A. M., Fisher, K. J., Bassok, M., Osterhout, L., DeWolf, M., & Holyoak, K. J. (2016). Conceptual integration of arithmetic operations with real-world knowledge: Evidence from event-related potentials. *Cognitive Science, 40*, 723–757.

Hafri, A., & Firestone, C. (2021). The perception of relations. *Trends in Cognitive Sciences, 25*, 475–492.

Hafri, A., Papafragou, A., & Trueswell, J. C. (2013). Getting the gist of events: Recognition of two-participant actions from brief displays. *Journal of Experimental Psychology: General, 142*(3), 880–905.

Halford, G. S. (1993). *Children's understanding: The development of mental models*. Erlbaum.

Halford, G. S., Bain, J. D., Maybery, M. T., & Andrews, G. (1998). Induction of relational schemas: Common processes in reasoning and complex learning. *Cognitive Psychology, 35*(3), 201–245.

Halford, G. S., & Busby, J. (2007). Acquisition of structured knowledge without instruction: The relational schema induction paradigm. *Journal of Experimental Psychology: Learning, Memory and Cognition, 33*(3), 586–603.

Halford, G. S., Cowan, N., & Andrews, G. (2007). Separating cognitive capacity from knowledge: A new hypothesis. *Trends in Cognitive Sciences, 11*(6), 236–242.

Halford, G. S., Wilson, W. H., Andrews, G., & Phillips, S. (2014). *Categorizing cognition: Conceptual coherence in the foundations of psychology.* MIT Press.

Halford, G. S., Wilson, W. H., & Phillips, S. (1998). Processing capacity defined by relational complexity: Implications for comparative, developmental, and cognitive psychology. *Behavioral and Brain Sciences, 21,* 803–831.

Halford, G. S., Wilson, W. H., & Phillips, S. (2010). Relational knowledge: The foundation of higher cognition. *Trends in Cognitive Sciences, 14,* 497–505.

Hawking, S. W., & Mlodinow, L. (2010). *The grand design.* Bantam.

Hare, B., & Woods, V. (2013). *The genius of dogs: How dogs are smarter than you think.* Dutton.

Hauptman, M., Blank, I., & Federenko, E. (2023). Non-literal language processing is jointly supported by the language and theory of mind networks: Evidence from a novel meta-analytic fMRI approach. *Cortex, 162,* 96–114.

Hayes, J. R., & Simon, H. A. (1977). Psychological differences among problem isomorphs. In N. J. Castellan, Jr., D. B. Pisoni, & G. R. Potts (Eds.), *Cognitive theory,* Vol. 2 (pp. 21–41). Erlbaum.

Heider, F., & Simmel, M. (1944). An experimental study of apparent behavior. *American Journal of Psychology, 57,* 243–249

Hemingway, E. (1964). *A moveable feast.* Charles Scribner's Sons.

Herrmann, R. J., Chaffin, R., Daniel, M. P., & Wool, R. S. (1986). The role of elements of relation definitions in antonym and synonym comprehension. *Zeitschrift für Psychologie, 194,* 134–153.

Hespos, S. J., Anderson, E., & Gentner, D. (2020). Structure-mapping processes enable infants' learning across domains, including language. In J. Childers (Ed.), *Language and concept acquisition from infancy through childhood: Learning from multiple exemplars* (pp. 79–104). Springer.

Hesse, M. B. (1963). *Models and analogies in science.* Sheed and Ward.

Hill, F., Santoro, A., Barrett, D., Morcos, A., & Lillicrap, T. (2019). Learning to make analogies by contrasting abstract relational structure. *Proceedings of the International Conference on Learning Representations.* https://arxiv.org/abs/1902.00120

Hobeika, L., Diard-Detoeuf, C., Garcin, B., Levy, R., & Volle, E. (2016). General and specialized brain correlates for analogical reasoning: A meta-analysis of functional imaging studies. *Human Brain Mapping, 37,* 1953–1969.

Hochmann, J.-R., Carey, S., & Mehler, J. (2017). Infants learn a rule predicated on the relation same but fail to simultaneously learn a rule predicated on the relation different. *Cognition, 177,* 49–57.

Hochmann, J.-R., Tuerk, A. S., Sanborn, S., Zhu, R., Long, R., Dempster, M., & Carey, S. (2017). Children's representation of abstract relations in relational/array match-to-sample tasks. *Cognitive Psychology, 99*, 17–43.

Hodges, A. (1983). *Alan Turing: The enigma.* Simon & Schuster.

Hoerl, C., & McCormack, T. (2019). Thinking in and about time: A dual systems perspective on temporal cognition. *Behavioral and Brain Sciences, 42*, e244.

Hofstadter, D. (2001). Epilogue: Analogy as the core of cognition. In D. Gentner, K. J. Holyoak, & B. N. Kokinov (Eds.), *The analogical mind: Perspectives from cognitive science* (pp. 499–538). MIT Press.

Hofstadter, D. R., & the Fluid Analogies Research Group (1995). *Fluid concepts and creative analogies.* Basic Books.

Hofstadter, D. R., & Mitchell, M. (1994). The Copycat project: A model of mental fluidity and analogy-making. In K. J. Holyoak & J. A. Barnden (Eds.), *Advances in connectionist and neural computation theory*, Vol. 2 (pp. 31–112). Ablex.

Hofstadter, D. R., & Sander, E. (2013). *Surfaces and essences: Analogy as the fuel and fire of thinking.* Basic Books.

Holland, J. H., Holyoak, K. J., Nisbett, R. E., & Thagard, P. R. (1986). *Induction: Processes of inference, learning, and discovery.* MIT Press.

Hollis, G., & Westbury, C. (2016). The principals of meaning: Extracting semantic dimensions from co-occurrence models of semantics. *Psychonomic Bulletin & Review, 23*, 1744–1756.

Holyoak, K. J. (1982). An analogical framework for literary interpretation. *Poetics, 11*, 105–126.

Holyoak, K. J. (1985). The pragmatics of analogical transfer. In G. H. Bower (Ed.), *The psychology of learning and motivation*, Vol. 19 (pp. 59–87). Academic Press.

Holyoak, K. J. (1991). Symbolic connectionism: Toward third-generation theories of expertise. In A. Ericsson & J. Smith (Eds.), *Toward a general theory of expertise: Prospects and limits* (pp. 301–355). Cambridge University Press.

Holyoak, K. J. (2012). Analogy and relational reasoning. In K. J. Holyoak & R. G. Morrison (Eds.), *Oxford handbook of thinking and reasoning* (pp. 234–259). Oxford University Press.

Holyoak, K. J. (2013). Thinking, broad and deep (review of *Surfaces and Essences* by D. Hofstadter & E. Sander). *Science, 340*, 550–551.

Holyoak, K. J. (2019). *The spider's thread: Metaphor in mind, brain, and poetry.* MIT Press.

Holyoak, K. J. (2023). Poet and psychologist: A conversation. *Metaphor and Symbol, 38*(2), 117–129.

Holyoak, K. J., & Cheng, P. W. (2011). Causal learning and inference as a rational process: The new synthesis. *Annual Review of Psychology, 62*, 135–163.

Holyoak, K. J., & Glass, A. L. (1975). The role of contradictions and counterexamples in the rejection of false sentences. *Journal of Verbal Learning and Verbal Behavior, 4*, 215–239.

Holyoak, K. J., Ichien, N., & Lu, H. (2022). From semantic vectors to analogical mapping. *Current Directions in Psychological Science, 31*(4), 355–361.

Holyoak, K. J., Ichien, N., & Lu, H. (2023). Analogy and the generation of ideas. *Creativity Research Journal.* https://doi.org/10.1080/10400419.2023.2232673

Holyoak, K. J., Junn, E. N., & Billman, D. O. (1984). Development of analogical problem-solving skill. *Child Development, 55*(6), 2042–2055.

Holyoak, K. J., & Koh, K. (1987). Surface and structural similarity in analogical transfer. *Memory & Cognition, 15*, 323–340.

Holyoak, K. J., & Lee, H. S. (2017). Inferring causal relations by analogy. In M. R. Waldmann (Ed.), *Oxford handbook of causal reasoning* (pp. 459–473). Oxford University Press.

Holyoak, K. J., Lee, H. S., & Lu, H. (2010). Analogical and category-based inference: A theoretical integration with Bayesian causal models. *Journal of Experimental Psychology: General, 139*, 702–727.

Holyoak, K. J., & Lu, H. (2021). Emergence of relational reasoning. *Current Opinion in Behavioral Sciences, 37*, 118–124.

Holyoak, K. J., & Monti, M. M. (2021). Relational integration in the human brain: A review and synthesis. *Journal of Cognitive Neuroscience, 33*(1), 341–356.

Holyoak, K. J., & Powell, D. (2016). Deontological coherence: A framework for commonsense moral reasoning. *Psychological Bulletin, 142*, 1179–1203.

Holyoak, K. J., Novick, L. R., & Melz, E. R. (1994). Component processes in analogical transfer: Mapping, pattern completion, and adaptation. In K. J. Holyoak & J. A. Barnden (Eds.), *Advances in connectionist and neural computation theory, Vol. 2: Analogical connections* (pp. 113–180). Ablex.

Holyoak, K. J., & Simon, D. (1999). Bidirectional reasoning in decision making by constraint satisfaction. *Journal of Experimental Psychology: General, 128*, 3–31.

Holyoak, K. J., & Stamenković, D. (2018). Metaphor comprehension: A critical review of theories and evidence. *Psychological Bulletin, 144*, 641–671.

Holyoak, K. J., & Thagard, P. R. (1989). Analogical mapping by constraint satisfaction. *Cognitive Science, 13*, 295–355.

Holyoak, K. J., & Thagard, P. R. (1995). *Mental leaps: Analogy in creative thought.* MIT Press.

Horne, Z., Powell, D., & Hummel, J. (2015). A single counterexample leads to moral belief revision. *Cognitive Science, 39*(8), 1950–1964.

Horne, Z., Rottman, J., & Lawrence, C. (2021). Can coherence-based interventions change dogged moral beliefs about meat-eating? *Journal of Experimental Social Psychology, 96*, 104160. https://doi.org/10.1016/j.jesp.2021.104160

Hoyos, C., Horton, W. S., Simms, N. K., & Gentner, D. (2020). Analogical comparison promotes theory-of-mind development. *Cognitive Science, 44*, e12891. https://doi.org/10.1111/cogs.12891

Hummel, J. E., & Holyoak, K. J. (1997). Distributed representations of structure: A theory of analogical access and mapping. *Psychological Review, 104*, 427–466.

Hummel, J. E., & Holyoak, K. J. (2003). A symbolic-connectionist theory of relational inference and generalization. *Psychological Review, 110*, 220–264.

Hunter, D. (2001). Reason is too large: Analogy and precedent in law. *Emory Law Journal, 50*(4), 1197-1264.

Ichien, N., Alfred, K. L., Baia, S., Kraemer, D. J. M., Holyoak, K. J., Bunge, S. A., & Lu, H. (2023). Relational and lexical similarity in analogical reasoning and recognition memory: Behavioral evidence and computational evaluation. *Cognitive Psychology, 141*, 101550.

Ichien, N., Lin, N., Holyoak, K. J., & Lu, H. (2024). Cognitive complexity explains processing asymmetry in judgments of similarity versus difference. *Cognitive Psychology, 151*, 101661.

Ichien, N., Liu, Q., Fu, S., Holyoak, K. J., Yuille, A. L., & Lu, H. (2023), Two computational approaches to visual analogy: Task-specific models versus domain-general mapping. *Cognitive Science, 47*, e13347. https://doi.org/10.1111/cogs.13347

Ichien, N., Lu, H., & Holyoak, K. J. (2022). Predicting patterns of similarity among abstract semantic relations. *Journal of Experimental Psychology: Learning, Memory, and Cognition, 48*(1), 108–121.

Ichien, N., Stamenković, D., & Holyoak, K. J. (2024). Large language model displays emergent ability to interpret novel literary metaphors. *Metaphor and Symbol.* https://doi.org/10.1080/10926488.2024.2380348

Ichien, N., Stamenković, D., Whatley, M. C., Castel, A. D., & Holyoak, K. J. (2024). Advancing with age: Older adults excel in comprehension of novel metaphors. *Psychology and Aging.* Advance online publication. https://dx.doi.org/10.1037/pag0000836

Ionescu, A., Lu, H., Holyoak, K. J., & Sandhofer, C. M. (2022). Children's acquisition of the concept of antonym across different lexical classes. In J. Culbertson, A. Perfors, H. Rabagliati, & V. Ramenzoni (Eds.), *Proceedings of the 44th Annual Meeting of the Cognitive Science Society.* Cognitive Science Society.

Inagaki, K., & Hatano, G. (1987). Young children's spontaneous personification as analogy. *Child Development, 58,* 1013–1020.

Jackendoff, R. (1990). *Semantic structures.* MIT Press.

Jackendoff, R., & Aaron, D. (1991). Review of Lakoff and Turner. *Language, 67*(2), 320–338.

Jacobs, B., Driscoll, L., & Schall, M. (1997). Life-span dendritic and spine changes in areas 10 and 18 of human cortex: A quantitative Golgi study. *Journal of Comparative Neurology, 386*(4), 661–680.

Jacobs, B., Schall, M., Prather, M., Kapler, E., Driscoll, L., Baca, S., Jacobs, J., Ford, K., Wainwright, M., & Treml, M. (2001). Regional dendritic and spine variation in human cerebral cortex: A quantitative Golgi study. *Cerebral Cortex, 11*(6), 558–571.

Jacobson, M. J., Goldwater, M. B., Markauskaite, L., Lai, P. K., Kapur, M., Roberts, G., & Hilton, C. B. (2020). Schema abstraction with productive failure and analogical comparison: Learning designs for far across domain transfer. *Learning and Instruction, 65,* 101222.

James, W. (1890). *The principles of psychology, Vol. 2.* Henry Holt.

Jamrozik, A., & Gentner, D. (2020). Relational labeling unlocks inert knowledge. *Cognition, 196,* 104146. https://doi.org/10.1016/j.cognition.2019.104146

Jee, B. D., Uttal, D. H., Gentner, D., Manduca, C., Shipley, T. F., & Sageman, B. (2013). Finding faults: Analogical comparison supports spatial concept learning in geoscience. *Cognitive Processing, 14*(2), 175–187.

Jiebert, S. A., Hosking, R. J., Taylor, A. H., & Gray, R. D. (2018). Mental template matching is a potential cultural transmission mechanism for New Caledonian crow tool manufacturing traditions. *Scientific Reports, 8*(1), 8956. https://doi.org/10.1038/s41598-018-27405-1

Jones, M., & Love, B. C. (2007). Beyond common features: The role of roles in determining similarity. *Cognitive Psychology, 55,* 196–231.

Jurgens, D. A., Mohammad, S. M., Turney, P. D., & Holyoak, K. J. (2012). SemEval-2012 Task 2: Measuring degrees of relational similarity. In *Proceedings of the First Joint Conference on Lexical and Computational Semantics (*SEM)* (pp. 356–364). Association for Computational Linguistics.

Kalandadze, T., Bambini, V., & Næss, K.-A. B. (2019). A systematic review and meta-analysis of studies on metaphor comprehension in individuals with autism spectrum disorder: Do task properties matter? *Applied Psycholinguistics, 40,* 1421–1454.

Karmiloff-Smith, A. (1992). *Beyond modularity: A developmental perspective on cognitive science.* MIT Press.

Keane, M. T. (1987). On retrieving analogues when solving problems. *Quarterly Journal of Experimental Psychology, 39A*, 29–41.

Kenett, Y.N. (2018). Investigating creativity from a semantic network perspective. In Z. Kapoula, E. Volle, J. Renoult, & M. Andreatta (Eds.), *Exploring transdisciplinarity in art and sciences*. Springer.

Khong, Y. F. (1992). *Analogies at war: Korea, Munich, Dien Bien Phu, and the Vietnam decisions of 1965*. Princeton University Press.

Kim, K. H. (2011). The creativity crisis: The decrease in creative thinking scores on the Torrance Tests of Creative Thinking. *Creativity Research Journal, 23*(4), 285–295.

Kintsch, W. (2000). Metaphor comprehension: A computational theory. *Psychonomic Bulletin & Review, 7*, 257–266.

Kittur, A., Hummel, J. E., & Holyoak, K. J. (2006). Ideals aren't always typical: Dissociating goodness-of-exemplar from typicality judgments. In R. Sun & N. Miyake (Eds.), *Proceedings of the Twenty-eighth Annual Conference of the Cognitive Science Society* (pp. 429–434). Erlbaum.

Klima, E., & Bellugi, U. (1979). *The signs of language*. Harvard University Press.

Kmiecik, M., Brisson, R., & Morrison, R. G. (2019). The time course of semantic and relational processing during verbal analogical reasoning. *Brain and Cognition, 129*, 25–34.

Knowlton, B. J., Morrison, R. G., Hummel, J. E., & Holyoak, K. J. (2012). A neurocomputational system for relational reasoning. *Trends in Cognitive Sciences, 16*, 373–381.

Koffka, K. (1935). *Principles of Gestalt psychology*. Harcourt, Brace.

Kotovsky, L., & Gentner, D. (1996). Comparison and categorization in the development of relational similarity. *Child Development, 67*, 2797–2822.

Kounios, J., & Beeman, M. (2015). *The Eureka factor: Aha moments, creative insight, and the brain*. Random House.

Kövecses, Z. (2020). *Extended conceptual metaphor theory*. Cambridge University Press.

Krawczyk, D. C., Morrison, R. G., Viskontas, I., Holyoak, K. J., Chow, T. W., Mendez, M. F., Miller, B. L., & Knowlton, B. J. (2008). Distraction during relational reasoning: The role of prefrontal cortex in interference control. *Neuropsychologia, 46*, 2020–2032.

Krawczyk, D. C., Hanten, G., Wilde, E. A., Li, X., Schnelle, K. P., Merkley T. L., Vasquez, A. C., Cook, L. G., McClelland, M., Chapman, S. B., & Levin, H. S. (2010). Deficits in analogical reasoning in adolescents with traumatic brain injury. *Frontiers in Human Neuroscience, 4*, 62. https://doi.org/10.3389/fnhum.2010.00062

Krawczyk, D. C., Holyoak, K. J., & Hummel, J. E. (2004). Structural constraints and object similarity in analogical mapping and inference. *Thinking & Reasoning, 10*, 85–104.

Krawczyk, D. C., Holyoak, K. J., & Hummel. J. E. (2005). The one-to-one constraint in analogical mapping and inference. *Cognitive Science, 29*, 29–38.

Krawczyk, D. C., Kandalaft, M. R., Didehbani, N., Allen, T. T., McClelland, M. M., Tamminga, C. A., & Chapman, S. B. (2014). An investigation of reasoning by analogy in schizophrenia and autism spectrum disorder. *Frontiers in Human Neuroscience, 8*, 517. https://doi.org/10.3389/fnhum.2014.00517

Krawczyk, D. C., McClelland, M. M., & Donovan, C. M. (2011). A hierarchy for relational reasoning in the prefrontal cortex. *Cortex, 47*(5), 588–597.

Krawczyk, D. C., Morrison, R. G., Viskontas, I., Holyoak, K. J., Chow, T. W., Mendez, M. F., Miller, B. L., & Knowlton, B. J. (2008). Distraction during relational reasoning: The role of prefrontal cortex in interference control. *Neuropsychologia, 46*(7), 2020–2032.

Kroger, J. K., Holyoak, K. J., & Hummel, J. E. (2004). Varieties of sameness: The impact of relational complexity on perceptual comparisons. *Cognitive Science, 28*, 335–358.

Kroger, J. K., Saab, F. W., Fales, C. L., Bookheimer, S. Y., Cohen, M. S., & Holyoak, K. J. (2002). Recruitment of anterior dorsolateral prefrontal cortex in human reasoning: A parametric study of relational complexity. *Cerebral Cortex, 12*, 477–485.

Kroupin, I. G., & Carey, S. E. (2022). You cannot find what you are not looking for: Population differences in relational reasoning are sometimes differences in inductive biases alone. *Cognition, 222*, 105007. https://doi.org/10.1016/j.cognition.2021.105007

Kubose, T. T., Holyoak, K. J., & Hummel, J. E. (2002). The role of textual coherence in incremental analogical mapping. *Journal of Memory and Language, 47*, 407–435.

Kubricht, J. R., Lu, H., & Holyoak, K. J. (2017). Individual differences in spontaneous analogical transfer. *Memory & Cognition, 45*, 576–588.

Kumar, A. A. (2021). Semantic memory: A review of methods, models, and current challenges. *Psychonomic Bulletin & Review, 28*, 40–80.

Kurtz, K. J., & Loewenstein, J. (2007). Converging on a new role for analogy in problem solving and retrieval: When two problems are better than one. *Memory & Cognition, 35*, 334–341.

Kurtz, K. J., Miao, C.-H., & Gentner, D. (2001). Learning by analogical bootstrapping. *Journal of the Learning Sciences, 10*(4), 417–466.

Kuwabara, M., & Smith, L. B. (2012). Cross-cultural differences in cognitive development: Attention to relations and objects. *Journal of Experimental Child Psychology, 113*, 20–35.

Kuznar, S. L., Pavlic, M., Glorioso, G. C., & Povinelli, D. J. (2020). Deconstructing the raven's theory of mind: An analysis of Bugnyar et al. (2016). *Animal Behavior and Cognition, 7*(4), 653–657.

Lakoff, G., & Johnson, M. (1980). *Metaphors we live by*. University of Chicago Press.

Lakoff, G., & Turner, M. (1989). *More than cool reason: A field guide to poetic metaphor*. University of Chicago Press.

Lassaline, M. E. (1996). Structural alignment in induction and similarity. *Journal of Experimental Psychology: Learning, Memory, and Cognition, 22*, 754–770.

Lee, D. G., & Holyoak, K. J. (2023). Transient value refinements during deliberation facilitate choice. *Decision.* https://doi.org/10.1037/dec0000215

Lee, H. S., DeWolf, M., Bassok, M., & Holyoak, K. J. (2016). Conceptual and procedural distinctions between fractions and decimals: A cross-national comparison. *Cognition, 147*, 57–69.

Lee, H. S., & Holyoak, K. J. (2008). The role of causal models in analogical inference. *Journal of Experimental Psychology: Learning, Memory, and Cognition, 34*, 1111–1122.

Levitin, D. J. (2008). *The world in six songs: How the musical brain created human nature*. Dutton/Penguin.

Lewis, C. I. (1929). *Mind and the world order*. Scribner.

Li, Y., Kenett, Y. N., Hu, W., & Beaty, R. E. (2021). Flexible semantic network structure supports the production of creative metaphor. *Creativity Research Journal, 33*(3), 209–223.

Lien, Y., & Cheng, P. W. (2000). Distinguishing genuine from spurious causes: A coherence hypothesis. *Cognitive Psychology, 40*, 87–137.

Linzen, T. (2016). Issues in evaluating semantic spaces using word analogies. *Proceedings of the 1st Workshop on Evaluating Vector-Space Representations for NLP* (pp. 13–18). Association for Computational Linguistics. https://doi.org/10.18653/v1/W16-2503

Loewenstein, J., Thompson, L., & Gentner, D. (1999). Analogical encoding facilitates knowledge transfer in negotiation. *Psychonomic Bulletin and Review, 6*, 586–597.

Loewenstein, J., Thompson, L., & Gentner, D. (2003). Analogical learning in negotiation teams: Comparing cases promotes learning and transfer. *Academy of Management Learning & Education, 2*(2), 119–127.

Lu, C., Krishna, R., Bernstein, M., & Fei-Fei, L. (2016). Visual relationship detection with language priors. In *Proceedings of the 14th European Conference on Computer Vision* (pp. 852–869). Springer.

Lu, H., Chen, D., & Holyoak, K. J. (2012). Bayesian analogy with relational transformations. *Psychological Review, 119*, 617–648.

Lu, H., Ichien, N., & Holyoak, K. J. (2022). Probabilistic analogical mapping with semantic relation networks. *Psychological Review, 129*(5), 1078–1103.

Lu, H., Liu, Q., Ichien, N., Yuille, A. L., & Holyoak, K. J. (2019). Seeing the meaning: Vision meets semantics in solving visual analogy problems. In A. Goel, C. Seifert, & C. Freksa (Eds.), *Proceedings of the 41st Annual Meeting of the Cognitive Science Society* (pp. 2201–2207). Cognitive Science Society.

Lu, H., Wu, Y. N., & Holyoak, K. J. (2019). Emergence of analogy from relation learning. *Proceedings of the National Academy of Sciences, USA, 116,* 4176–4181.

Lundie, M., Dasara, H., Beeghly, C., Kazmi, A., & Krawczyk, D. (2022). High-definition transcranial direct current stimulation over the left frontopolar cortex promotes analogical reasoning. *Mind, Brain, and Education, 16*(3), 209–220. https://doi.org/10.1111/mbe.12325

Mackey, A. P., Miller Singley, A. T., & Bunge, S. A. (2013). Intensive reasoning training alters patterns of brain connectivity at rest. *Journal of Neuroscience, 33,* 4796–4803.

Mackie, J. L. (1974). *The cement of the universe: A study of causation.* Clarendon Press.

Maclean, N. (1976). *A river runs through it and other stories.* University of Chicago Press.

Mahowald, K., Ivanova, A. A., Blank, I. A., Kanwisher, N., Tenenbaum, J. B., & Fedorenko, E. (2024). Dissociating language and thought in large language models: A cognitive perspective. *Trends in Cognitive Sciences.* arXiv:2301.06627.

Markman, A. B. (1997). Constraints on analogical inference. *Cognitive Science, 21*(4), 373–418.

Markman, A. B., & Gentner, D. (1993). Structural alignment during similarity comparisons. *Cognitive Psychology, 25*(4), 431–467.

Markman, A. B., & Stilwell, C. H. (2001). Role-governed categories. *Journal of Experimental and Theoretical Artificial Intelligence, 13,* 329–358.

Matlen, B., Gentner, D., & Franconeri, S. (2020). Spatial alignment facilitates visual comparison. *Journal of Experimental Psychology: Human Perception and Performance, 46,* 443–457.

McClelland, J. L., Rumelhart, D. E., & the PDP Research Group (1986). *Parallel distributed processing: Explorations in the microstructure of cognition: Vol. 2, Psychological and biological models.* MIT Press.

McNamara, T. P. (2005). *Semantic priming: Perspectives from memory and word recognition.* Psychology Press.

Medin, D. L. (1989). Concepts and conceptual structure. *American Psychologist, 44*(12), 1469–1481.

Medin, D. L., Goldstone, R. L., & Gentner, D. (1990). Similarity involving attributes and relations: Judgments of similarity and difference are not inverses. *Psychological Science, 1,* 64–69.

Meyer, D. E., & Schvaneveldt, R. W. (1971). Facilitation in recognizing pairs of words: Evidence for a dependence between retrieval operations. *Journal of Experimental Psychology, 90*, 227–234.

Meyer, M. L., Davachi, L., Ochsner, K. N., & Lieberman, M. D. (2019). Evidence that default network connectivity during rest consolidates social information. *Cerebral Cortex, 29*, 1910–1920.

Meyer, M. L., & Lieberman, M. D. (2018). Why people are always thinking about themselves: Medial prefrontal cortex activity during rest primes self-referential processing. *Journal of Cognitive Neuroscience, 30*(5), 714–721.

Mi, L., & Chen, Z. (2020). Hierarchical graph attention network for visual relationship detection. In *2020 IEEE/CVF Conference on Computer Vision and Pattern Recognition (CVPR)* (pp. 13883–13892).

Michotte, A. (1946/1963). *The perception of causality*. Basic Books.

Mikolov, T., Sutskever, I., Chen, K., Corrado, G., & Dean, J. (2013). Distributed representations of words and phrases and their compositionality. In C. J. C. Burges, L. Bottou, & M. Welling (Eds.), *Advances in Neural Information Processing Systems, 26*, 3111–3119.

Millay, E. St. V. (1922). *A few figs from thistles*. Harper & Brothers.

Minervino, R. A., Margni, A., & Trench, M. (2023). Analogical inferences mediated by relational categories. *Cognitive Psychology, 142*, 101561.

Minsky, M. (1975). A framework for representing knowledge. In P. H. Winston (Ed.), *The psychology of computer vision* (pp. 211–277). McGraw-Hill.

Misiewicz, R. (2020). Peirce on analogy. *Transactions of the Charles S. Peirce Society: A Quarterly Journal in American Philosophy, 56*(3), 299-325.

Mitchell, M. (1993). *Analogy-making as perception: A computer model*. MIT Press.

Mitchell, M. (2021). Abstraction and analogy-making in artificial intelligence. *Annals of the New York Academy of Sciences, 1505*(1), 79–101.

Monti, M. M., & Osherson, D. N. (2012). Logic, language and the brain. *Brain Research, 1428*, 33–42.

Monti, M. M., Parsons, L. M., & Osherson, D. N. (2009). The boundaries of language and thought in deductive inference. *Proceedings of the National Academy of Sciences, USA, 106*, 12554–12559.

Monti, M. M., Parsons, L. M., & Osherson, D. N. (2012). Thought beyond language: Neural dissociation of algebra and natural language. *Psychological Science, 23*, 914–922.

Moorjani, P., Amorim, C. E., Arndt, P. F., & Przeworski, M. (2016). Variation in the molecular clock of primates. *Proceedings of the National Academy of Sciences, USA, 113*(38), 10607–10612.

Morrison, R. G., & Knowlton, B. J. (2012). Neurocognitive methods in higher cognition. In K. J. Holyoak & R. G. Morrison (Eds.), *Oxford handbook of thinking and reasoning* (pp. 67–89). Oxford University Press.

Morrison, R. G., Krawczyk, D. C., Holyoak, K. J., Hummel, J. E., Chow, T. W., Miller, B. L., & Knowlton, B. J. (2004). A neurocomputational model of analogical reasoning and its breakdown in frontotemporal lobar degeneration. *Journal of Cognitive Neuroscience, 16*, 260–271.

Morsanyi, K., Hamilton, J., Stamenković, D., & Holyoak, K. J. (2022). Linking metaphor comprehension with analogical reasoning: Evidence from typical development and Autism Spectrum Disorder. *British Journal of Psychology, 113*, 479–495.

Morsanyi, K., & Holyoak, K. J. (2010). Analogical reasoning ability in autistic and typically-developing children. *Developmental Science, 13*, 578–587.

Morsanyi, K., Stamenković, D., & Holyoak, K. J. (2020a). Metaphor processing in autism: A systematic review and meta-analysis. *Developmental Review, 57*, article 100925.

Morsanyi, K., Stamenković, D., & Holyoak, K. J. (2020b). Analogical reasoning in autism: A systematic review and meta-analysis. In K. Morsanyi & R. M. J. Byrne (Eds.), *Thinking, reasoning, and decision making in autism* (pp. 59–87). Routledge.

Moyer, R. S., & Landauer, T. K. (1967). Time required for judgements of numerical inequality. *Nature, 215*, 1519–1520.

Murdoch, I. (1978). *The sea, the sea.* Chatto & Windus.

Murphy, G. L., & Hoffman, A. B. (2012). Concepts. In K. Frankish & W. M. Ramsey (Eds.), *Cambridge handbook of cognitive science* (pp. 151–179). Cambridge University Press.

Nagel, T. (1974). What is it like to be a bat? *Philosophical Review, 83*, 435–450.

Nagel, T. (1986). *The view from nowhere.* Oxford University Press.

Nee, D. E., Wager, T. D., & Jonides, J. (2007). Interference resolution: Insights from a meta-analysis of neuroimaging tasks. *Cognitive, Affective, & Behavioral Neuroscience, 7*, 1–17.

Nisbett, R. E., Krantz, D. H., Jepson, C., & Kunda, Z. (1983). The use of statistical heuristics in everyday inductive reasoning. *Psychological Review, 90*, 339–363.

Nisbett, R. E., & Ross, L. (1980). *Human inference: Strategies and shortcomings of social judgment.* Prentice-Hall.

Nokes-Malach, T. J., VanLehn, K., Belenky, D. M., Lichtenstein, M., & Cox, G. (2013). Coordinating principles and examples through analogy and self-explanation. *European Journal of Psychology of Education, 28*(4), 1237–1263.

Novick, L. R. (1988). Analogical transfer, problem similarity, and expertise. *Journal of Experimental Psychology: Learning, Memory, and Cognition, 14,* 510–520.

Novick, L. R., & Holyoak, K. J. (1991). Mathematical problem solving by analogy. *Journal of Experimental Psychology: Learning, Memory, and Cognition, 17,* 398–415.

Nowell, A. (2021). *Growing up in the Ice Age: Fossil and archaeological evidence of the lived lives of Plio-Pleistocene children.* Oxbow Books.

Oleynick, V. C., DeYoung, C. G., Hyde, E., Kaufman, S. B., Beaty, R. E., & Silvia, P. J. (2017). Openness/intellect: The core of the creative personality. In G. J. Feist, R. Reiter-Palmon, & J. C. Kaufman (Eds.), *Cambridge handbook of creativity and personality research* (pp. 9–27). Cambridge University Press.

Oden, D. L., Thompson, R. K. R., & Premack, D. (2001). Can an ape reason analogically? Comprehension and production of analogical problems by Sarah, a chimpanzee (*Pan troglodytes*). In D. Gentner, K. J. Holyoak, & B. N. Kokinov (Eds.), *The analogical mind: Perspectives from cognitive science* (pp. 471–498). MIT Press.

Ogundiran, A., & Saunders, P. V. (2011). Potters' marks and social relations of ceramic distribution in the Oyo Empire. *Azania: Archaeological Research in Africa, 46*(3), 317–335.

Oleynick, V. C., DeYoung, C. G., Hyde, E., Kaufman, S. B., Beaty, R. E., & Silvia, P. J. (2017). Openness/intellect: The core of the creative personality. In G. J. Feist, R. Reiter-Palmon, & J. C. Kaufman (Eds.), *Cambridge handbook of creativity and personality research* (pp. 9–27). Cambridge University Press.

Olsson, C., Elhage, N., Nanda, N., Joseph, N., DasSarma, N., Henighan, T., Mann, B., Askell, A., Bai, Y., Chen, A., Conerly, T., Drain, D., Ganguli, D., Hatfield-Dodds, Z., Hernandez, D., Johnston, S., Jones, A., Kernion, J., Lovitt, L., . . . Olah, C. (2022). In-context learning and induction heads. arXiv:2209.11895 [cs.LG].

OpenAI. (2023). GPT-4 technical report. arXiv:2303.08774.

Ouyang, L., Wu, J., Jiang, X., Almeida, D., Wainwright, C. L., Mishkin, P., Zhang, C., Agarwal, S., Slama, K., Ray, A., Schulman, J., Hilton, J., Kelton, F., Miller, L., Simens, M., Askell, A., Welinder, P., Christiano, P., Leike, J., & Lowe, R. (2022). Training language models to follow instructions with human feedback. *Advances in Neural Information Processing Systems, 36,* 4299–4307.

Patterson, K., Nestor, P. J., & Rogers, T. T. (2007). Where do you know what you know? The representation of semantic knowledge in the human brain. *Nature Reviews Neuroscience, 8,* 976–987.

Pearl, J., & Mackenzie, D. (2018). *The book of why: The new science of cause and effect.* Basic Books.

Peirce, C. S. (1931–1958). *Collected papers*, 8 vols. Edited by C. Hartshorne, P. Weiss, & A. Burks. Harvard University Press.

Penn, D. C., Holyoak, K. J., & Povinelli, D. J. (2008). Darwin's mistake: Explaining the discontinuity between human and nonhuman minds. *Behavioral and Brain Sciences, 31*, 109–130.

Penn, D. C., & Povinelli, D. J. (2007). Causal cognition in human and nonhuman animals: A comparative, critical review. *Annual Review of Psychology, 58*, 97–118.

Pennington, N., & Hastie, R. (1992). Explaining the evidence: Tests of the story model for juror decision making. *Journal of Personality and Social Psychology, 62*(2), 189–206.

Perrott, D. A., Gentner, D., & Bodenhausen, G. V. (2005). Resistance is futile: The unwitting insertion of analogical inferences in memory. *Psychonomic Bulletin and Review, 12*, 696–702.

Peterson, J. C., Chen, D., & Griffiths, T. L. (2020). Parallelograms revisited: Exploring the limitations of vector space models of simple analogies. *Cognition, 205*, 104440.

Piaget, J., Montangero, J., & Billeter, J. (1977). La formation des correlats. In J. Piaget (Ed.), *Recherches sur l'abstraction reflechissante I* (pp. 115–129). Presses Universitaires de France.

Pinker, S. (2007). *The stuff of thought: Language as a window into human nature.* Harvard University Press.

Planck, M. (1949). *Scientific autobiography and other papers.* Philosophical Library.

Plummer, P., DeWolf, M., Bassok, M., Gordon, P. C., & Holyoak, K. J. (2017). Reasoning strategies with rational numbers revealed by eye-tracking. *Attention, Perception, & Psychophysics, 79*, 1426–1437.

Popov, V., & Hristova, P. (2017). The relational luring effect: Retrieval of relational information during associative recognition. *Journal of Experimental Psychology: General, 146*, 722–745.

Postell, S. D. (2021). Jesus [not] as Moses in the Gospel of Matthew. In C. A. Evans & D. Mishkin (Eds.), *A handbook on the Jewish roots of the gospels* (pp. 82–93). Hendrickson.

Povinelli, D. J. (2000). *Folk physics for apes.* Oxford University Press.

Povinelli, D. J. (2011). *World without weight: Perspectives on an alien mind.* Oxford University Press.

Povinelli, D. J., Bering, J. M., & Giambrone, S. (2000). Toward a science of other minds: Escaping the argument by analogy. *Cognitive Science, 24*, 509–541.

Povinelli, D. J., & Giambrone, S. (1999). Inferring other minds: Flaws in the argument by analogy. *Philosophical Topics, 27*, 167–201.

Premack, D. (1983). The codes of man and beasts. *Behavioral and Brain Sciences, 6*(1), 125–136.

Premack, D., & Woodruff, G. (1978). Does the chimpanzee have a theory of mind? *Behavioral and Brain Sciences, 1*, 515–526.

Priniski, J. H., McClay, M., & Holyoak, K. J. (2021). Rise of QAnon: A mental model of good and evil stews in an echochamber. In T. Fitch, C. Lamm, H. Leder, & K. Teßmar-Raible (Eds.), *Proceedings of the 43rd Annual Meeting of the Cognitive Science Society*. Cognitive Science Society.

Pyers, J. E., & Senghas, A. (2009). Language promotes false-belief understanding: Evidence from learners of a new sign language. *Psychological Science, 20*(7), 805–812.

Ramnani, N., & Owen, A. M. (2004). Anterior prefrontal cortex: Insights into function from anatomy and neuroimaging. *Nature Reviews Neuroscience, 5*, 184–194.

Rapp, A. M., Mutschler, D. E., & Erb, M. (2012). Where in the brain is nonliteral language? A coordinate-based meta-analysis of functional magnetic resonance imaging studies. *NeuroImage, 62*, 600–610.

Rapp, M., Bassok, M., DeWolf, M., & Holyoak, K. J. (2015). Modeling discrete and continuous entities with fractions and decimals. *Journal of Experimental Psychology: Applied, 21*, 47–56.

Raven, J. C. (1938). *Progressive matrices: A perceptual test of intelligence, individual form*. Lewis.

Reed, S. K., Dempster, A., & Ettinger, M. (1985). Usefulness of analogous solutions for solving algebra word problems. *Journal of Experimental Psychology: Learning, Memory, and Cognition, 11*, 106–125.

Reed, S. K., Ernst, G. W., & Banerji, R. (1974). The role of analogy in transfer between similar problem states. *Cognitive Psychology, 6*, 436–450.

Reitman, W. R. (1965). *Cognition and thought: An information processing approach*. Wiley.

Richardson, H., & Saxe, R. (2020). Early signatures and developmental change in brain regions for theory of mind. *Neural Circuit and Cognitive Development, 2*, 467–484.

Richland. L. E., & Begolli, K. N. (2016). Analogy and higher order thinking: Mathematics as an example. *Policy Insights from the Behavioral and Brain Sciences, 3*(2), 160–168.

Richland, L. E., Chan, T. K., Morrison, R. G., & Au, T. K. (2010). Young children's analogical reasoning across cultures: Similarities and differences. *Journal of Experimental Child Psychology, 105*, 146–153.

Richland, L. E., & McDonough, I. M. (2010). Learning by analogy: Discriminating between potential analogs. *Contemporary Educational Psychology, 35*(1), 28–43.

Richland, L. E., Morrison, R. G., & Holyoak, K. J. (2006). Children's development of analogical reasoning: Insights from scene analogy problems. *Journal of Experimental Child Psychology, 94,* 249–271.

Richland, L. E., Stigler, J. W., & Holyoak, K. J. (2012). Teaching the conceptual structure of mathematics. *Educational Psychologist, 47*(3), 189–203.

Richland, L. E., Zur, O., & Holyoak, K. J. (2007). Cognitive supports for analogies in the mathematics classroom. *Science, 316,* 1128–1129.

Rittle-Johnson, B., Star, J. R., & Durkin, K. (2009). The importance of prior knowledge when comparing examples: Influences on conceptual and procedural knowledge of equation solving. *Journal of Educational Psychology, 101*(4), 836–852.

Robin, N., & Holyoak, K. J. (1995). Relational complexity and the functions of prefrontal cortex. In M. S. Gazzaniga (Ed.), *The cognitive neurosciences* (pp. 987–997). MIT Press.

Rogers, C. T. (1961). *On becoming a person: A therapist's view of psychotherapy.* Houghton Mifflin.

Rogers, T. T., & McClelland, J. L. (2014). Parallel distributed processing at 25: Further explorations in the microstructure of cognition. *Cognitive Science, 38,* 1024–1077.

Rosch, E. R. (1973). On the internal structure of perceptual and semantic categories. In T. M. Moore (Ed.), *Cognitive development and the acquisition of language* (111–144). Academic Press.

Ross, B. (1987). This is like that: The use of earlier problems and the separation of similarity effects. *Journal of Experimental Psychology; Learning, Memory, and Cognition, 13,* 629–639.

Ross, B. (1989). Distinguishing types of superficial similarities: Different effects on the access and use of earlier problems. *Journal of Experimental Psychology: Learning, Memory, and Cognition, 15,* 456–468.

Ross, B. H., & Kennedy, P. T. (1990). Generalizing from the use of earlier examples in problem solving. *Journal of Experimental Psychology: Learning, Memory, and Cognition, 16,* 42–55.

Rubin, R., & Strauss, N. (2023). *The creative act: A way of being.* Penguin.

Rumelhart, D. E., McClelland, J. L., & the PDP Research Group (1986). *Parallel distributed processing: Explorations in the microstructure of cognition: Vol. 1, Foundations.* MIT Press.

Rumelhart, D. E., Smolensky, P., McClelland, J. L., & Hinton, G. E. (1986). Schemata and sequential thought processes in PDP models. In J. L. McClelland, D. E. Rumelhart, & the PDP Research Group (Eds.), *Parallel distributed processing: Explorations in the microstructure of cognition: Vol. 2, Psychological and biological models* (pp. 7–57). MIT Press.

Samrani, G., Bäckman, L., & Persson, J. (2019). Interference control in working memory is associated with ventrolateral prefrontal cortex volume. *Journal of Cognitive Neuroscience, 31*(10), 1491–1505.

Santoro, A., Raposo, D., Barrett, D. G. T., Malinowski, M., Pascanu, R., Battaglia, P., & Lillicrap, T. (2017). A simple neural network module for relational reasoning. *Advances in Neural Information Processing Systems, 31*, 4974–4983.

Sarina, V., & Namukasa, I. K. (2010). Nonmath analogies in teaching mathematics. *Procedia Social and Behavioral Sciences, 2*, 5738–5743.

Schaeffer, B., & Wallace, R. (1969). Semantic similarity and the comparison of word meanings. *Journal of Experimental Psychology, 82*(2), 343–346.

Schank, R. C. (1982). *Dynamic memory: A theory of reminding and learning in computers and people*. Cambridge University Press.

Schauer, F. (2014). Analogy in the Supreme Court: Lozman v City of Riviera Beach, Florida. *Supreme Court Review, 1*, 405–432.

Schauer, F., & Spellman, B. A. (2017). Analogy, expertise, and experience. *University of Chicago Law Review, 84*(1), 249–268.

Schiff, W., Caviness, J. A., & Gibson, J. J. (1962). Persistent fear responses in rhesus monkeys to the optical stimulus of 'looming.' *Science, 136*, 982–983.

Schilpp, P. A. (Ed. and Trans.) (1979). *Albert Einstein: Autobiographical notes*. Open Court.

Scholl, B. J., & Tremoulet, P. D. (2000). Perceptual causality and animacy. *Trends in Cognitive Sciences, 4*(8), 299–309.

Schön, D. A. (1993). Generative metaphor: A perspective on problem-setting in social policy. In A. Ortony (Ed.), *Metaphor and thought* (2nd ed.) (pp. 137–163). Cambridge University Press.

Schneider, M., & Siegler, R. S. (2010). Representations of the magnitudes of fractions. *Journal of Experimental Psychology: Human Perception and Performance, 36*, 1227–1238.

Schunn, C. D., & Dunbar, K. (1996). Priming, analogy, and awareness in complex reasoning. *Memory & Cognition, 24*, 271–284.

Schustack, M. W., & Anderson, J. R. (1979). Effects of analogy to prior knowledge on memory for new information. *Journal of Verbal Learning and Verbal Behavior, 18*(5), 565–583.

Seifert, C. M., McKoon, G., Abelson, R. P., & Ratcliff, R. (1986). Memory connections between thematically similar episodes. *Journal of Experimental Psychology: Learning, Memory, and Cognition, 12*, 220–231.

Semendeferi, K., Armstrong, E., Schleicher, A., Zilles, K., & Van Hoesen, G. W. (2001). Prefrontal cortex in humans and apes: A comparative study of area 10. *American Journal of Physical Anthropology, 114*, 224–241.

Semendeferi, K., Teffer, K., Buxhoeveden, D. P., Park, M. S., Bludau, S., Amunts, K., Travis, K., & Buckwalter, J. (2011). Spatial organization of neurons in the frontal pole sets humans apart from great apes. *Cerebral Cortex, 21*(7), 1485–1497.

Shepard, R. N. (2004). How a cognitive psychologist came to seek universal laws. *Psychonomic Bulletin & Review, 11*(1), 1–23.

Shepard, R. N., & Metzler, J. (1971). Mental rotation of three-dimensional objects. *Science, 171*, 701–703.

Shu, T., Peng, Y., Zhu, S. C., & Lu, H. (2021). A unified psychological space for human perception of physical and social events. *Cognitive Psychology, 128*, 101398.

Sidney, P. G. (2020). Children's learning from implicit analogies during instruction: Evidence from fraction division. (2020). *Cognitive Development, 56*, 100956. https://doi.org/10.1016/j.cogdev.2020.100956

Siegler, R. S., & Opfer, J. E. (2003). The development of numerical estimation: Evidence for multiple representations of numerical quantity. *Psychological Science, 14*(3), 237–250.

Simms, M. K., & Richland, L. E. (2019). Generating relations elicits a relational mindset in children. *Cognitive Science, 43*, e12795.

Simon, D., Krawczyk, D. C., Bleicher, A., & Holyoak, K. J. (2008). The transience of constructed preferences. *Journal of Behavioral Decision Making, 21*, 1–14.

Singh, M., & Glowacki, L. (2022). Human social organization during the Late Pleistocene: Beyond the nomadic-egalitarian model. *Evolution and Human Behavior, 43*(5), 418–431.

Simon, D., Stenstrom, D. M., & Read, S. J. (2015). The coherence effect: Blending cold and hot cognitions. *Journal of Personality and Social Psychology, 109*, 369–394.

Sloman, S. A. (1996). The empirical case for two systems of reasoning. *Psychological Bulletin, 119*, 3–22.

Smirnova, A., Zorina, Z., Obozova, T., & Wasserman, E. (2015). Crows spontaneously exhibit analogical reasoning. *Current Biology, 25*(2), 256–260.

Smith, L. B. (1989). From global similarities to kinds of similarities: The construction of dimensions in development. In S. Vosniadou & A. Ortony (Eds.), *Similarity and analogical reasoning* (pp. 146–178). Cambridge University Press.

Smith, E. E., Shoben, E. J., & Rips, L. J. (1974). Structure and process in semantic memory: A featural model for semantic decisions. *Psychological Review, 81*, 214–241.

Smolensky, P. (1990). Tensor product variable binding and the representation of symbolic structures in connectionist systems. *Artificial Intelligence, 46*(1–2), 159–216.

Snow, R.E., Kyllonen, P.C., & Marshalek, B. (1984). The topography of ability and learning correlations. In R. J. Sternberg (Ed.), *Advances in the psychology of human intelligence*, Vol. 2 (pp. 47–103). Erlbaum.

Spearman, C. (1923). *The nature of intelligence and the principles of cognition.* Macmillan.

Spearman, C. (1927). *The abilities of man.* Macmillan.

Spearman, C. (1946). Theory of a general factor. *British Journal of Psychology, 36,* 117–131.

Spellman, B. A., & Holyoak, K. J. (1992). If Saddam is Hitler then who is George Bush? Analogical mapping between systems of social roles. *Journal of Personality and Social Psychology, 62,* 913–933.

Spellman, B. A., & Holyoak, K. J. (1996). Pragmatics in analogical mapping. *Cognitive Psychology, 31,* 307–346.

Spellman, B. A., Holyoak, K. J., & Morrison, R. G. (2001). Analogical priming via semantic relations. *Memory & Cognition, 29,* 383–393.

Spellman, B. A., Ullman, J. B., & Holyoak, K. J. (1993). A coherence model of cognitive consistency. *Journal of Social Issues, 4,* 147–165.

Squire, L. R. (2004). Memory systems of the brain: A brief history and current perspective. *Neurobiology of Learning and Memory, 82*(3), 171–177.

Stamenković, D., Ichien, N., & Holyoak, K. J. (2019). Metaphor comprehension: An individual-differences approach. *Journal of Memory and Language, 105,* 108–118.

Stamenković, D., Ichien, N., & Holyoak, K. J. (2020). Individual differences in comprehension of contextualized metaphors. *Metaphor and Symbol, 35*(4), 285–301.

Stamenković, D., Milenković, K., Ichien, N., & Holyoak, K. J. (2023). An individual-differences approach to poetic metaphor: Impact of aptness and familiarity. *Metaphor and Symbol, 38*(2), 149–161.

Star, J. R., Pollack, C., Durkin, K., Rittle-Johnson, B., Lynch, K., Newton, K., & Gogolen, C. (2015). Learning from comparison in algebra. *Educational Psychology, 40,* 41–54.

Starr, A., Leib, E. R., Younger, J. W., Project iLead Consortium, Uncapher, M. R., & Bunge, S. (2022). Relational thinking: An overlooked component of executive functioning. *Developmental Science*, e13320. https://doi.org/10.1111/desc.13320

Sternberg, R. J., & Lubart, T. I. (1995). *Defying the crowd: Cultivating creativity in a culture of conformity.* Free Press.

Stigler, J. W., Givvin, K. B., & Thompson, B. J. (2010). What community college developmental mathematics students understand about mathematics. *MathAMA-TYC Educator, 1*(3), 4–16.

Sunstein, C. R. (2021). Analogical reasoning. Harvard Public Law Working Paper No. 21-39. https://doi.org/10.2139/ssrn.3938546

Talmy, L. (1988). Force dynamics in language and cognition. *Cognitive Science, 12,* 49–100.

Terrace, H. S., Petitto, L. A., Sanders, R. J., & Bever, T. G. (1979). Can an ape create a sentence? *Science, 17*(4), 396–410.

Thagard, P. (1989). Explanatory coherence. *Behavioral and Brain Sciences, 12*(3), 435–502.

Thagard, P. (2021). *Bots and beasts: What makes machines, animals, and people smart?* MIT Press.

Thagard, P. (2022). *Balance: How it works and what it means.* Columbia University Press.

Thagard, P., Holyoak, K. J., Nelson, G., & Gochfeld, D. (1990). Analog retrieval by constraint satisfaction. *Artificial Intelligence, 46,* 259–310.

Thibaut, J. P., & French, R. M. (2016). Analogical reasoning, control and executive functions: A developmental investigation with eye-tracking. *Cognitive Development, 38,* 10–26.

Tik, M., Sladky, R., Luft, C. D. B., Willinger, D., Hoffmann, A., Banissy, M. J., Bhattacharya, J., & Windischberger, C. (2018). Ultra-high-field fMRI insights on insight: Neural correlates of the Aha!-moment. *Human Brain Mapping, 39,* 3241–3252.

Tohill, J. M., & Holyoak, K. J. (2000). The impact of anxiety on analogical reasoning. *Thinking & Reasoning, 6,* 27–40.

Tomasello, M. (2014). *A natural history of human thinking.* Harvard University Press.

Tomasello, M. (2019). *Becoming human: A theory of ontogeny.* Harvard University Press.

Trench, M., & Minervino, R. A. (2015). The role of surface similarity in analogical retrieval: Bridging the gap between the naturalistic and the experimental traditions. *Cognitive Science, 39,* 1292–1319.

Trench, M., & Minervino, R. A. (2020). *Distant connections: The memory basis of creative analogy.* Springer.

Tschirgi, J. E. (1980). Sensible reasoning: A hypothesis about hypotheses. *Child Development, 51,* 1–10.

Turkheimer, E., Haley, A., Waldron, M., D'Onofrio, B., & Gottesman, I. I. (2003). Socioeconomic status modifies heritability of IQ in young children. *Psychological Science, 14*(6), 623–638.

Turner, M. (1987). *Death is the mother of beauty: Mind, metaphor, criticism.* University of Chicago Press.

Turney, P. D. (2008). The Latent Relation Mapping Engine: Algorithm and experiments. *Journal of Artificial Intelligence Research, 33,* 615–655.

Turney, P. D. (2013). Distributional semantics beyond words: Supervised learning of analogy and paraphrase. *Transactions of the Association for Computational Linguistics, 1,* 353–366.

Tversky, B. (2019). *Mind in motion: How action shapes thought.* Basic Books.

Tversky, B., & Hemenway, K. (1984). Objects, parts, and categories. *Journal of Experimental Psychology: General, 113*(2), 169–193.

Tyumeneva, Y. A., Larina, G., Alexandrova, E., DeWolf, M., Bassok, M., & Holyoak, K. J. (2018). Semantic alignment across whole-number arithmetic and rational numbers: Evidence from a Russian perspective. *Thinking & Reasoning, 24,* 198–220.

Urbanski, M., Bréchemier, M.-L., Garcin, B., Bendetowicz, D., de Schotten, M. T., Foulon, C., Rosso, C., Clarençon, F., Dupont, S., Pradat-Diehl, P., Labeyrie, M.-A., Levy, R., & Volle, E. (2016). Reasoning by analogy requires the left frontal pole: Lesion-deficit mapping and clinical implications. *Brain, 139,* 1783–1799.

Utsumi, A. (2020). Exploring what is encoded in distributional word vectors: A neurobiologically motivated analysis. *Cognitive Science, 44,* e12844. https://doi.org/10.1111/cogs.12844

Utzon, J. (2002). *Sydney Opera House Utzon design principles* (pdf). Sydney Opera House Trust. https://web.archive.org/web/20090226042013/http://www.sydneyoperahouse.com/uploadedFiles/About_Us/The_Building/Content_AboutUs_UtzonDesignPrinciples.pdf

Valle, T. M., Bajo, M. T., & Gómez-Ariza, C. J. (2020). Cathodal transcranial direct current stimulation over the right dorsolateral prefrontal cortex cancels out the cost of selective retrieval on subsequent analogical reasoning. *Neuropsychologica, 141,* 107431. https://doi.org/10.1016/j.neuropsychologia.2020.107431

Van Overwalle, F. (2011). A dissociation between social mentalizing and general reasoning. *NeuroImage, 54*(2), 1589–1599.

Varley, R., & Siegal, M. (2000). Evidence for cognition without grammar from causal reasoning and "theory of mind" in an agrammatic aphasic patient. *Current Biology, 10,* 723–726.

Vartanian, O. (2012). Dissociable neural systems for analogy and metaphor: Implications for the neuroscience of creativity. *British Journal of Psychology, 103,* 302–316.

Vartanian, O. (2019). Neuroscience of creativity. In J. Kaufman & R. J. Sternberg (Eds.), *Cambridge handbook of creativity* (pp. 148–172). Cambridge University Press.

Vaswani, A., Shazeer, N., Parmar, N., Uszkoreit, J., Jones, L., Gomez, A. N., Kaiser, L., & Polosukhin, I. (2017). Attention is all you need. *Advances in Neural Information Processing Systems, 31*, 5998–6008.

Vendetti, M. S., Matlen, B. J., Richland, L. E., & Bunge, S. A. (2015). Analogical reasoning in the classroom: Insights from cognitive science. *Mind, Brain, and Education, 9*, 100–106.

Vendetti, M. S., Starr, A., Johnson, E. L., Modavi, K., & Bunge, S. A. (2017). Eye movements reveal optimal strategies for analogical reasoning. *Frontiers in Psychology, 8*, 932. https://doi.org/10.3389/fpsyg.2017.00932

Vendetti, M. S., Wu, A., & Holyoak, K. J. (2014). Far out thinking: Generating solutions to distant analogies promotes relational thinking. *Psychological Science, 25*, 928–933.

Viskontas, I. V., Morrison, R. G., Holyoak, K. J., Hummel, J. E., & Knowlton, B. J. (2004). Relational integration, inhibition and analogical reasoning in older adults. *Psychology and Aging, 19*, 581–591.

Volle, E., Gilbert, S. J., Benoit, R. G., & Burgess, P. W. (2010). Specialization of the rostral prefrontal cortex for distinct analogy processes. *Cerebral Cortex, 20*, 2647–2659.

Vonk, J. (2015). Corvid cognition: Something to crow about? *Current Biology, 25*(2), R69–R71.

Vosniadou, S. (2019). The development of students' understanding of science. *Frontiers in Education, 4*. https://doi.org/10.3389/feduc.2019.00032

Waldmann, M. R. (Ed.) (2017). *Oxford handbook of causal reasoning.* Oxford University Press.

Waldmann, M. R., & Holyoak, K. J. (1992). Predictive and diagnostic learning within causal models: Asymmetries in cue competition. *Journal of Experimental Psychology: General, 121*, 222–236.

Walker, J. M., Cheng, P. W., & Stigler, J. W. (2014). Equations are effects: Using causal contrasts to support algebra learning. In *Proceedings of the 36th Annual Conference of the Cognitive Science Society.* Cognitive Science Society.

Waltz, J. A., Knowlton, B. J., Holyoak, K. J., Boone, K. B., Back-Madruga, C., McPherson, S., Masterman, D., Chow, T., Cummings, J. L., & Miller, B. L. (2004). Relational integration and executive function in Alzheimer's disease. *Neuropsychology, 18*, 296–305.

Waltz, J. A., Knowlton, B. J., Holyoak, K. J., Boone, K. B., Mishkin, F. S., de Menezes Santos, M., Thomas, C. R., & Miller, B. L. (1999). A system for relational reasoning in human prefrontal cortex. *Psychological Science, 10*, 119–125.

Waltz, J. A., Lau, A., Grewal, S. K., & Holyoak, K. J. (2000). The role of working memory in analogical mapping. *Memory & Cognition, 28*, 1205–1212.

Wang, W.-C., Hsieh, L.-T., & Bunge, S. (2021). Transient neural activation of abstract relations on an incidental analogy task. *Journal of Cognitive Neuroscience, 33*(1), 77–88.

Wang, Y., Metoki, A., Xia, Y., Zang, Y., He, Y., & Olson, I. R. (2021). A large-scale structural and functional connectome of social mentalizing. *NeuroImage, 236*, 118115.

Ward, C., & Gimbel, S. (2010). Retroductive analogy: How to and how not to make claims of good reasons to believe in evolutionary and anti-evolutionary hypotheses. *Argumentation, 24*, 71–84.

Ward, T. B., Finke, R. A., & Smith, S. M. (1995). *Creativity and the mind: Discovering the genius within.* Plenum.

Wasserman, E. A., Castro, L., & Fagot, J. (2017). Relational thinking in animals and humans: From percepts to concepts. In J. Call, G. M. Burghardt, I. M. Pepperberg, C. T. Snowdon, & T. Zentall (Eds.), *APA handbook of comparative psychology: Perception, learning, and cognition.* American Psychological Association.

Wasserman, E. A., & Young, M. E. (2010). Same–different discrimination: The keel and backbone of thought and reasoning. *Journal of Experimental Psychology: Animal Behavior Processes, 36*(1), 3–22.

Watson, C. E., & Chatterjee, A. (2012). A bilateral frontoparietal network underlies visuospatial analogical reasoning. *NeuroImage, 59*, 2831–2838.

Webb, T., Fu, S., Bihl, T., Holyoak, K. J., & Lu, H. (2023. Zero-shot visual reasoning through probabilistic analogical mapping. *Nature Communications, 15*, 5144. https://doi.org/10.1038/s41467-023-40804-x

Webb, T., Holyoak, K. J., & Lu, H. (2023). Emergent analogical reasoning in large language models. *Nature Human Behaviour, 7*(9), 1526–1541. https://doi.org/10.1038/s41562-023-01659-w

Weinberger, A. B., Gallagher, N. M., Colaizzi, G., Liu, N., Parrott, N., Fearon, E., Shaikh, N. & Green, A. E. (2022). Analogical mapping across sensory modalities and evidence for a general analogy factor. *Cognition, 223*, 105029. https://doi.org/10.1016/j.cognition.2022.105029

Weir, A. A. S., Chappell, J., & Kacelnik, A. (2002). Shaping of hooks in New Caledonian crows. *Science, 297*, 981.

Weir, A. A. S., & Kacelnik, A. (2006). A New Caledonian crow (*Corvus moneduloides*) creatively re-designs tools by bending or unbending aluminum strips. *Animal Cognition, 9*, 317–334.

Wendelken, C. (2015). Meta-analysis: How does posterior parietal cortex contribute to reasoning? *Frontiers in Human Neuroscience, 21*(8), 1042. https://doi.org/10.3389/fnhum.2014.01042

Wendelken, C., Bunge, S. A., & Carter, C.S. (2008). Maintaining structured information: An investigation into functions of parietal and lateral prefrontal cortices. *Neuropsychologia, 46*, 665–678.

Wendelken C., Ferrer, E., Ghetti, S., Bailey, S. K., Cutting, L., & Bunge, S. A. (2017). Frontoparietal structural connectivity in childhood predicts development of functional connectivity and reasoning ability: A large-scale longitudinal investigation. *Journal of Neuroscience, 37*(35), 8549–8558.

Wendelken, C., Ferrer, E., Whitaker, K. J., & Bunge, S. A. (2016). Fronto-parietal network reconfiguration supports the development of reasoning ability. *Cerebral Cortex, 26*, 2178–2190.

Wharton, C. M., Holyoak, K. J., Downing, P. E., Lange, T. E., Wickens, T. D., & Melz, E. R. (1994). Below the surface: Analogical similarity and retrieval competition in reminding. *Cognitive Psychology, 26*, 64–101.

Wharton, C. M., Holyoak, K. J., & Lange, T. E. (1996). Remote analogical reminding. *Memory & Cognition, 24*, 629–643.

Whitaker, K., Vendetti, M. S., Wendelken, C., & Bunge, S. A. (2018). Neuroscientific insights into the development of analogical reasoning. *Developmental Science, 21*(2), e12531. https://doi.org/10.1111/desc.12531

Willems, R. M., de Boer, M., de Ruiter, J. P., Noordzij, M. L., Hagoort, P., & Toni, I. (2010). A dissociation between linguistic and communicative abilities in the human brain. *Psychological Science, 21*(1), 8–14.

Wilson, W. H., Halford, G. S., Gray, B., & Phillips, S. (2001). The STAR-2 model for mapping hierarchically structured analogs. In D. Gentner, K. J. Holyoak, & B. Kokinov (Eds.), *The analogical mind: Perspectives from cognitive science* (pp. 125–159). MIT Press.

Winston, P. H. (1975). Learning structural descriptions from examples. In P. H. Winston (Ed.), *The psychology of computer vision* (pp. 157–209). McGraw-Hill.

Winston, P. H. (1980). Learning and reasoning by analogy. *Communications of the ACM, 23*(12), 689–703.

Wolff, P., & Thorstad, R. (2017). Force dynamics. In M. R. Waldmann (Ed.), *Oxford handbook of causal reasoning* (pp. 147–167). Oxford University Press.

Wong, E. F., & Holyoak, K. J. (2021). Cognitive and motivational factors driving sharing of internet memes. *Memory & Cognition, 49*, 863–872.

Woolgar, A., Duncan, J., Manes, F., & Federenko, E. (2018). Fluid intelligence is supported by the multiple-demand system not the language system. *Nature Human Behaviour, 2*, 200–204.

Yang, Y., & Piantadosi, S. T. (2022). One model for the learning of language. *Proceedings of the National Academy of Sciences, USA, 119*(5), e2021865119. https://doi.org/10.1073/pnas.2021865119

Zhang, C., Gao, F., Jia, B., Zhu, Y., & Zhu, S.-C. (2019). RAVEN: A dataset for Relational and Analogical Visual rEasoNing. *Proceedings of the 2019 IEEE Conference on Computer Vision and Pattern Recognition*, 5312–5322.

Zhang, C., Jia, B., Gao, F., Zhu, Y., Lu, H., & Zhu, S.-C. (2019, 2019). Learning perceptual inference by contrasting. *Advances in Neural Information Processing Systems, 33*, 1075–1087.

Zhila, A., Yih, W., Meek, C., Zweig, G., & Mikolov, T. (2013). Combining heterogeneous models for measuring relational similarity. *Proceedings of the 2013 Conference North American Chapter of the Association for Computational Linguistics: Human Language Technologies* (pp. 1000–1009). Association for Computational Linguistics.

Zhou, J., Wei, C., Wang, H., Shen, W., Xie, C., Yuille, A. L., & Kong, T. (2022). iBOT: Image BERT pre-training with online tokenizer. *Tenth International Conference on Learning Representations*. arXiv:2111.07832v3.

Zhu, R., & Gopnik, A. (2023). Preschoolers and adults learn from novel metaphors. *Psychological Science, 34*(6), 696–704. https://doi.org/10.1177/09567976231165267

Index

Page number followed by *b* indicates boxed content, *f* indicates figures, and *t* indicates tables.